WEAKER SECTIONS

WEAKER SECTIONS
The Psycho-Social Perspective

Edited by
N. Hasnain

GYAN PUBLISHING HOUSE
NEW DELHI-110002

WEAKER SECTIONS
The Psycho-Social Perspective
(Psychology. Social Work. Sociology. Anthropology. Education. History)

ISBN : 81-212-0567-0

Published in 1998 in India by
Gyan Publishing House
5. Ansari Road
New Delhi 110 002

Laser Typeset at Grow Computers, Delhi.
Printed at Mehra Offset Press. New Delhi.

To
the philosopher and educationist
Dr. Zakir Husain
on his birth centenary

Contents

List of Tables

Preface

India is a pluralistic society consisting of many religions, castes, languages, regions, etc. Such multiplicities inherently bring with them enormous complexities and problem. No doubt, India has survived over the years with its massive capacity of adjustment keeping its basic ethos of 'unity in diversity'. Nonetheless, there is no denying the fact that certain sections of Indian society have been left to lag behind. The gaps between haves and have nots, privileged and deprived, affluent and poor, Hindus and Muslims, caste-Hindus and Scheduled Castes and Tribes, men and women, grown-ups and children have widened with time. It is ironical that a country like our in spite of its rich heritage of spirituality, tolerance, socialism and equality has suffered a lot because of the antagonistic forces. The concomitant result of such antagonism has been the disproportionate development of different sections of the society. Among those who got the short shrift are the minorities, women, children, Scheduled Castes and Tribes and aged people.

It is disheartening fact for a developing country that the majority of its population still live in deplorable socio-economic conditions. The psychological consequences of centuries deprivation of weaker sections surely puts an extra tax on them to be paid for their low self-esteem, low achievement, apathy and inferiority. This consequently has further negative influence on their global development. It doubles the burden of development with a probability of widening the gaps.

It becomes, therefore, the important duty of the social scientists to understand the causes and consequences of the deprivations of various kinds of these sections of society in order to find appropriate ways and means for their upliftment. This book is a modest attempt in this direction. It seeks to provide some of the important social, psychological, historical and agricultural dimensions of the weaker sections of the Indian society. In the galaxy of luminaries who championed the cause of the weak and downtrodden are Mahatma Gandhi, Pandit Jawaharlal Nehru, Maulana Abul Kalam Azad, Dr. B.R. Ambedkar, Jayaprakash Narain, Dr. Zakir Husain and many more enthusiastic and courageous persons. Jamia Millia Islamia, the baby of nationalism, reared and nourished by Maulana

Mohammad Ali Jauhar, Maulana Mahmoodul Hasan, Mahatma Gandhi, Hakeem Ajmal Khan, Dr. Mukhtar Ahmad Ansari, Saifuddin Kichlu, Abdul Majeed Khawaja, Dr. Zakir Husain, Professor Mohammad Mujeeb and others, always put the educational needs of the deprived and weaker sections of the society in the foreground. Established at Aligarh in 1920 in response to Gandhiji's call for 'non-cooperation' and the boycotting of all Government supported educational institutions it grew to become a central university in 1988 and celebrated its 75th anniversary in October, 1995 with a happy coincidence of 98th birth anniversary of Dr. Zakir Husain. To commemorate such a grand occasion, the Department of Psychology at the Jamia Millia Islamia with its modest resources and infantile weaker hands of an age of hardly ten years, organized a two-day national seminar 'Socio-Psychological Scenario of Weaker Sections' (21-22 October, 1995). Does the topic chosen for the seminar echo the laudable aims and purpose of the founders of Jamia and the Jamia itself ? This is a question left to be answered by the readers.

This book is a systematic collection and presentation of the papers presented at this seminar. In addition some other contributions were also included to make the picture more clear. Some papers could not be included as contributors failed to respond with revised versions. It is again a happy coincidence that the book is being published on the birth centenary of Dr. Zakir Husain and the 50th anniversary of India's independence. So, it has been humbly dedicated to this great son of India.

The seminar jointly sponsored by ICSSR and Jamia Millia Islamia was held under the directorship of myself. I am immensely thankful to both the organizations for their financial support. In conducting and organizing the seminar and preparing the book many people helped me. The foremost among them is Dr. M.G. Husain, Professor and then Head, Department of Psychology, Jamia Millia Islamia, New Delhi, at present Professor of Psychology, International Islamic University, Malaysia. It was under his supervision that the seminar was organized. I express my feeling of gratitude to him.

I am immensely indebted to Dr. Devaprasad Sen Mazumdar, Former Advisor, Defence Research and Development Organizations (DRDO), Ministry of Defence, Government of India for delivering the keynote address. Padma Bhushan Dr. Bindeshwar Pathak, Founder, Sulabh International Social Service Organization sent us his paper which was presented by Dr. S.P. Srivastava. I am thankful to both of them. I am also grateful to Professor R.S. Khan, Head, IASE and Dean, Faculty of Education, Jamia Millia Islamia for providing moral support and many of the facilities which made the organization of the seminar a success.

Thanks are also due to all the contributors whose papers form this book. I am grateful to my colleagues, Dr. M. Shafiq, Dr. K. Bharthi Kumari, Dr. Waheeda Khan, Dr. M.G. Shahnawaz, Mr. Naved Iqbal, and Mr. A.K. Mishra for their moral support. I would also like to thank the research scholars of the Department of Psychology, Dr. Neeru Singh, Mr. Meer Zafar Iqbal, Ms Sangeeta Sharma, Ms Talmeez Fatima and other students who helped in organizing the seminar. My thanks to Ms Talmeez Fatima for helping me to prepare the manuscript. The administrative staff of the department Mr. Shahnawaz Khan, Mr. Zishan Ahmad and Mr. Zafar Alam deserve appreciation for their active cooperation in the management and organization of the seminar. Mr. Nemat Ali and Mr. Mohd. Aslam, to them my thanks for computerizing and giving the manuscript its final shape. My wife, Ms Anjum Ara, son, Zafarul Hasnain and daughter, Sana were deprived of their dues many a time during the course of organization of the seminar and the preparation of the book. My late elder daughter Neshat Anjum will ever remain a source of inspiration for me. I pray to the Almighty to bestow peace upon her soul!

N. HASNAIN

Jamia Millia Islamia,
New Delhi

Jamia Millia Islamia
New Delhi

INTRODUCTION

There is no denying the fact that abilities and capacities are normally distributed in the population. It is not the religion, caste, sex or region. *Per se* responsible for the inferiority or superiority of abilities and capacities of the persons. It is the feelings of have not and helplessness resulting from global deprivation of the persons of religion and caste make them inferior. The treatment meted to persons belonging to the weaker sections in terms of inequality of opportunity, bias, prejudice and discrimination creates an interactional matrix which permits the norms of inequality and hatred to be grown, strengthened and blown up.

The vertical division of Indian society in terms of religion, caste, region and language brings with it all the prejudices and stereotyping and negative feelings. The horizontal division on the basis of political ideology, intelligence, and technological know-how is not accompanied by negative divisive psychological feelings attached to them. A case in view is the division of Indian history in terms of Hindu-Muslim periods which everybody knows has spread much hatred among people of two major religions of India. Much of the research clearly highlights the fact that the position of minorities, women, Scheduled Castes and Tribes is foregrounded with stigma, prejudice and stereotyping. All these are man-made and socially learnt and transmitted.

The cognitive processes are largely sharpened through experiential input. There are studies which reveal the close relationship of cognitive processes with sensory deprivation (Zubek 1969), and cultural background (Broota and Ganguli 1975; Segall, Cambell, and Herkovits 1966; Triandis 1964), Deprivation puts a limit on the experiential breadth and therefore mars the psychological functionings. The general low socio-economic status of minorities, Scheduled Castes and Tribes, the weak and poor position of children and the general low social status of women in society have brought poor socio-cultural environment compelling them to constitute 'the weaker sections' of society. The lack of equality of opportunity, unemployment, poverty and illiteracy have made their conditions worse . The socio-cultural, economic and psychological conditions and environment of scavengers are more than worse. The legislative and administrative measures to ensure their equality and eradicate discrimination against them and certain privileges of reservations in jobs and education tó speed up their development and progress in order to bring them up to the level of other social groups do not seem to give wanted results. Consequently their socio-psychological scenario is still pregnant with inequality and discrimination. Nonetheless, they are slowly and gradually becoming aware of their rights and shares in the corporate life of society. However, much remains to be done.

The problems of these sections of society are multifaceted. The roots seem to be penetrated deep into the socio-religious fabric but consequences are undoubtedly psychological in nature. It is the prime duty of social scientists to investigate and understand these socio-religious roots and their psychological consequences so that ways and means can be suggested and concerted efforts can be made to ameliorate the socio-psychological conditions of these sections of society.

Lewis Oscar (1966) has proposed that "Culture of Poverty" is responsible for the poverty and backwardness of people. He opines that culture of poverty is different from the culture of affluence and to adapt to the harsh realities of life the poor protects himself with a philosophy of life which is characterized by fatalism, impulsiveness, present time orientation, inability to delay gratification, concrete as opposed to abstract thinking, inferiority, aggression and authoritarianism. However, cultural deprivation (Kogan 1970; Rath and Dash, 1972; Wright *et al.* 1970), social deprivation (Rankin 1970; Tulkin 1972), educational deprivation (Getzels 1969), economic deprivation (Symmonds 1968), affective deprivation (Gerwirtz 1961), cognitive deprivation (Green *et al.* 1967) all tell almost the same story. All the said conditions deprive the individuals of opportunities and consequently bring restrictions to them for the optimal development of cognitive, emotional and behavioural spheres of their personality.

Scheduled Castes and Tribes, women and minorities which form the major portion of weaker sections of society have been living under conditions of various kinds of deprivation. Their poor living conditions, insufficient intake of food and calories, poor schooling, lack of facilities of modern amenities, and poor interactional matrix could not be changed in spite of the legislative and administrative measures to bring them at par the other sections and communities of society. The reason being two-fold, discrimination, partisan attitude and prejudice of the administrative machinery; and a lack of will, prevalent apathy and defeatist tendency on their part to ameliorate their conditions.

The deprived, weakers feel threat and challenge to their lives and properties. The feeling of suspicion and insecurity prevails among them. The suspicion becomes sharper in case of denial of the legitimate rights. Threat to religion, identity and culture is resisted with retaliation and greater vigour. In such conditions ethnocentrism and prejudice are strengthened. The gap and lack of communication give rise to social tension and conflict. The frequent eruption of caste and communal riots are the results of such partisan attitudes. These and other such problems need real zeal and actual secular and socialist approaches. But on the contrary, political mileage and gains and games of capturing vote and power are played by fanatics and some short-sighted political leaders. The prejudice and conflict bring hindrances in way of nation-building and national development.

The achievement of the independence of the country was a common goal fought together and achieved together by all the communities—ethnic, religious, regional and linguistic—but the denial of freedom to the access of opportunities and sectarian and discriminative behaviour made the scheduled caste, scheduled tribe and minorities helpless and alienated. This alienation gradually made them apathetic and irresponsive. Belief in luck and fate came to their rescue in such desperate conditions making their capacities, strengths and capabilities defunct and paralyzed. They could not get rid of this apathetic condition until the new awakening came to them by 'Mandal vis-à-vis Kamandal' conflict. Though Kamandal got immediate momentum but Mandal could not lose its importance and significance. It got its share in the form of 11th Lok Sabha elections of June, 1996. The social and political deprivation of the weaker sections brought them together to fight against sectarian and communal forces. However, much remains to be done.

The prevailing apathy and defeatism in these sections of society seem to be equally responsible for their socio-educational backwardness and poverty. Though, the apathetic conditions of the weaker sections of society seem to be largely a result of the treatments meted to them, their conditions is not going to change in any way if they do not seek to understand their own exploitation. The weaker sections have to accept the hard core realities so as to put double efforts and surpass those who had been their masters. There is a need to make them aware that there is no place for the feeling of inferiority, shame and repentance in the development process of a people as in the psychological sense the weaker sections are not inferior to anybody as far as the abilities, cognitive and psychological resources are concerned. Therefore, the need of the hour is that these sections of society should work out themselves the strategies to overcome age-old stigmas.

Keeping these ends in view a Three-day national seminar was organized on 21-23 October, 1995 by the Department of Psychology, Jamia Millia Islamia, New Delhi as a part of 'Platinum Jubilee Celebrations' of the Jamia.

This book is an outcome of this seminar. The papers presented in the book speak for the main weaker sections of our society. The attempt is to provide a wholesome presentation of major weaker sections of the Indian society. They delicately touch some of the important psycho-social and historical aspects of the weakest of the weakers, scavengers and others, Scheduled Castes and Tribes, Muslims, women, children, aged and farmers. Nonetheless, the sections on children and aged are relatively small and because of the paucity of papers only three or four papers could be included in them. However, these articles have touched and explained very important aspects of children's personality and life of the aged.

The keynote address was delivered by Professor Devaprasad Sen Mazumdar. In his keynote address Professor Mazumdar elucidated the concept and criteria of the weaker section and systematically mentioned the negative consequences—educational, health and cognitive—of poverty, socio-economic hardship, lack of facilities and opportunities of the weaker sections of the Indian society. He expressed apprehension that some of the cognitive deficits due to malnutrition may be *transgenerational* in character. Quoting Murray and Hernstein's book *The Bell Curve* Dr Mazumdar remarked that USA is gradually getting divided into two classes: 'cognitive elite' and growing sub-class of 'low IQ Blacks'. To him, there exists a large chunk of disadvantaged people in India other than Scheduled Castes and Tribes, minorities and other Backward Castes who may also suffer from the cognitive deficit and therefore, demarking these disadvantaged people on the basis of caste is not appropriate. In his opinion the weaker section is a group of deprived people and obviously something is lacking in their cultural and educational milieu. This milieu needs enrichment with a greater thrust on education, healthcare, recreation and vocational training. He has emphasized the need of concerted efforts and suggested long-term planning for their upliftment.

The book consists of five sections. It needs to be mentioned that these sections are not exclusive, for many of the papers overlap. These sections have been made for the convenience of systematic presentation of the materials and are not exclusive. The first section deals with the social psychological aspects of Scheduled Castes and Tribes. There are eight articles in this section. The first paper was presented as keynote address and its introduction has already been given in previous paragraph. In the second article, Dr. Bindeshwar Pathak thoroughly discusses the socio-economic and psychological problems of the most neglected section of the Indian society, the scavengers. Through his first-hand experiences of doing social work with them Dr. Pathak has seen and felt the hardships faced by scavengers. Enumerating various problems and difficulties of this section of society and critically evaluating the efficacies of various government programmes for their benefit and upliftment he has discussed the contributions of Sulab International, a movement of rehabilitation of scavengers launched, cherished and developed by him. This programme includes: training and rehabilitation, Sulabh Public School, social upgradation programme, and social adoptation programme. In their article Akbar Husain and M.G. Husain have empirically measured the psychological and social well-beings of scavengers and have concluded that they are not psychologically as unhealthy as socially deprived and rejected. Mohd. Rafique Alam has compared in his article the quality of life of Scheduled Castes vis-à-vis Caste-Hindu and has obtained significantly better quality of life of caste-Hindu than Scheduled Caste and urban than rural subjects for obvious reasons.

G.S. Gupta and Asha Arora have gauged and compared the modernization of Scheduled Caste subjects vis-à-vis Brahmin, Vaishya and Kshatriya subjects in their article. They have obtained that Brahmins are significantly least modernized for the reasons of their religious orientation. The Scheduled Caste subjects are placed next on the modernization scale. They have held the poor economic conditions of Scheduled Caste to be responsible for their less modernized conditions. They have also discussed the results in the light of reservation policy for Scheduled Caste persons in jobs in relation to modernization. In his article, N. Hasnain has presented the psychological scenario of Scheduled Tribes of Kumaun Hills of Uttar Pradesh. Describing the general socio-economic and cultural conditions of two important tribes, Shauka (Bhotia) and Tharu, he has systematically presented that though these tribes have psychological potentials of academic achievement, creativity and operational thoughts, they suffer from a greater degree of alienation, feelings of insecurity, defeatism and have lesser adjustment capacity than caste-Hindu subjects. Hence, they remained unable to utilize and exploit the social and psychological conditions for the development of their psychological resources. N. Hasnain and Dipendra Singh Maher in their article present and compare the self-concept of subjects of Bhotia (Shauka) and Tharu tribes and non-tribe subjects. They concluded that because of the better socio-cultural conditions non-tribe subjects have had significantly the best self-concept and because of socio-cultural inhibitions and economic affluency the subjects of Shauka tribe (Bhotia) have significantly better self-concept than Scheduled Caste but poorer than caste-Hindu subjects. In the last paper of this section, Qamar Jahan has compared the prejudice of high and low self-disclosee Tharu tribe and Scheduled Caste females and has obtained high self-disclosee Scheduled Tribe females to be lesser prejudiced than their counterparts.

Section 2 presents the socio-psychological and historical conditions of minorities with special reference to Muslims. There are six papers in this section. In the first paper Mujeeb Ashraf presenting the historical perspectives of legacy and dilemma of Indian Muslims has reviewed their conditions in present international scenario. Describing the past of the Indian Muslims he has tried to awaken the Muslims from the unrealistic dreams of past and to face the socio-political realities of the day. Asghar Ali Engineer has systematically analyzed the concepts of fanaticism and communalism in his paper. Quoting examples from world over Engineer has held the Indian socio-political and economic conditions responsible for the development of fanaticism and communalism. For him, fanaticism is not related to religion but to human psychological type. He has rightly mentioned that in fact religion per se is neither fanatical nor liberal. It is what its follower makes it out to be. In the same way religion for him is not the fundamental cause of communalism. Rather, it is an instrumental cause. In India, both fanaticism and communalism are the products of a competition for power between Hindu and Muslim elites. He has viewed fundamentalism as the product of modern American society. He has defined fundamentalism as the attempt to achieve secular goal through religious means. Communal violence gets intensified during the period of political crises or economic downturn generating high rates of unemployment or intense economic competition, he asserts. Sheema Aleem in her paper has presented the concept of communalism and its vicarious effects on the development of identity in Muslims. In his article Mohammad Ghufran has empirically traced the relationship of prejudice with feeling of insecurity in Hindus and Muslims of social tension-prone and social tension-free areas. He has obtained significant effect of insecurity and social tension on prejudice. However, religion of the subjects was found to be an uninfluential factor for prejudice. Significant two-way interactional effect of social tension and feeling of insecurity, and three-way interactional effect of the three variables on prejudice were obtained. Mohd. Intekhabur Rahman in his paper has described the perceived reactions of Muslims towards police. He has given ways and means to rebuilt the image of police in the eyes of Muslims. In the last article of this section Sanwat Singh has measured and compared the altruistic behaviours of Muslim and Hindu adolescents of city, town and village. He has obtained significant effect of locale, and religion on altruistic behaviour. However, the interactional effect of the two variables was found to be insignificant. His statistical analysis showed Hindus to be more altruistic than Muslims.

Section 3 of the book deals with women. There are six articles in this section. In the first article N. Hasnain presenting empiritical findings establishes that women are not inferior to men in achievements. He has given explanation that socio-cultural factors and child-rearing practices are responsible for the differences, if any, in achievement of men and women. Navita Daga and Akbar Husain in their article have compared sources and effects of stress among working and non-working women. They have also presented different approaches to stress. They obtained insignificant differences among stress sources, stress effects and stress behaviours of working and non-working women. On the basis of findings, they have concluded that women of both categories are very often affected by stress and use it positively. Describing the concept and areas of adjustment S.K. Srivastava has measured and compared the adjustment of male and female Scheduled Caste and non-Scheduled Caste adolescents in his article. He has obtained significantly better adjustment among males than females in all the five areas : home, health, social, emotional and educational and also in total adjustment. He has also shown significantly better adjustment for Non-Scheduled Caste than Scheduled Castes subjects in all the areas as well as total adjustment. P.N. Arora and Dileep Kapoor in their article have compared the self-disclosure of maritally adjusted and unadjusted Scheduled Caste women. They have shown that maritally adjusted Scheduled Caste women are significantly more self-disclosee than non-adjusted self-disclosee women. On the basis of the findings they have advocated for more provisions of facilities and job avenues for Scheduled Caste women to make them able to disclose themselves in a greater way. In the next article Meera Singh and N.C. Verma have compared the gain of nutrition knowledge among Santhal tribe women as a result of training for fifteen days. They have obtained that older participants could not get as much advantage of the training as younger ones. Moreover, education, size of land holding and type of family were found to be influential factors in gaining knowledge of nutrition among Santhal tribal women. Level of education emerged as the most influential factor. Hence they suggested the need for education of the Santhal tribe. S.P. Sinha and Neelima Mukherjee in the last article of this section have empirically measured the personal space orientation among conventional Hindu wives. They have obtained that personal space requirements differed significantly for different dyads: for Wife-Husband dyad least personal space was required followed by Wife-Female, Husband-Male, Husband-Female, and Wife-Male dyads.

Section 4 on 'children' consists of four papers. M. Akhtar Siddiqui in the first paper of this section has discussed an important issue—equality of opportunity of education for children of different sections of society. He has pointed to the ways and forms of inequality in opportunity. To him, the educational facilities are unevenly distributed in districts, regions, and persons of different economic strata, sexes, rural-urban areas, castes and minorities. He has also suggested ways and means to lessen the gaps between the educational opportunities of affluent and the aforesaid sections of society. Ataur Rahman Khan in his article has given comparative state of affairs regarding enrolment and literacy rate of girls in various countries at the secondary level. He has mentioned that most of the underdeveloped countries face the problems of resources and well-equipped teachers. By presenting structure of enrolment at secondary level in various countries he has given a comparative view of Indian scene. The third article of S.N. Dubey deals with the measurement and comparison of a very important aspect of deprived caste-Hindu and Scheduled Caste children, the cognitive functioning. He has used the Intelligence Quotient, short-term memory, and Bender-Gestalt test of visual-motor functions as measures of cognitive functioning. He found a significant impacts of socio-cultural deprivation and locale on the three measures. The interactional effects of the two independent variables on all measures were also significant. He has discussed his results in terms of lack of orientation of children in such tasks in rural and low socio-economic conditions. Pradeep K. Khattri in his article has given a useful technique based on principles of operant conditioning to modify abusive verbal behaviours of Scheduled Caste and non-Scheduled Caste children. He has found insignificant difference between abusive word usage of Scheduled Caste and non-Scheduled Caste children. Operant conditioning was found to be equally effective technique to change the abusive behaviours of children of both castes. Socially disadvantaged Scheduled and non-Scheduled Caste children react to various types of reinforcement in similar ways. Negative reinforcement was always better for both groups as compared to positive reinforcement.

The last section is a miscellaneous type which deals with the aged and others. In this section, three papers are related with aged persons, one with mass-media and one with farmers. In the first paper related with old age N. Hasnain, Neeru Singh and Sangeeta Sharma have dealt with the concept of the old age and its problems in a psycho-social perspective. The second paper dealing with old age is related with comparison of the feelings of insecurity and alienation among aged persons of four categories: persons living with spouse, persons whose spouse is dead, widows, and widowers. In this article Mohd. Ghufran and N. Hasnain have obtained significantly greater insecurity among aged whose spouse is dead than the aged whose spouse is alive; and among widowers than widows. In the same way significantly greater feeling of alienation in widowers than widows has been reported. They have discussed the results in terms of family set-up and cultural aspects of the Indian society. In the third paper, Neeru Singh and M.G. Husain have empirically investigated the internal and external dimensions of locus of control of pre-retired and retired aged belonging to the middle and high economic classes. Their findings revealed significantly greater internal locus of control of pre-retired persons from high and middle economic status than the retired persons from the two socio-economic status, significantly greater external locus of control of retired aged from both socio-economic status than pre-retired aged from the two status, and no any significant difference in powerful/others of pre-retired and retired aged of the two status.

The fourth paper of N. Hasnain and Talmeez Fatima posits systematic description of how false half truths and stereotyped projections of persons of weaker sections are being given by television through different programmes and serials. Such stereotyped presentations from negative images of the people of these sections in the minds of viewers which pile harmful effects on their self-respect and self-concept. The fifth paper of Sohrab Ali gives a description of rural farmers as weaker section. To him, though, Government is providing various subsidies on agricultural inputs, the subsidies are ineffective, and not benefiting to the rural poor farmers due to various lacuna in the policies. He has also suggested some important measures to uplift the socio-economic conditions of these farmers.

Taken together, the articles included in this book present the weak and strong psycho-social aspects of the weaker sections of Indian society, and hint the need for serious plans for intervention to remove the hindrances responsible for weak points of these sections.

REFERENCES

Broota, K.D. and Gangulai, H.C. (1975). Cultural difference in perceptual selectively. *Journal of Social Psychology,* 95, 157-163.

Gerwirtz, J.L. (1961). A learning analysis of the effect of affective privation and childhood. *Acta Psychotogia,* 19, 404-405.

Getzels, J.W. (1969). A Social Psychology of Education. In Lindzey, G. and Aronson, E. (Eds). *The Handbook of Social Psychology,* Vol. 5, N.Y. : Addison Wesley, 459-537.

Green, R.L. Hofmann, L.T. & Morgan, R. (1967). Some effects of deprivation on intelligence, achievement and cognitive growth. *Journal of Negro Education,* 36, 5-14.

Kogan, T.P. (1970). Socio-economic community variables as predictors of cognitive test performance of school children. *Dissertation Abstracts,* 31, 29-59.

Levis Oscar. (1966). The culture of poverty. *Scientific American,* 215, 19-25.

Rankin, N.O. (1970). The effects of selective social deprivation in a natural setting. *Dissertation Abstracts,* 30, 4820-4821.

Rath, R and Dash, A.S. (1972). Cognitive growth and classroom hearing of naturally deprived children in the primary schools. *Paper presented at the East West Centre for Cross-Cultural Studies,* Honolulu.

Segall, Cambell and Herkorits, M.J. (1966). The influence of culture on visual perception. *Indianapolis : Bobbs-Merrill.*

Symmonds, M. (1968). Disadvantaged children growth in a climate of hopelessness and despair. *Journal of Psychoanalysis,* 28, 15-24.

Triandis, H.C. (1964). Cultural influences upon cognitive processes. In Berkowetz, L. (Ed.). *Advances in Social Experimental Psychology,* 1, 2-41.

Tulkin, S.R. (1972). An analysis of the concept of cultural deprivation. *Development Psychology,* 6, 326-339.

Wright, B.W. Gleniger, M.F. & Keene, P.J. (1970). Cultural deprivation : Operational definition in terms of language development. *American Journal of Orthopsychiatry,* 40, 77-86.

Zubek, J.P. (1969). Sensory deprivation : *Fifteen years of Research.* N.Y. : Appleton-Century-Crofts, 296.

List of Contributors

Akbar Husain
Reader
Department of Psychology
A.M.U., Aligarh.

Akbar Hussain
Ex-Lecturer
Department of Psychology
Jamia Millia Islamia, New Delhi.

Asghar Ali Engineer
Director
Institute of Islamic Studies
9/B, Ist Floor, Himalay Apartment
Santacruz (East), Mumbai -400 055

Asha Arora
Lecturer
Government Khursheed Girls' College
Rampur (U.P.).

Ata-ur-Rehman Khan
Faculty Member
Department of Humanities and Social Sciences
Faculty of Engineering
Jamia Millia Islamia, New Delhi.

Bindeshwar Pathak *(Padam Bhushan)*
Founder of Sulabh International Social
Service Organisation
Mahavir Enclave,
Palam, Dabri Road
New Delhi-110 045.

Devaprasad Mazumdar
Former Advisor
Defence Research and Development
Organizations (DRDO)
Government of India
Ministry of Defence
New Delhi.

Dileep Kapoor
Lecturer in Physical Education
Government Raza Postgraduate College
Rampur (U.P.).

Dipendra Singh Maher
Department of Psychology
Government Postgraduate College
Pithoragarh (U.P.).

G.S. Gupta
Reader and Head
Department of Psychology
Government Raza Postgraduate College
Rampur (U.P.).

M. Akhtar Siddiqui
Professor
Institute of Advanced Studies in Education
Faculty of Education
Jamia Millia Islamia, New Delhi.

Meera Singh
Asstt. Professor
Department of Extension Education
Faculty of Home Science
R.A.U., Pusa, Bihar.

M.G. Husain
Professor of Psychology
Faculty of Revealed Knowledge and Human Sciences
International Islamic University
Malaysia.

Mohd. Ghufran
Lecturer in Psychology
Government M.B. Postgraduate College
Haldwani (Nainital).

Mohd. Intekhab-ur-Rehman
Lecturer in Psychology
Millat College
Darbhanga, Bihar.

Mohd. Rafique Alam
Reader in Psychology
H.D. Jain College
(Veer Kunwar Singh University)
Arrah.

Mujeeb Ashraf
Professor
Department of History and Culture
Jamia Millia Islamia
New Delhi.

Navita Daga
Research Scholar
Department of Psychology
A.M.U., Aligarh.

N.C. Verma
Associate Professor
Department of Extension Education
Faculty of Agriculture
R.A.U., Pusa, Bihar.

N. Hasnain
Head
Department of Psychology
Jamia Millia Islamia
New Delhi.

Neelima Mukherjee
Scientist, CRRI, Delhi.

Neeru Singh
Senior Research Assistant
Department of Psychology
Jamia Millia Islamia, New Delhi.

P.N. Arora
Reader
Department of Psychology
Government Raza Postgraduate College
Rampur (U.P.).

Pradeep K. Khattri
Reader and Head
Department of Psychology
National College, Lucknow.

Qamar Jahan
Ex-Lecturer in Psychology
Gargi College
New Delhi.

Sangeeta Sharma
Research Scholar
Department of Psychology
Jamia Millia Islamia, New Delhi.

Sanwat Singh
Reader
Department of Psychology
Government Raza Postgraduate College
Rampur (U.P.).

Sheema Aleem
Lecturer
Department of Psychology
Jamia Millia Islamia
New Delhi.

S.K. Srivastava
Reader
Department of Psychology
Gurukul Kangri University
Hardwar.

Sohrab Ali
Reader
Institute of Advanced Studies in Education (IASE)
Faculty of Education
Jamia Millia Islamia
New Delhi.

S.P. Sinha
Reader and Head
Department of Psychology
Dayalbagh Educational Institute
Dayalbagh, Agra.

Surendra Nath Dubey
Reader
Department of Psychology
Saket College, Faizabad.

Talmeez Fatima
Research Scholar
Department of Psychology
Jamia Millia Islamia
New Delhi.

SECTION I

Scheduled Castes and Tribes

1

The Weak and the Strong*

Devaprasad Sen Mazumdar

The theme topic of "Psycho-social scenario of Weaker Sections" is timely and relevant, eventhough quite a few people may think that the end part 'weaker sections' has appeared in different garbs on many occasions at different forums and often highlighted by the mass media and political parties over last 15 to 20 years. It gathered momentum with (Late) Mrs. Indira Gandhi's slogan of *Garibi Hatao* (Remove poverty). Poverty and weaker section were considered to be soulmates. Each one needed the other for making any kind of discussion exciting and impressive. Cynics considered it to be a vote-catching slogan. Yet, with willing suspension of disbelief, 'poverty' and 'weaker section'—one may call this section as the poor as well—still remain as grim reminders and bitter testimony of our failure to raise the bottom of our populace to a minimal decent standard of living or providing a quality of life of which every Indian can be proud of,—and that after half a century of earning independence from our British masters.

According to Human Development Report, 1995, by the United Nation's Development Programme (UNDP), India ranks 134 on Human Development Index (HDI) 0.439 lower than Pakistan (HDI - 0.483), Myanmar (0.457), Maldives (0.554), Sri Lanka (0.704) but higher than Bangladesh (0.364) and Nepal (0.343) in the family of 174 nations. India's HDI falls in category of 'Low Human Development.' HDI is based on three indications. First is the life expectancy which represents the health status, the second is the education — representing the knowledge and the third is the real GDP purchasing power parity in dollars, indicates standard of living. The first five places on HDI index are occupied by Canada

---

* Keynote address

Profile of Human Development **Developing Countries**

		ACCESS TO								
	Life Expect 1992	Health Service % 1985-93	Safe Water % 1988-93	Sanitation % 1988-93	Daily Calorie Per Cap. 1992	Adult Literacy % 1992	Daily Newspaper (Per 100 per) 1992	TV (per 100 per.) 1992	Realg GDP Per Cap. (US $) 1992	GNP Per Capital (US $) 1992
High Dev.										
23. CYPRUS	77.0				3,782		11	15	15,050	10,300
24. HONG KONG	78.6	99	100	88	3,144	91.2	82	28	20,340	15.710
Medium Dev. Excluding China										
70. IRAN	67.5	80	89	71	2,861	64.9	2	6	5,420	2.230
97. SRI LANKA	71.9	93	60	50	2,275	89.3	3	5	2,850	560
111. CHINA	68.5	90	69	16	2,729	79.3	-	3	1950	480
Low Dev. Excluding India										
134. INDIA	60.4	85	79	27	2,395	49.9	3	4	1,230	310
151. NEPAL	53.5	"	42	6	1,937	25.6	1	4	1,170	170
153. CAMBODIA	51.6	53	36	14	2,021	-	-	1	-	-
146. BANGLADESH	53.6	45	84	31	2,019	36.4	1	-	1,230	220

(.950), U.S.A. (.937), Japan (.937), Netherland (.936) and Finland (.934). India's record, as such, does not look impressive even though during the last five decades considerable progress has been made.

The pertinent question is whom we should call weaker section of the society. The nomenclature has proved to be highly debatable during the last six years because of inclusion of other backward class (OBC), as if the older 'backward class' term was not good enough. Perhaps the intention was to make the term more comprehensive. Now comprehensiveness has reached such absurd length that many religious, ethnic, regional and host of small communities are crying to include themselves into same class or other with an eye on the reservation factor. So the earlier Scheduled Caste/Scheduled Tribe concept of weaker class, as envisaged by founding fathers of our constitution, including late Dr. Ambedkar—has lost its meaningfulness and relevance. By gradually broadbasing and expanding the scope of the weaker section in an already caste-ridden society, we are only reinforcing the artificially described 'sub-classes' and stoking the fire of sub-nationalism and class conflict, but obviously not Marxian in the style of classical Marxian 'class-struggle'. If we go on with this preposterous high-mindedness of safeguarding the interest of every tiny caste or class with an eye on the slice of cake of 'reservation' and associated facilities and fringe benefits, the quota system will cross 100 per cent and we have to invent some new mathematical symbol or model which is larger than 100 per cent and what we may call larger than life reality. As such, the concept of weaker section of the society has been so ill-defined by naive labelling of caste and class that we cannot make much of it except making the confusion worse confounded. No doubt, some political mileage can be always obtained out of this ambiguity in the coming election year. But is it desirable? Can't we social scientists frame some empirically desired criteria—which can provide an objective base for identifying the 'real' weaker section of the society without raising a lot of emotion? A seminar of national magnitude, like the one today, can bring a lot of sense in the confused and partisan scenario.

A guideline has been already enunciated, and universally accepted and reaffirmed by the Vienna declaration in 1993. It was adopted by 171 states of the World Conference on Human Rights in 1993, including India. One of its major emphases has been equal enjoyment of human rights by women and men. It stresses upon :

(i) Equal access to basic social services like education and health

(ii) Equal opportunities for participation to decide about economic and political issues

(iii) Wage and reward to be equal towards work performed
(iv) Same and equal protection under law
(v) Elimination of discrimination by gender and violence against women
(vi) Equal rights of people at work place and home, i.e., both public and private.

You will notice that on all these dimensions the affluent and educated get the cream, whereas, the poor and uneducated are left miles behind, and most of the opportunities like health care and education necessary for upward social mobility are either not available or meagerly available to people. No doubt, the world is richer today, but while more than 75 per cent of the world population live in developing countries, they only enjoy 16 per cent of the world's income—while the richest 20 per cent have 84 per cent of world's income. In this respect, when we talk of 'weaker section' it should mean the section of society which is subjected to continued deprivation. Human deprivation can always mar the quality of life. Deprivation of humankind is now a global problem for most of the developing countries. The countrywise scenario varies considerably. Regional imbalances are marked.

Another important thing is the cognitive deficit resulting from malnutrition—particularly protein and calorie malnutrition—leading to kwashiorkor or Marasmus in early childhood. Both of them result in arrested mental development, and in many cases the damage is irreversible. It is one of the most serious nutritional diseases. "It has been estimated that more than half of all the children in the world are at risk" (Rose). It is interesting to note that longitudinal researches show that small baby size is correlated with low economic status and large family size. Rose writes further "Once again the critical question is how far actual performance is affected by poverty and malnutrition. Whilst it becomes extremely difficult to sort out many of the other related variables in such studies, the longitudinal studies suggest that low scores are also associated with low socio-economic background of the parents, large family size and poor maternal state of health during pregnancy". He quotes from research studies of Passamanick and his associates, as to how deficiency of diet associated with low income can cause complications in pregnancy followed by intellectual retardation and behaviour disorder of children. Rose also mentions the studies of Harrell that when nutritional dietary supplement was given to pregnant mother, it raised I.Q. of children at the age of 2-4, compared to mothers not given the supplement diet. It appears, therefore, quite likely that performance deficit of children from such deprived backgrounds (one may call it from the weaker section environment) are related to long-term impoverishment of this kind.

Profile of Human Deprivation

HDI Rank	*Illiterate (million) Adults (Age 15 & Above) 1992*	*Illiterate Females 1992*	*Children not in Primary School 1992*	*Malnourished Children under 5 (thousand) 1992*	*Children dying before Age of 5 (thousand) 1992*
High					
24. HONG KONG	0.4	0.3	-		1
Medium Excluding China					
70. IRAN	11.4	7.2	200	4,145	130
97. SRI LANKA	1.2	0.8	-	762	7
Low Excluding India					
128. PAKISTAN	43.8	25.2	-	3,725	687
134. INDIA	271.8	169.9		69,345	3102
151. NEPAL	8.2	4.8	1,100	1,665	99
146. BANGLADESH	46.00	23.1	4,785	11,480	536

Wealth, Poverty, Social Investment

	Income Share lowest 40% Households % 1981-92	*Ratio of highest 20% to lowest 20% 1981-92*	*People in Poverty (%) Urban 1990*	*People in Poverty (%) Rural 1990*	*Social Security benefit expend. (% of GDP) 1985-90*	*Public Expend. on Education (% of GNP) 1990*	*Public Expend. on Health (% of GDP) 1990*
High							
24. HONG KONG	16.2	8.7	-	-	-	3.0	1.1
Med. Excluding							
111. CHINA	17.4	6.5	-	12	3.4	2.3	2.1
134. INDIA	21.3	4.7	38	49	0.5	3.5	1.3

Educational Imbalance **Developing Countries**

	Pupil Teacher Ratio		Secondary Technical Enrolment (% of total Secondary)	Scientists, and Technicians, (per 1000 people)	Public Expenditure on Education (in % of GNP)	Education in % total Government Expenditure	Primary & Secondary Education (as % of all levels)	Higher Education (as % of all levels)
	Primary 1990	Sec. 1990	1988-1991	1988-92	1960-1990	1990	1990	1990
High								
HDI								
24. HONG KONG	27	23	10	-	- 3	17.4	71	29
31. KOREA REP.	34	25	18.6	2.3	2 3.6	22.4	79	7
Medium Excluding China								
107. EGYPT	24	18	20.9	0.8	4.1 6.7	-	70	30
111. CHINA	22	15	9.1	1.6	1.8 2.3	12.4	67	19
Low Excluding India								
128. PAKISTAN	43	19	1.6	0.1	1.1 3.4	-	70	18
134. INDIA	47	-	1.6	0.3	2.3 3.5	11.2	71	17
146. BANGLADESH	63	27	0.7	-	0.6 2.0	10.3	88	9

Demographic Profile

	Estimated Population (million)			Annual Population Growth Rate %		Population Doubling Date (at Current Growth Rate)	Crude Birth Rate	Crude Death Rate	Total Fertility Rate	Contraceptive Prevalence Rate. Any Method (%)
	1960	1992	2000	1960 1992	1992 2000	1992	1992	1992	1992	1986-93
High										
HONG KONG	3.1	5.8	6	2.0	0.4	2118	11.2	5.6	1.2	81
Medium Excluding China										
CHINA	457.5	1183.6	1284.6	1.9	1.0	2054	18.5	7.2	2.0	83
Low Excluding India										
PAKISTAN	56.0	129.3	161.8	8.0	2.8	2016	40.9	9.3	6.2	12
INDIA	442.3	884.4	1022.0	2.2	1.8	2028	29.1	10.0	3.0	43

What is more alarming, however, is that some of the cognitive deficits due to malnutrition may be 'transgenerational' in character. Animal studies show that undernutrition of mother is reflected in the reduced brain weight of its litters. Harlow's work with monkeys adds further evidence in this direction. Social behaviours in monkey reared under deprived condition turned out to be abnormal and this was reflected in the rearing of its own infants. If we generalise it to human level, we tend to conclude that children brought up in deprived condition are at risk in two ways. They are likely to be affected by the malnutrition during pregnancy of the mother, they are likely to grow and stay in the same adverse condition as their mother. The environment and the out come appears to perpetuate itself. This point has been previously brought to the fore by Richards, Richardson and Spears (1976).

Recently, one book *The Bell Curve* (Murray and Herrnstein, 1994) has added to the excitement and controversy about 'cognitive class' and 'cognitive deficiency' related to I.Q. tests. The book is the product of eight years of painstaking research and more than 400,000 copies have been sold and still being sold in large number. Their findings have immediate implication and relevance in the area of employment, education, welfare dependency, illegitimacy, crime and poverty. In their view, U.S.A. is ruled by a "cognitive elite" selected by I.Q. tests, the Scholastic Aptitude Test (SAT) and admitted to top institutions and universities. The large cognitives middle class lies between the I.Q. of 90-100 whereas at the left-hand tail of the normal distribution curve there are 12.5 million people, who are deficient in intellectual capacity, by and large, to go up in employment or social ladder. It does not mean that there are no black Americans with higher I.Q., but the average I.Q. of a black American is found to be less (85) than the whites (100). In other words, there are proportionately more 'dull' and 'very dull' among the coloured people than in whites. The logic of their findings veers towards the inference that I.Q. is largely inherited. Blacks are unlikely to overcome their social pathology, and one should not dream of an equal and integrated society or culture in U.S.A.

Herrnstein had stated earlier that "dumb" people (dull) outbreed "clever" people, and the country is gradually getting divided into two classes—*Cognitive elite*—and the growing sub-class of low I.Q. blacks. People belonging to "Cognitive elite" like business tycoons, political leaders and other professionals are misleading the country by expensive efforts to raise the class of cognitively disadvantaged out of poverty and pursuing similar other policies and programmes—which is a meaningless

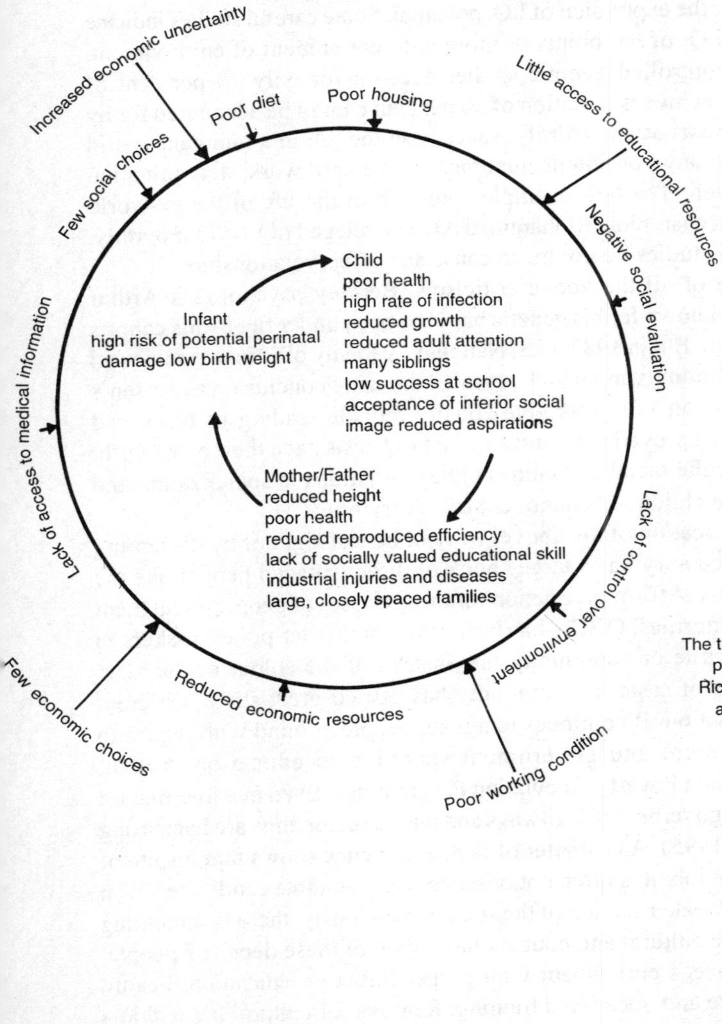

The transgenerational deficits of poor environment
Richards, Richardson and Spears, 1972

exercise. It is not likely to yield any result in the long run. On the contrary, a fierce form of racism may arise in the future.

The above thesis has been said to suffer from many logical contradictions like subscribing to Flynn Effect (rise of 3 points of I.Q. in every decade) and at the same time arguing that there is reduction of I.Q. by dysgenesis among 'dumb' people. The second criticism is that influence of environment cannot be ignored totally. Adequate environment is necessary for the expression of I.Q. potential. Some careful studies indicate increase of I.Q. of ten points or more with enrichment of environment. Even well controlled genetic studies account for only 70 per cent of variation. That means variation of 30 per cent cannot be accounted for by genetic elements at all. Thirdly, success on the job in a mundane world depends on many non-intellectual factors like hard work, determination and motivation. The best example comes from the life of the ex-world Heavyweight champion, Mohammad Ali with alleged I.Q. of 78. Fourthly, correlational studies do not mean cause and effect relationship.

Because of all the above criticisms, Berkley psychologist Arthur Jensen, well-known for his genetic bias, has been under fire by his cohorts time and again. But in 1982, U.S. National Academy of Sciences reviewed his data and findings and which revealed the same conclusion as Jensen's that questions on I.Q. tests give equally reliable reading of black and white ability. It proved substantively that I.Q. tests have their own worth. It cuts across the racial and cultural line. Variations in socialization and upbringing in childhood cannot explain everything.

The implication of the above, will not be lost sight of by discerning people. Our country has a large chunk of disadvantaged people like the Black in U.S.A. Affirmative action for these classes of people—call them S.C./S.T., minorities, OBC—has been taken up by our policy-makers in India along caste or community line instead of the colour of the skin. This criterion of caste or community has caused great stir in different parts of the nation. It continues to agitate people's mind with regard to special treatment and government spending in education, health, employment and Poverty Alleviation Programmes. Even in a free-market economy the government, Railways and public sector units are hamstrung (Mazumdar, 1995). As a matter of fact, experience shows that inspite of reservation on job, it is often not possible to get suitable candidates from the so-called weaker section of the society, Obviously, there is something wanting in the cultural and educational milieu of these deprived people. This milieu needs enrichment with proper thrust on education, health, recreation care and vocational training. Removal of cultural lag within a targeted period will be difficult. It may take decades but the impetus has to be sustained.

Even in the most affluent countries there are pockets of poverty and misery. But removal of poverty, even with adequate social security measures, needs a sound economic infrastructure. The East European countries and the former USSR had taken total care of primary needs of its citizens like food, health-care, education, employment, etc. Yet, inspite of control planning, their economies could not sustain, and everything blew-off like a house of cards when the crunch came in the USSR in 1991. Where is the Poverty Alleviation Programme now in Russia and CIS? Everything has been thrown out of window. An economy has to be activated by increase in production of goods and services. Otherwise, if only crores of rupees are pumped in as welfare measures, it is likely to fuel the inflationary spiral or it may end up in stagflation (stagnant economy with inflationary pressure). Increasing budget deficit will create the same volatility in the money-market as witnessed in the first half of November, 1995 from the end of October, 1995. The present scenario is not only a psycho-social scenario for the weaker section of society, it is more of a reflection of the eco-psycho-social environment.

In this connection a long-term strategy is called for and the then Prime Minister Narasimha Rao's (18 Nov. 1995) call for participation in implementing the Integrated Urban Poverty Eradication Programme covering 345 Class II cities in the country with a population between 50,000 and 100,000 is a step in the right direction. The Centre assisted programme sponsored by the Union Ministry of Urban Affairs and Employment is aimed at preventing the migration of people from villages to urban areas in search of employment under the five-year time-bound programme to be implemented between 1995-2000. An amount of Rs. 6500 crores would be spent. The all-India programme would benefit 47 lac urban poor and with whole town approach, benefit 23.6 million people in these towns.' The programme's chief emphasis will be to encourage underemployed and unemployed urban youth to set-up small micro-enterpreneurs to servicing, petty business and manufacturing for which there is plenty of scope in urban areas.

Another interesting part of programmes at the national level is that it is proposed to establish a National Urban Poverty Eradication Fund in which private enterprises can contribute with tax-saving incentive. The local-bodies covered under the Panchayat Nagar Palika Act, it is claimed, will have a greater role to play in implementation of programme. It has been further announced that during the year 1995-96 an overall investment of Rs. 700 crore would be made available. One can only add a word of caution that mere intention and funding is not good enough in Indian situation. It is the monitoring and implementation part which often go awry. Often the monitoring units do not exist or exist in name alone. Most often these monitoring units are slow to respond or they may have to depend on unreliable data. So is the problem with funding. Funding vested with local bodies must be constituted of men with unimpeachable honesty. It is desirable to associate reputed men from public life or former Govt. professionals who have imagination, foresight, experience and no vested interest except the interest in the alleviation of poverty of the urban poor and weaker section of the society. They need not be hard core activists. Activists have usually emotionally charged tunnel vision. They may miss the wood for trees. A certain amount of objectivity, candour, dispassionate determination and elan is called for. Such men are still available in India, but we are often afraid of utilizing them because their association is likely make a project succeed, and they may tread on too many toes of the vested interest class. Such a blinkered attitude is to be avoided from the very beginning, because once we start with wrong assumptions and implicit perversity, it does not take a long time to corrupt any system beyond redemption. Another factor to consider is the psychology of clientele who are going to be beneficiaries of this programme. Some of them may not be cutout at all for this kind of micro-level enterpreneurship except collecting the project money against five percent of his contribution as margin money.

The psycho-social and economic scenario of the poor or weaker section of society has considerably changed over the last five decades. The changes have been slow but nothing of radical nature has occurred so far. The weaker section has now become more articulate, aggressive and organized under different kinds of leadership. The scheduled caste, scheduled tribe, backward class, other backward class and others constituting the weaker section of society offer a substantial vote-bank to contending political parties in a democratic India. These parties are embroiled at time mores in struggle for power than upliftment of the weaker section. As a result, conflicts, violence and tension is rife. Many of the weaker sections have now become affluent. But their numbers are small. Their relative affluence sometimes elevate them to the position of leadership of being spokesman of the weaker section. Time only will tell when we are going to reach a stable and acceptable level of standard of living so that the stigma of poor is removed. We need to address ourselves also to the question whether our country is to be run by meritocracy or special privileged groups sanctified by constitution, and how to adjust the conflicting interest.

It is a pity that social, psychological and political scientists have very little to say or exercise authority in the allotment of resources for the poor. It is said that their so-called objectives understanding does not lend itself to value judgement, ethics, and morality since science is supposed to be neutral in revealing truth or understanding a phenomenon. Their value-free considerations or views can never ensure total commitment for the success of a programme for the upliftment of the poorer section of people. Because, success of a programme requires committed people with relatively strong value judgement. This is a kind of intellectual impasse—but not unresolvable. Practicality and prediction of an empirical pay-off with certain amount of accuracy may transform a valueless scientist into a value-added scientist in the future.

REFERENCES

Human Development Report (1995). Published for the United Nations Development Programme (UNDP). Delhi : Oxford Press.

Mazumdar, D.P. Sen (1995). *Riddle of Human Potential and Its Use.* Paper read at Seminar on "personnel selection" sponsored by Defence Institute of Psychological Research (DIPR), R and D Organisation, Ministry of Defence. 25-26 Oct., 1995.

Murray. C. and Herrnstein. R. (1994). *Bell Curve*. New York: New York Press.

Rose, S. (1971). Environmental Effect on Brain and Behaviour. I.K. Richardson. D. Spears. M. Richard. (Eds.) *Race. Culture and Intelligence.* Middlesex. England. Penguin Books.

2

The Psycho-Social Scenario of Scavengers and the Role of Sulabh International

Bindeshwar Pathak

Sociologists, social activists and voluntary action groups more often operate on fixed premises while dealing with subjects integrally connected to the welfare and well-being of the weaker sections of society. Discussions on the theme usually border on the considerations of educational and economic well-being; the modalities of empowerment, the flaws in the implementation of the policies and the programmes of the government, the inadequacy of voluntary action and the obvious weaknesses of the welfarist approach towards resolving the problems and predicaments of the weaker and vulnerable of our society. I have no intention of belittling the importance of current discussions on weaker sections of our society, but I do feel that we should first understand and explain the social and psychological context of the oppressed in our midst. That understanding, I believe, should precede the examination of our welfarist orientation to tackling the problems of the weak and vulnerable, dispossessed and the disadvantaged.

Sufferings of Scavengers

Before I develop the central theme of my discussion, let me make a submission. While I am fully conversant with the problems and predicaments of several segments of the weaker sections in our society, I have concentrated all my energy and attention basically to uplift one of the weakest of the weaker sections of society — SCAVENGERS — to be precise. As I have worked for the liberation of scavengers for two and a half decade, I am most qualified to speak about their silent social and psychological sufferings, their trials and tribulations, their problems and predicaments, and finally their disabilities and disappointments. My close understanding of the suffering "psyche" of the scavengers, has indeed helped me to set-up Sulabh International to redeem them from intense social and psychological deprivation, from situations of psychic distress and from the stranglehold of a disabling social context.

In this article, I would mainly deal with the exceedingly poignant existential reality of the scavengers (in effect, their psycho-social scenario), highlighting (a) the agony of the scavengers and (b) the redeeming role of Sulabh International Social Service Organisation.

The Agony of the Scavengers

Scavengers constitute a minuscule minority amongst the Scheduled Caste population, comprising of about 8 to 12 lakh scavengers (figures vary in different official estimates). They are regarded as the weakest in the social and economic sense, because of their lowest position in the caste hierarchy. They are untouchables even amongst the entire array of the untouchables of the scheduled castes. Unlike other Scheduled Castes they are not politically organized, and hence have no political clout. This deprives them of the patronage of any political party. They have no national or State-level organised forum where their needs and aspirations could be effectively articulated and voiced.

Scavengers have been given scant attention by social science scholars in terms of research and writing. While there exist enormous literature on almost all segments of weaker sections in our society —Scheduled Castes, Scheduled Tribes, minorities, women and children— there are few focused writings on scavengers. Their untold miseries have not been extensively documented. However, the writings of Ambedkar (1977), Crook (1986), Fuchs (1981), Ghurye (1957), Issacs (1965), Malkani (1960), Pathak (1991), and Shyam Lal (1984) are of direct relevance in terms of the context and coverage of the problems of scavengers. The report of Seven Commissions/Committees/Task Force appointed by Central and State governments for examining the working and living conditions of scavengers (including their liberation) further augment the information on the subject.

On the basis of the available material on scavenging and scavengers, as also on the basis of my own writings on the subject (see my book—*Road to Freedom : A Sociological Study on the Abolition of Scavenging in India,* 1991), there emerges an agonising scenario — a very pathetic picture about the psycho-social situation of scavengers, depicting a distressing existential reality of their life and living. A few generalised statements will speak about the social status of scavengers:

1. Scavengers constitute an underprivileged social group treated as "Impure" and consequently ritually avoided.
2. Like "Piriah" groups, they are treated as inferior and often regarded as less than human. They live on the fringe of society. Often excluded from social contact, though their services are accepted as highly valuable.
3. They are socially ostracized because of their ritual impurity and for certain peculiar objectionable habits and ritually polluting profession.
4. They are backward, and often oppressed, not because they are racially, socially and culturally inferior than others, but simply because they have been assigned the lowest of the low status in social hierarchy.
5. As outcasts and rejects of the Indian society, scavengers have suffered condemnable human indignities throughout the ages.
6. They have been treated like dreaded contagious disease calling for a disdainful distance and the most minimal social contact.
7. Because of their social degradation, scavengers have been compelled to live their life as socially disadvantaged persons reluctantly resigned to accepting their social degradation and discrimination as part of their fate.
8. Besides social backwardness; scavengers are economically backward too. Most scavenger families, therefore, live in situations of abject poverty because of both structural and personal factors. Structural factors being the low family income on account of engagement in low paying occupation, and personal factors being their large-family size and the male members' indulgence in smoking, drinking and gambling.
9. Most scavengers are illiterate and thus educationally backward. In spite of the facilities for their free education, children are not sent to schools in an overwhelming number of cases, and female education is not considered to be at all important.
10. The economic and educational backwardness has deprived many scavenger families from taking advantage of the constitutionally conferred privileges meant for the welfare of the dispossessed.
11. Politically too, scavengers are little organised as compared to people of other low-born sub-castes, commonly called the disadvantaged sections of society.
12. While in the recent years there has been some change in the traditional occupational structure of the scavengers, a large majority of them is still tied up with traditional hereditary occupations.

The Father of the Nation, Mahatma Gandhi summed up the scavengers' social situation best when he said :

"Socially they are lepers and economically they are worse than slaves".

Mahatma Gandhi was so moved with the agonizing social situation of scavengers that he wrote :

"I may not be born again, but if happens, I would like to be born in the family of scavengers so that I may relieve them of the inhuman, unhealthy and hateful practice of carrying nightsoil".

Here, I would also like to reproduce certain excerpts from my own writings on scavengers. These would illustrate their agony and sum-up their social and psychological distresses.

1. "To be sure, scavengers have always been Harijans among Harijans, the poorest among the poor. This has been the continuing fact of Indian social life and has remained unchanged".
2. "The scavengers need not be introduced; we know them but refuse to mention their names. We quietly dismiss them at the backdoors after flinging at them the day's left over of the kitchen. In small towns, these mysterious figures materialise in the dark shadows early in the morning; stealthily scurring between lanes and by-lanes, cleaning dry latrines and collecting human excreta on the head to the tankers which cart it away to disposal spots".
3. "The social degradation of scavengers is revolting to the conscience of any civilized society which is set wondering if in the past there had been any cruelty more hurting to the dignity of man than scavenging which is practised in India without flinch or apology".
4. "Scavenging has many linkage — social, economic, historical and attitudinal. These have to be snapped one by one before last of the scavengers is freed and rehabilitated in other professions".
5. "Socially, scavengers are untouchables among untouchables. They are completely sealed off from the mainstream of social life. The law (Articles 17 and 42 of the Constitution and the Protection of Civil Rights Act, 1955) does not help in this respect at all. The sporadic attempts of private persons, or social organizations have not changed the situation either. The question of social acceptability is not a matter of law; it is an attitudinal problem which has to be solved differently".
6. "The problem of liberating scavengers is too big to be solved with efforts that are inadequate and sporadic. It is time to organise our national efforts and energy in order to abolish scavenging once and for all. The nation must pool all its resources and borrow, if necessary,

from international lending agencies to obliterate this stigma from Indian society which hurts our claim to civility and culture".

7. "The scavengers go about practising their profession of carrying human excreta on the head, generation after generation, without protest or representation to the power that be. They have no forum, no union, nor any caste leader to plead for their salvation. These are the defenseless people, almost perpetually waiting for a redeemer, who does not seem to be coming".
8. "In no other country scavenging is amalgamated with the evil structure of caste and untouchability as is the case in India. The communities engaged in scavenging are at the lowest bottom of the social hierarchy. Caught in the quagmire of miserable working and living conditions, they reside in separate localities, segregated from the main settlements".
9. "Notwithstanding the socialistic rhetoric of our politicians, scavengers do not have full access to the state-sponsored welfare schemes, either due to official apathy or their locational isolation".
10. "Although the eradication of scavenging and rehabilitation of scavengers have now been included in the revised 20-point programme, the approach of the authorities to the problem remains muddled".

National Concern on Scavenging

The national concern on scavenging was expressed in number of the reports of the Government appointed Commissions/Committees right from the days of independence. Reports have expressed anguish on the working and living conditions of the scavengers, voiced strong sentiments on the question of untouchability, caste differentiation, the age-long suppression, privations and afflictions suffered by scavengers. The report of a Committee of the National Labour Commission on the Working and Service Condition of Sweepers and Scavengers (1968-69) went to the extent of saying that "a section of humanity should be condemned to such degrading condition is a slur on our culture and disgrace to our society." Both Indira Gandhi and Rajiv Gandhi had condemned the practice as inhuman and degrading. They had resolved to undertake a planned programme to eradicate this national disgrace as early as possible.

While there is no denying the fact that some significant work has been done in the post-independent india, especially after the commencement of the Gandhi centenary year, in respect of liberating the scavengers from the social bondage, the problem, without doubt, persists as a continuing disgrace for the nation. Many welfare schemes launched by the Ministry of Welfare, Government of India (National Scheme of Liberation and Rehabilitation of Scavengers (1992) and the appointment of National Commission of Safai Karamcharis, have not made much significant dent into the problem. The latest Annual Report of the Ministry of Welfare, Government of India (1994-95) admits this fact. In reference to the National Scheme for the Liberation and Rehabilitation of Scavengers the Report says : "While the Scheme has been in operation for the last three years, the progress is extremely dismal barring few exceptions. Even the survey of scavengers is still not complete" notwithstanding the fact that survey conducted in many States suffers from several deficiencies.

The evaluation studies made to assess the impact of these governmental programmes revealed that the efforts have fallen short of what is really required to liberate the scavengers, mainly because of the absence of priority to the programmes in the Government's planning process. The studies have revealed that despite the emphasis by all political leaders and efforts made by the Government since independence, and inclusion of eradication of scavenging in the revised 20-point programme of 1986, not much tangible improvement could be made.

The Contribution of Sulabh International

Sulabh International Social Service Organisation (formerly, Sulabh Shauchalaya Sansthan), a NGO, set up in 1970 at Patna, Bihar to eradicate manual scavenging and improve the environmental sanitation, shares the credit of devising and popularising a low-cost sanitation technology known as Sulabh Shauchalaya. The Sulabh technology has offered a viable alternative to scavenging. The hand-flush pit privy represents an innovation in the field of low-cost sanitation in India. The toilets built on Sulabh technology do not require the services of scavengers and thus free them from a defiling occupation. With the advent of this technology, more than 700,000 bucket privies have been converted into Sulabh Shauchalayas so far, and about 37,000 scavengers have been relieved from their defiling and degrading hereditary occupation, and have been settled in other jobs.

Sulabh International Social Service Organisation in its journey of more than two-and-half decades has now expanded its area of operation, and has assumed the shape of a social movement. The Sulabh Movement, as it is known now, is a nation-wide movement in the area of low-cost sanitation, liberation of scavengers, social transformation, upgradation of the down-trodden, prevention of environmental pollution, creation of non-conventional source of energy, training of change-agents for voluntary action and diffusion of innovations for promoting inexpensive and affordable technology in sanitation, health, hygiene and rural development. Like other important social movements in India, the ideology of Sulabh Movement is rooted in the ideas and ideals of Mahatma Gandhi and other renowned social reformers of the country. The integration of the socially ostracized people of low-castes, especially the scavengers, into the mainstream of modern Indian society colours the ideology of Sulabh Movement.

The major ideological stands of Sulabh Movement are :

1. Removal of inequitions caste structure
2. Elimination of social discriminations
3. Abolition of the abhorrent practice of untouchability
4. Social upgradation and mainstreaming of the down-trodden
5. Conferring self-respect and dignity on such sections of society who are economically marginalised and socially and culturally backward
6. Fight against social evils which divide people on narrow considerations of caste and creed
7. Rejection of caste identity and consciousness and appeal to adopt a rational approach on issues connected with broader intents and purposes of social integration.

Sulabh Movement has successfully completed its social mandate by liberating 37,000 scavengers. The movement has succeeded in its social transformation endeavours by adopting a two pronged approach : introduction of appropriate technology and initiation of a social upgradation programme of reformist nature. The mass movement has now spread all over the country with a cadre of 35,000 Sulabh Volunteers in nineteen states and two Union Territories, catering to low-cost sanitation requirements in 999 towns.

With the conversion of 700,000 bucket latrines into scavenging free Sulabh Shauchalayas in individual households, 269 towns have been made scavenging free. Sulabh has already built and maintains 3,000 public toilets and bath complexes. These are being used by about ten million people everyday.

While Sulabh's contribution to the low-cost sanitation is unparalleled, its accomplishments in the liberation and rehabilitation of scavengers and their wards have been nationally and internationally recognised. The endeavours of Sulabh International in respect of scavengers fall under the following heads :

(A) Training and Rehabilitation

For the training and rehabilitation of the sons and daughters of scavengers, Sulabh started three training institutes, one each in the state of Bihar, Maharashtra and Rajasthan. The Institutes impart training in different trades — tailoring, mechanics, typing, driving, manufacture of cane materials, manufacture of leather goods, latrine pan manufacturing, carpentry, electrician and TV repairs. Through Sulabh's training and rehabilitation programme, about four thousand children of scavengers have been trained to take up economically rewarding occupations. Most of them have been employed in the formal and informal sectors of business and industry. Sulabh International has also formulated a scheme for the self-employment of the youths trained from its three Institutes with the financial and technical support from the Government of India.

(B) Sulabh Public School

Realising that education is a key to human development, Sulabh has set-up a school, first of its kind, in Delhi to provide quality education to the children of scavenger families and to those belonging to other socio-economically weaker sections of society. The school can be matched with any other school for the children of the elite groups. But the merit of the school lies in not being an elite educational institution, which are too many in the country, it lies in breaking the tradition of setting up the Government run school that impart inferior education to the children of the weaker sections of society.

The Sulabh School in Delhi is a pace-setting institution. It intends to equip the traditionally disadvantaged sections of society with the instrument of education (a real social leveler) for their upward social mobility in the emerging class structure. By opening up the gates of the school to the children on non-scavenger families the school avoids segregation. This has been done with a definite purpose to enable the children of scavenger families mix freely with the children of the higher castes and grow up as equals in society.

(C) Social Upgradation Programme

To further widen the outreach of the programme for the liberation of scavengers, Sulabh has embarked upon a novel strategy of scavengers' social upgradation. The central idea behind the strategy is that liberation from an unclean occupation is not enough; what is essential in the assimilation of scavengers in the social mainstream. The strategy entails frequent organising of inter-caste, inter-community get-togethers, eating and socialising with liberated scavengers, holding of seminars and conferences to generate public opinion.

(D) Social Adoption Programme

A very significant dimension of Sulabh Movement is its recent programme of persuading the nation's elites to select one scavenger family each for social interaction. This programme is consistent with the Movement's overall strategy of social absorption of scavengers. The national and international print media had hailed this programme as a landmark, and a novel concept. In a write-up captioned — Elite Adoptions, *Indian Express,* (April 16, 1994) referred to the programme "as an attempt to undo the social injustice done to Balmikis (the scavengers)". One such elite adopter, the noted Supreme Court Lawyer, Sri Lalit Bhasin, said, "the idea of adoption by the elite is revolutionary. Of course, things progress at a snails pace, but some one has to take the lead. And Dr. Pathak did". Another elite adopter, Dr. (Mrs) Chitra Naik, the Member of Planning Commission, said, "The idea of this kind of adoption is obviously a positive step. It would help in socially redefining images."

The lower-castes would no longer remain at the fringe but would be incorporated and accepted into the advanced society.

Sulabh's adoption programme answers the question whether after liberation, training and education, scavengers and their children will enjoy social respectability and status in society at par with the so-called upper caste people of India? By linking scavenger families to persons committed to their welfare, the intention is not only to provide them a status, but also to inspire others to shed social prejudices and embrace scavengers as their equals. This programme is an attempt to undo the social injustice done to the members of the scavenging caste. The programme is of critical significance because scavenging is not entirely a problem of money technology and law to solve. It is also a cultural and attitudinal problem which begins in the minds of men. Hence, through persuasion, it seeks to link defenseless scavengers to eminent people so as to enable the social outcast fight the battle for social justice with the support of the elites families whose most important obligation is to work in their own quiet ways to end this inhuman practice and save society from being split into another hostile class. The response to Sulabh's appeal has been fairly encouraging and the programme has taken off very well. So far 5,000 scavenger families have been adopted by high caste people, including judges, advocates, journalists, Members of Parliaments, Ministers at the Central level, the businessmen and academics.

Conclusion

The Sulabh Movement is a well-organized institutional attempt to change society through reforms, education and persuasion to restore human dignity to the under-privileged people, especially to about half a million scavengers who still physically clean and carry human excreta. The Movement seeks to achieve reforms through non-militant modes and methods. The reform it tries to seek is backed by social, economic, educational and technological measures, as well as by ameliorative programmes and policies of the Government. The technological measures comprise of low-cost sanitation technology as devised, developed and implemented by Sulabh International. The ameliorative measures comprise of efforts made by governmental and non-governmental organisations working for the elimination of manual scavenging and the liberation of scavengers and their wards from cleaning and carrying human excreta. The Movement's agenda of action also includes rehabilitation of liberated scavengers in gainful employment after training, their social upgradation, opening up of residential schools for providing quality education to the children of scavengers, prevention of environmental pollution caused by open-air defecation, energy from human waste and integrated rural and human resource development. The Gandhian principles and precepts provide an ideological backbone in Sulabh Movement, justify its operational perspective and facilitate mobilization of Sulabh volunteers for purposes of collective action.

The Sulabh Movement is essentially a reformist movement. It is a movement against iniquitous caste structure, social discrimination and untouchability. It seeks social upgradation of scavengers, bestowal of full religious rights to the untouchables, social absorption (social mainstreaming) self-respect for scavengers within the Hindu fold, breaking of social barriers between numerous castes and fight against several evils in religious customs and caste practices. The movement is an answer to the unfulfilled desire of Mahatma Gandhi, who wanted liberation of scavengers from social bondage.

3

Psycho-Social Well-being of Scavengers

Akbar Hussain **and** ***M.G. Husain***

In Indian society scavenging has never been a voluntary occupation. A particular section of the society was called *Chandal* or *Bhangi* who performed the tasks of scavenging under the dictates of tradition and later on sacred sanctions. Irrespective of the religion followed scavenging is demeaning occupation. Scavenging an age-old occupation existed from early historical time. Scavenging was done by a particular hereditary group known as *Chandals*. This was an enslaved group dictated to do scavenging work generation after generation and thus scavenging became a hereditary occupation.

On the other hand in western countries there was no specific class or group of scavengers. Scavenging was done on voluntary basis and for serving self-interests. The rural population used night soil as manure. From villages they brought commodities for selling or supplying them to urban people and before returning to the village they collected the night soil in the containers meant for the purpose and took human excreta to the rural areas for the fertilization purpose. But in India the situation was different. Most of the people lived in villages do not need night soil deposited in the urban habitats to be used as manure. The rural people defecated in the field and the night soil deposited was converted into good manure. In this way problem of producing night soil did not arise in Indian rural areas. Hence scavenging was required for the disposal of night soil defecated inside the service latrines in the urban habitat. It was difficult to take up the work voluntarily. Thus the job of cleaning lanes, roads, removing dead animals, cleaning garbage and night soil was allowed to a particular section of people who were initially defeated by Aryans. It is just possible that in course of time due to being associated with dirty and inferior jobs they were declared as polluted and it was believed that those who will be touched by them would also become polluted. Hence they were restrained and forbidden from coming into physical touch with the members of the ruling race and gradually they became untouchable.

Referring to this fact Bindeshwar Pathak (1991) has pointed out "the scavengers were placed at the lowest rung of the caste ladder. The nature of job or work traditionally associated with them, or imposed upon them pushed them to the lowest stratum of the social hierarchy of exterior castes. The task of cleaning night soil was the most inferior job because this involved the touching of human excreta by the scavengers. Consequently they did not get social justice and the humane treatment. Being economically poor and socially backward, they could neither revolt against the unjust sanctions nor could get rid of the scavenging works". The magnitude of the problem is also reflected from the following observations made by the famous daily *'Indian Express'*, New Delhi in its issue of September 24 ,1980. "The primitive methods of removing human excreta still being used in India are a disgrace to the country".

It appears from the above remarks that the condition of scavengers is most pathetic and miserable. After viewing the pathetic condition of scavengers and the treatment they receive from people at large, interest generated in the mind of the researchers to examine the psycho-social status of the scavengers. These status can be understood by their level of development on psychological and social indicator of well-being.

The psychological development or well-being has only one prominent sign. It speaks of a mind that is peaceful and quiet (Krishnamurti, 1986). According to Hindu thought well-being unfolds at three levels, namely, cognitive, conative and affective. At the cognitive level it has to be realised that the source of all the problems is within the self and one has to recognize the lustful inclination of the self-haunted by desires and heading for attachment. At the conative level a person's well-being will manifest in performance of duty and fulfillment of one's wordly obligations. At the affective level there has to be the expansion of the self beyond the ego and dawning of the finest form of humility.

Similarly it is argued that a socially sensitive person would be a socially developed individual. In other words, having a liberal, accepting, fair and sympathetic attitude towards certain larger social issues could be a pointer to an individual's social maturity and socially developed outlook. Social sensitivity speaks of a particular humane quality namely, empathy for other people and indicates concern for problems at the societal level.

A socially sensitive person has potentials for evolving into a selfless person who may offer his/her services for the common good.

Development that addresses to human beings must include an indicator that refers to happiness in interpersonal relationship. The social support available at home buffers all kinds of real and psychological stresses and strains that the individual might suffer while making frantic efforts for acquiring material prosperity, successful social life and personal achievements.

In sum, an individual who experiences satisfaction in interpersonal relationship with the family members, is likely to be happy and enjoy a better quality of life. On the other hand the scope for his/her overall development and psychological well-being becomes more promising in such favourable circumstances.

Thus, to know the mental health and social interaction of the scavengers the study was designed to assess their psychological as well as social well-beings.

Methodology

Sample

200 scavengers (100 males and 100 females) were selected from different localities of Patna by using purposive method of sampling. Out of which 100 were Hindus and 100 Muslims.

Tools

Two questionnaires by Varma and Husain (1990) were used for measuring psychological and social development.

Results and Discussion

Obtained scores were analysed separately for each group (Hindu, Muslim, Males, Females) and for each of the scales by computing, mean, S.D. and 't'. The results are presented in the tables to follow :

Table 1

Results of 't' between Mean Psychological and Social Well-being of Hindu-Muslim Scavengers.

Well-being	*Mean* (Hindus)	*S.D.* (Hindus)	*Mean* (Muslims)	*S.D.* (Muslims)	*'t'*
Psychological Well-being	66.98	8.29	67.85	9.13	0.99
Social Well-being	34.11	8.01	33.55	2.85	0.87

Table 2

Results of 't' between Mean Psychological and Social Well-being of Male and Female Scavengers.

Well-being	Mean	S.D.	Mean	S.D.	't'
	Male		Females		
Psychological Well-being	67.92	8.12	66.91	9.01	0.92
Social Well-being	34.06	8.11	33.60	7.79	0.88

After groupwise analysis of the data it was found that Muslim scavengers were little superior to their Hindu counterparts with regard to their psychological development (Mean = 67.85 and 66.98 respectively). So far as the social well-being or development was concerned the finding was reverse (Table 1). In this case Hindus group had little dominance over the Muslim scavengers (Mean = 34.11 and 35.55 respectively).

Similarly, it was also evident from the results (Table 2) that males groups had edge over the female scavengers on both measurements of development (psychological and social). However, none of the differences either between Hindu and Muslim scavengers or between male and female scavengers was found statistically significant (t = .99 and .87; and .92 and .88 >.05 respectively).

On the basis of above findings it can be said that scavengers in general were not found to be as much socially developed as they were psychologically. Their level of psychological satisfaction or well-being was higher than that of social satisfaction. It indicates that scavengers were neither mentally dissatisfied with their occupation nor they perceive their occupation as much derogatory as other people think. But it is society which creates problem for them. It is generally observed that society not only had negative feelings towards the scavengers rather it perceives them as untouchable and subhuman. Because of this feeling scavengers perceive themselves as alienated and disregarded section of society that leads to sense of dissatisfaction in their social life.

On the other hand it can also be said that the quality of life or psycho-social well-being of scavengers were almost similar irrespective of their relation or sex. Marginal differences were found between the psycho-social development of Hindu and Muslim and also between male and female scavengers. It indicated that scavengers as a whole denote a particular class or caste. They all perceive their job in a particular way and get similar treatment from other sections of society.

Thus, it can be concluded that scavengers were not as much psychologically unhealthy as they were socially deprived and rejected. They had higher psychological satisfaction than social satisfaction irrespective of their caste, religion and sex.

REFERENCES

Indian Express (1980). 24 September, Delhi edition.

Krishnamurti, J. (1956). *Commentaries on living,* Rajgopal, D. (Ed.), New Delhi: B.J. Publications.

Pathak, Bindeshwar. (1991). *Road to Freedom : A Sociological Study of Scavenging in India,* New Delhi.

Verma. J. and Hussain, A. (1990), Collectivism as correlate of Indigenous Development', ICSSR Project Report, New Delhi.

4

Quality of Life of Scheduled Caste and High Caste Youths

Md. Rafique Alam

The quality of life is a composite measure of the physical, mental and social well-being, happiness and satisfaction of an individual and as such is a multi-faceted concept dealing with a range of factors such as health, marriage, family, work, financial situation, educational opportunities, self-esteem, creativity, sense of belonging and trust. Very often terms like subjective well-being, happiness, life satisfaction and quality of life are used interchangeably. Cutter (1986) stated that quality of life is broadly defined as an individual's happiness or satisfaction with life and environment including needs and desires, aspirations, life-style, preferences and other tangible and intangible factors which determine overall well-being. When an individual's quality of life is aggregated to the community level, the concept is linked to existing social and environmental conditions, such as economic activity, climate or the quality of cultural institutions (Campbell *et al* 1970).

India is committed to provide better quality of life to her every citizen. The Preamble of the Constitution of India prescribes that the people of the country would try to secure (i) social, economic and political justice, (ii) liberty of thought, expression, belief, faith and worship, (iii) equality of status and of opportunity, and (iv) a sense of fraternity to assure the dignity of the individual and the unity of the nation. According to Article 14 of the Constitution the state shall not deny to any person equality before the law or the equal protection of laws within Indian territory. Article 15 prohibits discrimination on grounds of religion, race, caste, sex or place of birth. No citizen can, on any of these grounds, be subjected to any disability or restriction with regard to access to shops, public restaurants, hotels and places of public entertainment and resort or the use of wells, tanks, bathing ghats, roads maintained by state funds. Article 16 guarantees equality of opportunity in matters of public appointment. But there are specific exemptions. A legislature can make special provisions for women and children, for the advancement of socially and educationally backward classes and for Scheduled Castes and Tribes. The Parliament may limit employment under a state or local authority to the local residents. Under Article 42, the States may also provide for reservations in appointments to posts for backward classes. In spite of these constitutional provisions, the state is unable to protect and provide justice to many members of the weaker sections, who are victim of riot, arson, loot, rape, molesting and killings.

Psychology as a discipline is most competent to deal with behavioural dimensions of weaker sections. While other aspects are neither ignored nor their importance minimized, it should be emphasized that ignoring the psychological variables may lead ameliorative programmes to unexpected and undesirable consequences. Understanding the psychological characteristics of the weaker sections is as important as the analysis of the system that brought in the condition of weaker position .

For psychology, the phenomenon can best be viewed in ecological perspective. The economic and socio-cultural environment of the weaker section is characterized by low income, inequality, socio-cultural disadvantage arising from his (her) position in terms of class and caste hierarchy. These disadvantages take the form of familial deprivation, early separation from family, illiteracy or inadequate schooling, low educational level of parents, inadequate housing such as residence in slums or remote rural areas. These factors cumulatively give rise to a phenomenon of extreme deficit.

Sinha (1979) holds that, the psychological problems of the weaker sections of society — the underprivileged, backward classes, the Scheduled Castes and Tribes—which largely constitute the poor can be viewed in terms of concentric layers of ecology. For example, general poverty and the attendant congestions of living space, the limitations and roles enjoined by caste, and the meagre facilities provided by the civic authorities to these areas can be viewed as the surrounding layer of ecology. The condition and facilities prevalent at home, the role relationships prevalent therein, and the activities encouraged or discouraged would constitute the outer and visible layer of ecology. Similarly, the conditions of the school and the nature and quality of schooling, as well as the nature of the child's peer groups would be regarded as other factors of outer layer of ecology. The contrast between both layers of ecology is easily understood by comparing children from caste-Hindu families with those from the Scheduled Caste families. For centuries, the Scheduled Castes have been living under conditions of intense social disadvantages and prevented from sharing in the mainstream of socio-cultural and economic life of the Hindu Society. The socio-culture disadvantages under which the weaker sections exist is referred to by Indian psychologists as cultural deprivation (Sinha,1979).

Whiteman *et al.* (1968) have observed that social deprivation implies that the association between social grouping and specific environmental factors is not directly causal, but is mediated by more basic societal conditions such as unemployment, poverty, and inequality of opportunity in various areas.

Chatterjee (1980) has reported that social-economic conditions exercise a powerful impact upon children's cognitive functioning, or achievements in school subjects. However, it becomes complicated producing somewhat different outcomes in rural and urban areas.

Singh *et al.* (1980) argue that poverty and prejudice are the two sides of the coin of social disadvantage, one economic and other social. They distort and prevent the development and growth of the potentialities of the individual. Most important indices of social disadvantage are low income, low caste, tribe status, female sex and rural residence. Social disadvantage adversely affects intelligence and academic achievement in direct proportion . Even when intelligence is matched, social disadvantaged children are academically inferior to the advantaged ones. The parental support significantly influences the academic achievement of the child and even compensates for certain lack of I Q points.

Tripathi and Pande (1976) found that Scheduled Caste students perceive their school climate more supportive in minority school rather than in majority school. Scheduled caste students in majority school showed low need for achievement, poor academic self-concept, high fear of failure and unrealistic aspirations as compared to Scheduled Caste students in minority school. Teachers expected better academic performance from students belonging to Non-Scheduled Caste as compared to Scheduled Caste.

Rath *et al.* (1972) have studied intellectual and other cognitive manifestations of three groups of children in Orissa. These groups consisted of samples taken from the student population belonging to three castes i.e., the Brahmin, the Scheduled Tribe and the Scheduled Caste children studying together in the same class. The results indicated that with regard to intelligence, Brahmin children were highest, followed by Scheduled Tribe and Scheduled Caste children, respectively. The results of concept formation test showed that Brahmin children were superior to the other two groups.

Many other studies on cognitive and intellectual consequence of poverty have indicated that apart from economic deprivation, the poor are also the victims of many socio-cultural disadvantages whose psychological consequences are harmful. Misra (1977) remarks that ecological factors provide the source and variety for sensory stimulation and thereby enriching or impoverishing the experiential content of the individual. It has been suggested that all the deficiencies are due to the ecocultural factors that surround the poor.

According to Shukla and Singh (1974) socio-economic status, caste, age, nature of schooling facilities and rural-urban background play important roles in shaping cognitive abilities. In the lower age groups the scores of higher castes and the Scheduled Castes were similar if not slightly in favour of the Scheduled Castes. But with advancing age and years of schooling the differences got reversed, and accentuated in favour of higher castes, producing a kind of 'broomstick' or 'torchlight' effect.

Many researchers have suggested that poverty produces some motivational and personality characteristics that result in various kinds of inadequacies (Coleman1971; Bronfenbrenner 1974; Bee 1974; Adams 1963; Alam 1992). The socially disadvantaged children are characterized by low need for achievement and low educational and vocational aspirations. They are pessimistic, and indifferent to their future. Various studies confirm that these tendencies are found in both western and Indian societies.

Maslow (1970) has stated that under conditions of deprivation deficiency needs usually predominate, but after they have been met satisfactorily, human beings become more concerned with meeting higher-order needs. Deprivation keeps individuals more occupied with meeting deficiency needs, and that their higher needs would not get adequate opportunities for proper growth.

Bee (1974) has argued that the need for achievement is influenced by a capacity for taking pride in accomplishment, which is socially learnt. The social disadvantaged group does not learn this capacity and is unable to judge its performance by internalized standards of excellence. Coleman (1971) has reported that the poor Negro boys had internalized a most effective mechanism for self-discouragement. They were 'socialized to self-imposed failure'. He also observed that the low need for achievement was related to perceptions of low parental acceptance and high parental punitiveness..

It has been generally found that Scheduled Caste and Scheduled Tribe students have a strong tendency to refer success to external factors (God, fate, kindness of teachers, etc.). They are thankful for their beneficience rather than ascribe success to their own ability and efforts and thus take pride in their accomplishment and experience a sense of fulfilment, which would be reinforcing to their behaviour. This externalization of success factor reduces its reinforcing value. The mediating mechanism that they adopt of ascribing success to external agencies frequently leads to superstitious behaviour, perpetuation of fatalistic outlook, and produces superstitious ritualism, i.e., performing the same rites before undertaking a big task. It also sometimes leads to the ingratiation of the significant others (Sinha 1979).

Rath (1974) has reported significantly low aspiration levels for income, occupation and education of the poor and under privileged tribal students in comparison to those of higher castes. There was also a high and significant positive correlation between the low aspiration of the parents and their school going children of lower caste and tribal groups. It was contended that aspirations of children were nothing other than internalized projections of similar aspirations of their parents.

Sinha (1969) has found that the residents of highly backward and undeveloped villages when compared with those from the advanced villages, were overwhelmingly concerned with immediate needs of subsistence and had static levels of aspiration. They frequently construed their hopes and aspirations in fanciful and unrealistic terms and were unable to conceptualize the needs under a wider frame of reference of a village community or a country. Their behaviour was characterized by extreme caution, absence of risktaking and failure avoidance.

Pareek (1970) psychologically defines poverty in terms of deprivation and helplessness and elaborates the motivational pattern induced by it. Apart from orientation to helplessness and feeling of powerlessness, he suggests a paradigm of culture of poverty, that is, poverty as a structural component produces a three-fold motivational pattern characterized by low need for achievement, low need for extension and high need for dependency. He contends that dependency motivation is expressed through lack of initiative, avoidance syndrome, excessive fear of failure, seeking favours of superior, overconformity and aggressive rejection of authority. This dependency is often reflected in over dependence on governmental and other external agencies and almost total lack of self-help.

Numerous foreign and Indian studies have shown a negative relationship between social disadvantage and academic achievement (Rath, 1974; Coleman, 1971; Shukla *et al.* 1974; Sinha, 1979; Bee, 1974; Chatterjee, 1980). The poor academic performance of the socially disadvantaged children is the cummulative result of a large number of obstructing and handicapping factors in their personality, families, schools and the larger society.

Some studies have examined the relationship of academic achievement with self-concept and some personality traits. Since there are social class differences in self-concept and personality traits, these studies become relevant to our discussion of social disadvantage and academic achievement. It has been found that high self-esteem enhances academic achievement, because characteristics such as sense of responsibility, self-assurance and conscience strengthen academic motivation. There is positive correlation between intelligence, achievement and environmental conditions. Over-achieving sdudents had better self-concept than the under-achieving ones. Some studies have reported linear relationship between positive self-concept and academic achievement, some have shown curvilinear relationship while others have shown no relationship at all. On the whole, there seems to be a clear tendency of linear relationship between positive self-concept and academic achievement (Whiteman *et al.* 1968; Singh *et al.* 1980; Tripathi *et al.* 1976).

Indian and foreign researchers have examined the relationship of social disadvantage and personality traits, psychiatric disorders, crime and delinquency. It has been found that lower social class, low caste, Scheduled Castes and Tribes are more prone to mental illness. Coleman (1971) has reported eight times higher rate of incidence of schizophrenia in low socio-economic class. The patients from lower socio-economic group spend longer time in the hospital than those from higher socio-economic group. Hussain (1985) found a positive relationship between personality adjustment and socio-economic status even when intelligence, family size, parents' income, education, age, and age of the child were controlled. There was better adjustment (home, health, social, emotional and overall) in the high socio-economic group.

Alam (1981) has observed that socio-economic status is related with neuroticism, psychoticism and anxiety. Subjects of low socio-economic status were high on neuroticism, psychoticism and anxiety. The poor were found to be more anxious. Rath (1974) has also reported higher incidence of psychopathic traits like neuroticism and insecurity in low caste group than in high caste ones. The fantasies of adolescent boys and girls from low socio-economic status reflected anxiety, aggression, punishment, depression as dominant themes. The adolescent boys from low socio-economic status were characterized by high sensitivity, anxiety, sleep difficulties and neurasthenic tendencies. Social disadvantage has also been found to be associated with crime and delinquency. Delinquency is associated with broken homes. Parental absence and inadequacy resulting from poverty contributes to delinquency (Coleman, 1971). Hassan (1975) found negative correlation between socio-economic status and prejudice. He has also reported positive correlations between religious and caste prejudices and between prejudice and conservative social attitudes. He further observed that prejudice was positively correlated with attitudes to family, social customs, and politics.

Bronfenbrenner (1974) has shown social class differences in familial conditions, child-rearing practices, parent-child interactions, parental roles and value system. These differences have been related to attitudinal and personality differences in the children from low and high socio-economic status. Socialization is the intervening and mediating variable between the socio-economic conditions and their psychological consequences. He has reported that the middle class parents are more receptive, egalitarian in their relationship with their children and more accessible to them than the lower class parents. In lower social class the repressive and the indulgent patterns of upbringing alternate which make the child confused and ambivalent to parents. The husbands are more dominant in upper class, the wives are more dominant in lower class, and there seems to be equality of status in the middle class. The upper class parents emphasize on the internalization of values of honesty, self-control, consideration and curiosity. The working class mothers emphasize conformity whereas upper-class mothers emphasize child's growth and development, affection and satisfaction. In middle class families, compared to lower class, there is more emphasis on independence in early childhood, higher expectations of academic achievement and greater belief in the availability of success.

Yarrow (1972) has reported that the high incidence of father-absence among the lower class families contributes to the ineffective and faulty socialization of the child and harms their personality development. He pointed out that a father-deprived child particularly a male child, lacks a masculine model to identify with. The child shows more underlying faminine traits and tries to compensate for it by demonstrating extreme masculinity. He is characterized by immature dependency and impulsiveness.

Father-absence also influences language development. It has been found that boys who identify with mothers are poor performers on differential analytic tasks. Bernstein (1964) has demonstrated interfacing of language with other forms of social behaviour and association of social class differential with linguistic skills. He shows that the linguistic code developed by the poor is restricted, relatively undifferentiated, simplex, lacking in modifiers, implicit and aimed at reinforcing and implementing the social structure rather than conveying information. In contrast, the linguistic code of middle and upper class strata is elaborated.

The relationship of deprivation with cognitive, motivational and personality development has also been examined. The tragedy of the deprived child perhaps begins with his conception. Deprived mother is likely to be malnourished. She does not get pre-natal care available to mothers in upper socio-economic status. Nor does she receive proper post-natal care. Like the mother, the child is also malnourished and does not receive the necessary careful handling during birth and afterwards. Therefore, the present study was undertaken with a view to measure the effects of residence and caste on the quality of life.

Methodology

Sample

The sample comprised 200 undergraduate male students (100 urban comprising 50 high caste and 50 Scheduled Caste and 100 rural comprising 50 high caste and 50 Scheduled Caste) selected through stratified random sampling technique from the urban and rural colleges of the Patna district. The mean age of the subjects was 18.5 and SD 4.3.

Design

The study was conducted using 2X2 factorial design. The two independent variables studied were varied at two levels each, i.e., urban and rural, and high caste and Scheduled Caste. Subjects were equally distributed in the four cells. The different dimensions of quality of life as measured by Quality of Life Scale served as dependent variable in the study.

Tools

Personal Data Sheet

Informations regarding residence and caste were collected through personal data sheet.

Quality of Life Scale

Yousuf's (1994) quality of life scale was administered. The quality of life scale consists of 197 items in Hindi. It has been developed on the basis of some a-priori clusters. These a-priori clusters were generated, adopted and developed on the basis of interviews, discussions and literature review. A set of 31 a-priori clusters were developed. These are: (1) health and quality of food intake, (2) material and financial securities, (3) physical health and personal safety, (4) perceiving oneself physically and mentally competent and equal to others, (5) relation with parents, (6) relation with siblings, (7) relation with close friends, (8) offering help to friends and others, (9) activities related to helping or encouraging other people, (10) activities related to forming or contributing in any formal organization, (11) activities related to solving the problems of cripple, (12) activities related to State (local) or Central Government, (13) personal education, (14) intellectual development, (15) personal planning, (16) occupational role, (17) need for learning and doing quality work, (18) personal understanding, (19) personal expression, (20) creative ability, (21) sharing joy with family members, (22) socializing, (23) passive recreational activities, (24) observing recreational activities outside home, (25) participatory recreational activities, (26) active recreational activities, (27) duration of marriage and number of dependents, (28) relation with spouse, (29) age of the respondent at the birth of first child, (30) actual and expected family size, and (31) having and raising children.

On an average the interview took about fifty minutes. For eliciting responses a binary response pattern has been considered appropriate. Some of the items are negatively worded to counter response set. Its high correlations with other scales, indicate its meaningfulness and reasonable degree of construct validity. In this scale higher the score means better quality of life and vice versa.

Procedure

Each respondent was contacted individually at his house or at the testing centre depending upon the mutual convenience of the investigator and the respondent. Both the tools required approximately one hour to complete. First of all personal data sheet was administered and then respondents were asked to respond to each of the statement of the quality of life scale.

Results

Data was analyzed keeping in mind the objectives of the present study. Differences in the quality of life on the two independent variables (residence and caste) were analyzed by ANOVA. There is a significant main effect of residence ($F = 89.18$, $p<.01$) indicating that rural and urban youths differ significantly in their quality of life. There is also a significant main effect of caste (F=15.91, p<.01) indicating that high caste and Scheduled Caste youths differ significantly in their quality of life. The interaction effect does not emerge as significant (F=0.33. >.05).

Table 1

Two-way ANOVA of the Quality of Life Scores

Source	*Sum of squares*	*df*	*Mean squares*	*F*	*P*
A. Residence	2575.67	1	2575.67	89.18	<.01
B. Caste	459.58	1	459.58	15.91	<.01
Interaction (AXB)	9.62	1	9.62	.33	>.05
Between group	3044.87	3	1014.95	35.14	<.01
Within group	5661.72	196	28.88	-	-
Total	8706.59	199			

Discussion

The results indicate that residence and caste status have a significant effect on the quality of life. In the sample examined, it has been observed that the quality of life of urban youths are better than the rural youths. In Indian villages a large number of families live below the poverty line, which makes a decent human existence impossible. What is needed is not the abuses and vulgarity of affluence, which is as self-destroying as poverty, but the minimum material, physical, sanitary, nutritional and educational resources and a social climate of equality and justice absolutely necessary for the development of the rural youth. The findings are consistent with the findings of Mukherjee (1980), Flanagan (1978), Liu (1976) and Zinam (1989).

Moreover, high caste enjoyed better quality of life than the Scheduled Caste. Many low caste members are still treated with latent contempt and have only nominal contact with the members of upper castes. There is general social avoidance for lower caste people in villages. Degrees of admission to group ceremonies also vary as a function of the caste of the person. Scheduled Castes are still excluded from entries to a variety of socio-cultural activities. The majority of the people of this caste seek out their livelihood as agricultural, industrial labourers or employed in low status professions. Most of them have their dwellings on the outskirt of villages and in the slum areas of cities. In villages they work as traditional wage earners of the land owners (zamindars) on a full time or part time basis. Their cultural, social and religious life is quite different from those belonging to higher castes. For centuries, the Scheduled Castes have been living under conditions of intense social disadvantages and prevented from sharing in the mainstream of socio-cultural and economic life of the Hindu society. Thus, these findings are consonant with the findings of Sinha (1979) and Mukherjee (1981).

In recent years, a number of attempts have been made at enriching the lives of the weaker sections. In Indian society which is in largely a disadvantaged society, organization of remedial programmes involves huge amounts of money, resources and personnel. In view of diverse societal and ecological conditions the problem of deprivation and enrichment in India has to be tackled in a different manner. They should be trained to become more active and aspiring so that they themselves may be able to procure the enriching facilities for better quality of life.

REFERENCES

Adams, J.S. (1963). Toward an understanding of inequality, *Journal of Abnormal and Social Psychology*, 67, 422-36.

Alam M.R. (1992). *Occupation Choice of Indian Youths.* New Delhi ; Uppal Publishing House.

Alam, M.R. (1981). Cognitive difference in relation to certain psycho-social factors. *Unpublished Ph.D. thesis,* Patna University, Patna.

Bee, H. (1974). *Social Issues in Developmental Psychology.* New York : Harper.

Bernstein, B. (1964). Elaborated and restricted codes : their social origins and some consequences. In J. Gumperz and D. Hymes (eds.), *The Ethnography of Communication. American Anthropologist.* 66, Part 2.

Bronfenbrenner, U. (1974). Development research, public policy, and ecology of childhood. *Child Development,* 45, 1-5.

Campbell, A., Converse, R., and Rodgers, W. (1970). *The Quality of American Life.* New York : Russel Sage.

Chatterjee, B.B. (1980). Effect of social deprivation : Some contradictory findings. *Social Change.* 10, 9-14.

Coleman, J.C. (1971). *Psychology and Effective Behaviour.* Bombay : D.B. Tarporevala.

Cutter, S. (1986). Measuring the quality of life. *Futurist,* 20, 58-59.

Flanagan, J.C. (1978). A research approach to improving our quality of life. *American Psychologist,* 33, 138-47.

Hassan, M.K. (1975). Social prejudice among college students. *Ph.D. Thesis,* Ranchi University, Ranchi.

Hussain, S. (1985). *Adjustment and Its Measurement.* New Delhi : S. Chand.

Liu, B.C. (1976). *Quality of Life Indicators in US Metropolitan Areas :* A statistical analysis. New York : Praeger Publishers.

Maslow, A.H. (1970). *Motivation and Personality.* New York : Harper Row.

Misra, G. (1977). Cognitive functioning and ecological factors. Paper presented to the symposium on *Ecological Factors in Cognitive Development. Annual Convention of U.P. Psychological Association.*

Mukherjee, R. (1981). On the study of quality of life in India. In UNESCO Quality of Life: Problems of Assessment and Measurement. *Socio-Economic Studies No. 5*, UNESCO.

Mukherjee, R. (1980). On the appraisal of quality of life. In A. Szalai and F.M. Andrews (eds.), *The Quality of Life : Comparative Studies.* California : Sage Publication.

Pareek, U. (1970). Poverty and motivation : figure and ground. in V.L. Allen (ed.), *Psychological Factors in Poverty.* New York : Academic Press.

Rath, R. (1974). Teaching and learning problems of the disadvantaged tribal children. Presidential Address, *Twelfth Annual Conference of the Indian Academy of Applied Psychology,* Utkal University, Bhubaneshwar.

Rath, R. and Dash, A.S. (1972). Cognitive growth and classroom learning of naturally deprived children in the primary schools. Paper presented at the *East West Centre for Cross-Cultural Studies,* Honolulu.

Singh, A.K. and Jaiswal, M. (1980). Parental influences, intelligence and scholastic achievements. Paper presented at the Department of Psychology, Ranchi University, Ranchi.

Sinha, D. (1979). Poverty, ecology, cognitive and motivational factors in adolescents. Theme paper presented to *All India Conference.* Zakir Hussain College, University of Delhi.

Sinha, D. (1969). *Indian Villages in Transition : A Motivational Analysis.* New Delhi: Associated Publishing House.

Shukla, P. and Sinha, D. (1974). A developmental study of the relative efficacy of different cues in depth perception. *Indian Journal of Psychology,* 49, 220-30

Tripathi, R.C. and Pande, N. (1976). Motivational consequences of educational climate. Paper presented at the Fourteenth Annual Conference of the IAAP, III, Kharagpur,

Whiteman, M. and Deutsch, M. (1968). Social disadvantage as related to intellective and language development. In M. Deutsch *et al.* (eds). *Social Class, Race and Psychological Development.* New Youk : Holt Rinehart.

Yarron, L.J. (1972). Enrichment and deprivation : Towards a conceptual and empirical differentiation of the early environment. In F.J. Monks *et al.* (eds.) *Determinants of Behavioural Development.* New York : Academic Press.

Yousuf, S.M.A. (1994). Quality of Life: Some psychometric properties. *Journal of the Indian Academy of Applied Psychology,* 20, 153, 162.

Ziman, O. (1989). Quality of life, quality of the individual technology and economic developments. *American Journal of Economics and Sociology,* 48, 55-68.

5

Modernization among Male Adolescents of Different Castes

G.S. Gupta and *Asha Arora*

Manu had categorized the Hindus into four groups on the basis of the nature of job opted or allotted to them in society. For centuries this job culture worked as an identification mark for a particular class e.g., (i) Brahmins, the intellectual class of society, (ii) Vaishyas, the trading class, (iii) Kshatriyas, the warrior class, and (iv) Shudras, indulged in manual work. The personality patterns of persons belonging to these four castes and their offsprings developed on the basis of the work carried out by a particular group. Its reflection can be seen in attitudes, values, prejudices, likings and dislikings and in behaviour of members of these groups even today. Over time the caste system created a great chasm between persons of different castes. The Shudras were being considered as "Untouchables" and had to face several socio-economic and religious problems. Leaders like Gandhiji fought to remove the social evil of untouchability. But, caste system was deep rooted in Indian society and it became an important determinant of the socio-economic structure. It has been observed that caste affects the perception, thinking, emotion, power motivation, n-ach and other behavioural characteristics. India like all developing countries is passing through a period of social change; as a result with the advancement of education and the increasing effect of western culture, a modern outlook is gradually replacing traditional ways of life. Describing the nature of this change, Rath (1973) stated that whatever may be the socio-cultural factors of change, on the psychological plane, it involves a great conflict between the old and the new, the aged and the youth and tradition and modernity. Rogers (1969) defines the term 'modernization' as a process by which an individual moves from a traditional way of life to a more complex, technologically advanced and rapidly changing life-style. In present society, factors which determine nature of modernization are literacy rate, mass media (like, radio, T.V., films, newspapers, magazines), exposure, Cosmopolitan attitudes, empathy, motivation achievement, fatalism and aspirations. Caste characteristics also plays an important role in this process. Studies by sociologists have established that caste shapes personality and can affect perception to a great extent.

Psychologists have tried to explore the role of caste in the modernization process. Myrdal (1970) tried to correlate modernization with the caste system. In India, Srivastava (1976), Kumar (1991) and Chitra (1993) have tried to work out a similar correlation. Chitra (1992) does not find any significant relationship between caste system and modernization. Srivastava (1976) concluded that higher castes are moving towards modernity and while lower castes are moving towards the traditions. Kumar (1991) found a significant and key role played by the caste system in the modernization. Max Weber (1958) in his book, *The Religion of India* wrote that the Hindu religious value system, combined with its rigid caste system is the main reason for the economic backwardness of the Indian people. This economic backwardness in turn negatively affects the process of modernization. However, the institution of caste itself *per se* does not affect modernization. Rather, the poverty and lack of facilities associated with the weaker sections such as the Scheduled Castes are more important and obvious obstacles to modernization.

The purpose of this study is to explore the impact of caste characteristics on the process of modernization among literate urban male adolescents. It was hypothesized that the adolescents of various Hindu castes do not differ significantly in their mean modernization scores.

Methodology

Sample

The study was conducted on a randomly selected sample of 156 literate urban male adolescents (ranging in age from 12 to 20 years) of Rampur district in Uttar Pradesh. On the basis of their caste, the entire sample was categorized into the four caste groups, i.e., Brahmin, Vaishya, Kshatriya and Scheduled Castes. Each group was comprised of thirty-nine subjects. Education, religion, socio-economic status and intelligence, of these groups were controlled.

Tool

'Modernization Scale' constructed and standardized by Singh,

Tripathi and Lal (1979) was administered to the sample. The scale consists of thirty-two items in simple Hindi language. The items included in the scale give a clear picture of subject's attitude towards modernization in all the spheres of personality and behaviour. It reveals both their acceptance and rejection of modernity. It takes approximately twenty-five minutes in its completion. The reliability of the tool is 0.78 and validity ranges between 0.61 to 0.97.

Results and Discussion

Analysis of variance technique was applied to find out the significance of difference in the modernization scores of four testing groups. Data with statistical measure have been shown in Table 1.

Table 1

Caste Variations in Modernization of Adolescents

Group	*Mean*	*F-ratio*	*P*
Brahmin	93.03		
Vaishya	168.63		
		4.89	0.01
Kshatriya	162.86		
Shudra	152.47		

NOTE : Sample base for each group is 39.

Value of F-ratio significant at .01 level of confidence with 3/152 degree of freedom is 3.92.

Table 1 reveals a significant difference in the mean modernization scores of four groups taken into consideration. The obtained F-ratio value is 4.89 which is quite higher than that of table value 3.92, significant at 0.01 level of confidence. Hence, the null hypothesis is rejected and it can be stated firmly that caste affects modernization positively. The results reveal that even today when equal facilities are available to members of all castes there is a significant difference in the perception towards adoption of modernization. This difference can be ascribed to varying caste background. The mean modernization score of Brahmins is 93.03, while that of Vaishyas is 168.63, Kshatriyas is 162.86 and that of Scheduled Castes is 152.47. The vast difference in mean modernization score between Brahmin and other castes may be attributed to orthodox nature of Brahmins, who because of their religious and cultural inclination do not approve permit modernization in their community. Our society also gives a clear picture of it. Results of the present study also show that there is not a great difference in the mean modernization score of Vaishya and

Kshatriya community. To the mind of researchers its one of the main reason may be that both the communities are enjoying higher social status, since long. The subjects of the Vaishya community have the power of wealth, while the Kshatriya's have the power of muscle. Both of them have major plus point and moreover they are members of open group. So, there is not a great difference in their perception and admission of modernization in their life-style.

As regards Scheduled Castes and Backward Castes their ancestors passed a miserable life. But through the efforts of leaders like Gandhiji, Dr. B.R. Ambedkar before independence and Pandit Nehru after independence Scheduled Castes and Backward Castes are continuously striving for a respectable position in the society and national life. The rapid rate of socio-economic change among this community have changed their perception to a great extent. Now they are leaving traditional ways of life and adopting modern outlook in all the fields of life, e.g., education, economic, material and scientific changes, etc. whole heartedly.

Reservation policy of Government of India framed during post-independence era by our leaders and approved by honourable Supreme Court of India has also contributed a lot to the upliftment of poor and downtrodden, especially the weaker section of society (Scheduled Caste and backwards share a lot in this class of society). This reservation policy has contributed much in the process of attitude change of weaker sections of society. It has also helped in the restoration of confidence among the weaker section of society. In nutshell reservation policy has contributed to a great extent in the process of acceptance and achievement of modernization.

A brief look on the studies conducted to explore the role of caste characteristics on the process of modernization of Indian people show that some are in favour and some are contrary to the results obtained in present study e.g., Trivedi (1973). Srivastava (1976) and Kumar (1991) reported changes generated by modernization are caste oriented. While the results obtained by Chitra (1993) in her study are contrary to the results obtained in this study.

India is passing through a transitional state of social change. With the advancement of scientific and technological knowledge and remarkable progress in the field of agriculture, industrialization and all round progress on economic front, a change is being observed in the attitude and values of the people belonging to different castes and religions of Indian society. Consequently our old prejudices and stereotyped values are ending and a new era of world brotherhood, patriotism, self-respect and respect to others, competition *vs* cooperation, divergent thinking and foresightedness are gradually developing in the personality traits of people of all sections of our society, with a common objective of achievement of national prestige and national progress.

REFERENCES

Chitra, N. (1992), Universal primary education. *The Journal of Education and Social Change,* 10-12.

Chitra, N. (1993), Modernization : As a Function of Family Structure, Caste, Age and Sex. *Unpublished Ph.D. Thesis.* Meerut : Meerut University, Meerut.

Kumar, V. (1991). *Family Life and Socio-Economic Problems of the Aged.* New Delhi : Efficient Offset Printers.

Myrdal, G. (1970). *Asian Drama : An Inquiry into the Poverty of Nations.* London : Harper & Row.

Rath, R. (1973). *Psycho-Social Problems of Social Change,* Bombay: Allied Publishers.

Rogers, C. (1969). *Modernization among Peasants : The Impact of Communication,* New York: Holt Rinehart and Winston.

Singh, R.; Tripathi, A.N. and Lal, R.G. (1979). *Modernization Scale.* Kushi Nagar : Budha P.G. College.

Srivastava, S.K. (1976). *Tradition and Modernization : Process of Continuity and Change in India.* Indian International Publications.

Trivedi, D.N. (1973). Caste, modernization and institutionalization of change, *The Eastern Anthropologist,* 26.

Weber, M. (1958). Social Change. *Journal of Council for Social Development,* 21, 21-26.

6

Scheduled Tribes in Kumaun Hills: Potentials and Welfare

N. Hasnain

Of the Scheduled Tribes inhabiting Kumaun hills are important in terms of population, socio-cultural heritage and psychological investigations. They are Bhotia or Shauka tribe of Pithoragarh district and Tharu of Nainital district.

Bhotia or Shauka Tribe

Pithoragarh is located in north-western side of Uttar Pradesh. It is surrounded by Nepal in east, China (Tibet) in north, Almora district of Kumaun and Chamoli district of Garhwal in west. Its southern side is surrounded by district Nainital. There are six tehsils in Pithoragarh district. They are : Champawat, Gangolihat, Dharchula, Didihat, Munsiyari, and Pithoragarh. The Shauka tribe inhabit Dharchula, Didihat, and Munsiyari tehsils. According to 1981 census, the total population of Pithoragarh district in 1981 was 489267 in which 17337 were Scheduled Tribes. The total population of the district rose to 560442 in 1991 (Census, 1991). However, the break-up of population of Bhotia tribe in 1991 Census is not known.

Traditionally, the name Bhotia has been applied for the people inhabiting the trans-Himalayan valleys of Gori, Dhauli, Kuthiyangti and their tributaries along the northern most mountainous part of Kumaun. But due to prejudices, stereotypes and stigma attached with the word 'Bhotia' it has taken a negative meaning. Therefore, the word 'Shauka', is preferred in its place. The Shauka tribe claims to be a Rajput race who dwelt originally in the hill provinces of snowy range and migrated to Tibet, whence, after a residence of several generations, they again crossed the Himalayas and established themselves in the districts which they now inhabit, officially they are the members of a 'Mongoloid border tribe' (Srivastava, 1978). Writers, like Atkinson (1886), Walton (1911) and Pant (1935) are also of the opinion that they are 'Mongoloid people.' They, originally struggled for recognition as Rajput, but from 1953 because of dwindling trade with Tibet, which was finished after China war they demanded to be included in the list of 'Scheduled Tribes.' This was accepted by Uttar Pradesh Government in 1967.

The four Shauka valleys (Byans, Chaudans, Darma, and Johar) are flanked by ridges covered with perpetual snow. These valleys have an elevation of more than 10,000 feet above the sea level and the altitude of Shauka valleys ranges from 10,000 feet to 19,000 feet above the sea level. These valleys are wholly covered with snow for half the year. In this sense they are undoubtedly hard-working and have wonderful capacity to resist cold and difficult geographical conditions. They are simple natured, happy, easy-going, good humoured and orderly race. Srivastava (1953) has written that the level of interaction between the Shauka valleys has been fairly high. Marriages between the Chaudansi and Byani Shaukas are frequent. The traditions of the different valleys though differ in detail but form the main outlines of the same story.

The heads of Shauka villages are often remarkably sensible and well informed. Their make of life gives them more experience of the world than other people of hills. They take a much greater interest in matters not immediately affecting that is commonly found amongst eastern people. Writers are of the opinion that it appears that this tradition is not of very modern origin. They have well-knit religions beliefs, folk dances, and songs. The literacy and general awareness level of Shauka tribe is appreciably high.

Tharu Tribe

The frontiers of Nainital district are surrounded by the districts of Almora in north, Garhwal and Bijnor in west, Moradabad, Rampur and Pilibhit districts in south. Its eastern side is surrounded by Nepal and district Pithoragarh. There are eight tehsils in Nainital district. They are : Dhari, Haldwani, Kashipur, Khatima, Kichcha-Kutoli, Nainital, and Sitarganj. The later five tehsils are situated in tarai region and Tharu tribe inhabit Khatima and Sitarganj tehsils. The total population of Nainital district in 1981 was 1136523 in which 73,998 were Scheduled Tribes. The total population of the district according to 1991 Census has gone upto 1585325. Some of the tehsils of Nainital district have now been included in the newly carved district of Udham Singh Nagar. Many interpretations prevail regarding the origin of Tharu tribe, Sherring (1938) is of the opinion that the Tilpur Pargnah near the tarai was once in the possession of this tribe, who were expelled by Tilvikram Sen with the help of Banjaras. Buchman supports the view that originally they were Rajputs and they came from Chittor. They belonged to the family of Jaimal and Patta. They were driven from their home and settled in the tehsils of Nainital where they presently inhabit. The reference seems to indicate the third siege of Chittor by Akbar in 1567 A.D. Nesfield says that they are a kin to tribe known as Meecha living on the bank of Kosi river on the forest hills of Himalayas (Quoted by Verma, 1983).

According to Majumdar (1961) the Tharu tribe of tarai is of Mangoloid extraction from the shape of the eyes and of the high cheek bones, the nose and their yellow - brown complexion. Some say that they are descents of Rajputs but others are of the opinion that they are Mangoloid tribe from Mid Asia. Others are of the opinion that they are not Aryans (Singh, 1982).

Tharus who resemble the artisan caste in body characteristics the Bhauta and the Habura in facial characteristics and some of the higher castes in nasal characterisation, claim Rajput origin on the mother side and Bhil on the father's. Majumdar (1961) is of the opinion that Tharus are Mangoloid tribe with mixed non-Mangoloid traits.

The Tharu families are at liberty to migrate from one village to another. The village community maintains law and order by observing their traditions or customs. All the customs are preserved in folk tales, songs and stories. The members of the village community live together. They jointly face the problems and calamities. It also maintains disciplines by social approval. The village community's administration is looked after by village officials who enjoy a high position. They are the Pradhan (village chiefmen), the Mustajar (contractor and sole proprietor of the village), the Sarwarkar (spokesman of Pradhan or Mustajar), and the Kotwar (the village peon). The Pradhan has to perform administrative, social, and religious duties of the village. He has to report to the tehsildar or the police regarding violation of law and order in the village. Srivastava (1958) says that he performs all those duties by satisfying the Government officials with his hospitality and general assistance.

The Tharus are example of female dominance. They allow inordinate latitude to their women in all matters and the later are so dominant that men are often heard of complaining maltreatment by their wives. In cases of maltreatments by the wife often the husband has no alternative but to pray for redress. In Tharu society, women choose their partners in marriage. Many of the principal occupations of Tharus are denied to men and innumerable prohibitions hedge the daily routine of Tharu life (Majumdar, 1961). It is said that formerly Tharu did not allow husbands or any male to enter into their kitchen and touch their water pots but these restrictions have now been relaxed and have almost been given up.

Tharu religion is based on belief in ghosts, demons and spirits of the dead whom they fear. According to Knoles, the Tharus worship Mahadev and possess some idea of the supreme being known as Narayan who provides sunshine, rain and harvests. Majumdar (1937) says that there is a Hindu impact over Tharus. So they worship Satnarayan and Hindu gods and goddesses. It is, however, observed that Tharus have borrowed gods and goddesses from amongst Hindu Pantheons, Muslim Pirs, Saints and Sikh Gurus who find a place in their religion. They believe in spirits. They try to control these spirits by worship, threat or offerings. Some of the spirits regularly receive offerings according to seasons and time, while others are to be placed by casual sacrifices at the time of sickness or repeated misfortune.

Psychological Researches

In the above socio-cultural perspectives of Shauka and Tharu tribes some studies were carried out by the author and his Ph.D. Students under his guidance in the Department of Psychology, Govt. P.G. College, Pithoragarh (Kumaun University, Nainital). These studies shed lights on the psychological make-up of the personalities of these important tribes of Kumaun Hills. The studies cover the cognitive and non-cognitive aspects of the two tribal groups.

Studies on Cognitive Aspects

A study on creativity of Shauka and non-tribal male and female students was carried out by Ramesh Singh Bisht in 1986. He selected 160 Shauka tribal and 160 non-tribal Intermediate students from general population. Among each group there were 80 males and 80 females. The samples were taken from a randomly selected initial sample of 400 Shauka and 400 non-tribal samples. The samples were taken from various Intermediate colleges of Pithoragarh district. He used Mehdi's (1973) Verbal and Non-verbal creativity tests. Non-tribal subjects obtained significantly more mean verbal and composite creativity scores than Shauka tribal subjects. The mean non-verbal creativity score of non-tribal students was greater than that of tribal subjects but it did not reach to the statistical significance. Males obtained significantly greater mean verbal, non-verbal and composite creativity scores than females. Another study was undertaken by Dipendra Singh Mahar in 1993 on the relationship of academic achievement and self-concept; and academic achievement and alienation of Shauka tribal, Tharu tribal and non-tribal Intermediate students. He randomly selected 200 subjects from each group from different Intermediate colleges of Pithoragarh district and tarai region of Nainital district. Mahar used in his study Mohsin's (1979) Self-Concept Inventory to measure the self-concept of the subjects. It is a 48 item inventory consisting of positive and negative items equally balanced in number about abilities and strength pertaining to the cognitive, affective and conative areas. He used Dutt and Kureshi's (1976) 21 item alienation scale. It is a Likert-type five-point scale. The scale is structured on five factors of alienation, namely, Despair, Disillusionment, Unstructures Universe, Narcissism and Psychological Vacuum.

Mahar obtained significantly positive correlationship between academic achievement and self-concept, insignificant positive relationship between academic achievement and alienation, and significantly negative relationship between self-concept and alienation of Shauka tribal adolescents. Negligible positive relationship between academic achievement and self-concept, significant positive relationship between academic achievement and alienation, and self-concept and alienation of Tharu adolescents were obtained.

Significantly positive relationship between academic achievement and self-concept, negative significant relationship between academic achievement and alienation, and significantly positive relationship between self-concept and alienation of non-tribal subjects were obtained.

Another study was carried out by Meena Kumari Kharkwal in the year 1988 on the development of formal operational thought of Tharu and non-tribal boys. Formal operational thought was measured by Sandhu's (1979) 'Piaget-type Task Test'.

Piaget's (1953a and 1954b) theory of cognitive development assumes four stages of cognitive development. They are : sensorimotor period, preoperational period, concrete operational period, and formal operational period. The last stage starts from 11 to 12 years in most of the young Children and completes upto 15 years of age. Piaget's theory accepts that cognitive development occurs through a sequence of stages that are thought to be universal, and cultural factors affect only the age at which the stages are attained (Desen and Haron, 1984). Piaget (1970) has pointed out that cultural differences, language and education are expected to accelerate or delay the average chronological ages at which the stages are attained.

At the stage of formal operational thought people begin to develop a new set of mental abilities that Piaget terms 'formal operation.' These new operations are 'formal' in the sense that they permit young people to operate upon or think about concrete operations. Formal operations are, thus, second order operations that permit the manipulation of first order operations. In a sense formal operations are to concrete operations what algebra is to arithmetic. At this stage the child is able to handle hypotheses and reasoning with propositions removed from the concrete and the present. This is the stage of spontaneous development of experimental mental transformation in reality. By thinking in abstract terms and by manipulating abstract symbols, the child is able to solve problems and reason in an abstract manner. He considers alternative solutions without going through concrete trial and error procedures. Hypotheses are formed, considered, and substantiated or discarded. At this stage contradictions in the world can be dealt with and resolved at least in the sense of arriving at a balance or a perspective.

Kharkwal (1988) took 120 Tharu tribal and 120 non-tribal subjects from various educational institutions of Khatima and Sitarganj tehsils of Nainital district. The subjects in each major group belonged to four age groups : 11-12, 13-14, 15-16, and 17-18 years of age each consisting of 30 subjects. In each of these age groups of Tharu and non-Tharu groups, 10 subjects were of below average I.Q., 10 of average I.Q. and 10 of above average I.Q. These groups were formed out of an initial sample of 400 Tharu and 400 non-Tharu randomly selected subjects. Jalota's (1976) 'Group Test of General Mental Ability' (revised) was administered to the subjects for the measurement of their I.Q.

Comparisons of Tharu and non-Tharu subjects at none of the age levels except at the age of 17-18 years emerged to be significant but Tharu subjects in all age groups except at 11-12 years lagged behind the non-Tharu subjects in the development of formal operational thought.

The comparison of Tharu and non-tribal subjects showed that the degree of development of formal operations thought in Tharu subjects at the age of 11-12 years was a bit greater than the non-Tharu subjects. However, the degree of development in Tharu subjects in all the other age groups was lesser than the non-tribal subjects. Moreover, the difference between the two cultures became sharper with the advancement in age. The degree of development from 15-16 to 17-18 in Tharu subjects decelerates but in non-Tharu subjects it accelerates making the difference very vast.

Studies on Non-Cognitive Aspects

A U.G.C. financed research project was undertaken by the author (Hasnain, 1989) on alienation, adjustment and security-insecurity among

Scheduled Tribe, Scheduled Caste and Caste-Hindus. He selected 200 class XI and XII students from each Shauka tribe, Scheduled Caste and caste-Hindu groups. The subjects were randomly selected from Intermediate Colleges of Dharchula and Pithoragarh tehsils of district Pithoragarh. He used Dutt and Kureshi's (1976) "Alienation Scale", Srivastava's (1976) "Short form of Maslow's security-insecurity inventory" and Kumar's (1985) "Revised Adjustment Inventory" to measure alienation, security-insecurity and adjustment of the subjects respectively.

The results of alienation showed insignificant difference between the means of Scheduled Tribe and Scheduled Caste subjects. However, both Scheduled tribe and Scheduled Caste subjects were found to be significantly more alienated than caste-Hindu subjects. Insignificant difference was obtained between the mean security-insecurity scores of Scheduled Tribe and Scheduled Caste subjects. However, Scheduled Tribe and Scheduled Caste subjects were found to be significantly more insecure than caste-Hindu subjects. The results of adjustment revealed insignificant difference between the mean adjustment scores of Scheduled Tribe and Scheduled Caste subjects. However, both groups were found to be significantly less adjusted than the caste-Hindu subjects.

In his study Mahar (1993) found that the mean self-concept score of non-tribal group was significantly highest and that of Tharu subjects was significantly lowest. The Shauka subjects came in between the two. The non-tribal subjects were significantly most alienated and Tharus the least alienated groups.

Hasnain (1994) carried out another study on defeatism of Shauka Scheduled Tribe, Scheduled Caste and caste-Hindu subjects. He took 50 Intermediate students from each group. The subjects were randomly selected from different Intermediate College of Dharchula and Pithoragarh tehsils. They were administered author's (Hasnain, 1987) 'Defeatism Scale' in order to measure their defeatist attitude. Shauka Scheduled Tribe subjects were found to be significantly more defeatist than caste-Hindu subjects. However, insignificant differences between the defeatism of Scheduled Tribe and Scheduled Caste; and Scheduled Caste and Caste-Hindu subjects were obtained. Nonetheless, the Schedule Caste subjects were more defeatist than Caste Hindu subjects.

Discussion

The findings on creativity suggest that Shauka subjects lag behind the non-tribal subjects in verbal and composite creativity but they are a bit better than non-tribal subjects in non-verbal creativity. The Shauka tribal culture seem to lack in providing verbal mechanisms and strings but its non-verbal cultural aspect seems to be rich which needs appreciation. So far as the verbal aspect of creativity of Shauka tribal group is concerned it seems that this culture lacks interactional spectrum, the necessary mechanism of verbal expression. The reluctant attitude of the group in mixing with the general population and sharing the ideas may be detrimental to the development of verbal creativity and creativity as a whole. But the interactional process is a two-way traffic. Therefore, the attitude of general population towards them may also count for the deficit in their creativity.

Positive significant relationship between academic achievement and self-concept of Shauka subjects is a healthy trend indicating thereby the realistic knowledge about themselves. But it is lacking in Tharu tribal and non-tribal groups. This is further confirmed by the negative correlationship between self-concept and alienation in Shauka group and positive significant correlationship between the two of Tharu and positive though insignificant relationship between the two variables in non-tribal subjects.

The results of correlationship between academic achievement and alienation are intriguing for, negative though insignificant correlationship between the two was found only in non-tribal group. It was positive in both Shauka and Tharu groups. Tharu students perhaps being ignorant of the importance of study and academic achievement seem to be equally ignorant of their social, political and ethnological importance. This inference is further confirmed by the significant positive relationship between self-concept and alienation in their (Tharu's) case. The causes of positive relationship between academic achievement and alienation seem to lie in their feeling of worthlessness and a bit harsh and tense treatment meted to them by the general population of the region.

The results of Meena Kharkwal's (1988) study clearly indicated the deficit in formal operational thought of Tharu subjects. As a social group they seem not to emphasize and practise the values and importance of cognitive development. It should be kept in mind that though, I.Q. of Tharu and general students were equal, yet the operational thought involved in handling hypotheses and reasoning, experimenting and manipulating abstract symbols are not developed in them upto the level it is developed in their non-tribal counterparts. Perhaps their beliefs in ghosts, demons and spirits of dead ones hinder the development of scientific outlook hindering thereby the development of cognitive aspects necessary for scientific enquiry. Therefore, schemes and programmes for the development of scientific approach in Tharu tribal group should be chalked out for, this is the only way of their progress, development and prosperity.

Hasnain's (1989) study revealed almost equal degree of alienation in the Shauka tribal and Scheduled Caste subjects. They were significantly more alienated than caste-Hindu subjects. Socially and psychologically this is an unhealthy condition and detrimental to the development of wholesome and integrated outlook which may cut them off the main stream. They, however, do not seem to be much responsible for such a condition. Rather, the responsible factors might be the socio-political conditions prevailing in the region. Not only this but significantly greater insecurity feeling and poorer adjustment was found in them. All these negative psychological developments are explosive and unhealthy. Hasnain's (1994) study revealed greater defeatist feeling in Shauka tribal students than the students of general population. All these must be taken into considerations while framing the policies of development of the region and the country.

Mahar's (1993) study revealed a kind of poorer self-concept both in Shauka and Tharu subjects. This poor self-concept brings in them a kind of ignorance about their real strength and abilities. A person ignorant of his self is like a blind person throwing the arrow without knowing and taking the aim. So ways and means for the development of right kind of self-concept in tribal subjects should be considered seriously in any developmental scheme meant to them.

Epilogue

These findings pose challenge to the social scientists and planners. The psychological scenario of the two major tribes, viz., Shauka and Tharu of the Kumaun hills is surely not appreciable. In fact we have to play major role in providing them social, political and psychological environment and opportunities for the expression and development of their psychological potentials. The behaviours and treatments meted to them by and large are predisposing conditions for their deteriorating psychological well-being. Integrated and multipronged well-thought programmes for their psychological welfare is the need of the hour. Else the present psychological conditions might prove expensive and easily convertible into repulsive tendencies. Therefore, I submit and suggest to start work immediately for, late in this case may be expensive. After all precaution is better than cure.

REFERENCES

Atkinson, E.Y (1886). *The Himalayan Districts of North Western Provinces of India.* Allahabad, Vols. I, II, III.

Bisht, Ramesh Singh (1986). A study of creativity as a function of academic achievement, sex and socio-economic status in tribal and non-tribal students. *Unpublished Ph.D. Thesis.* Nainital : Kumaun University.

Desen, P.R. and Heron A. (1984). Cross-cultural test of Piget's theory. *Journal of Developmental Psychology,* 4, 295-341.

Mahar, Dipendra Singh (1993). Self-concept, alienation and academic achievement in Bhotia and Tharu adolescents. *Unpublished Ph.D. Thesis.* Nainital : Kumaun University.

Dutt, M. and Kureshi, A. (1976). Towards developing an alienation scale : a factor analytical approach. Abstracts of papers accepted for reading in the *'Section of Psychology and Educational Sciences' at Indian Science Congress.*

Faunce, W, (1979). Social Problems of an *Industrial Civilization.* New York : Mc Graw-Hill.

Hasnain, N. (1989). A study of alienation, adjustment and security-insecurity among Scheduled Tribe, Scheduled Caste and upper Caste Hindus of Kumaun hills. *An unpublished summary of a research project.* New Delhi, University Grants Commission.

Hasnain, N. (1994). Defeatism in Scheduled Tribes, Scheduled Caste and caste Hindus, *Proceedings of the Eighty first session of the Indian Science Congress.*

Jalota, S.S. (1976). *Test of General Mental Ability* (Hindi) Revised. Chandigarh.

Jersild, A.T. (1965). Social and individual origins of the self. In D.E. Hamachek (Ed.) *'The Self in Growth, Teaching and Learning.'* New York : Prentice Hall.

Josephson, E. and Mary, M.A. (1962). *Man Alone : Alienation in Modern Society.* New York : Dell Publishing Company.

Kumar, P. (1985). *Revised Adjustment Inventory (RAI).* Deptt. of Psychology. Sardar Patel University. Vallabh Vidyanagar.

Majumdar. D.N. (1937). *A Tribe in Transition : A Study in Culture Pattern.* London : Longmans Green.

Majumdar, D.N. (1961). *Races and Cultures of India.* Bombay : Asia Publishing House.

Mc. David. J.W. and H. Harari (1986). *Social Psychology : Individuals. Groups. Societies,* Delhi : CBS Publishers and Distributors.

Meena K. Kharakwal (1988). Development of formal operational thought in Tharu and Non-Tharu boys. *Unpublished Ph.D. Thesis.* Nainital : Kumaun University.

Mehdi. B. (1973). Verbal and non-verbal tests of creative thinking. Aligarh : Fatima Qamar.

Mohsin. S.M. (1979). *Mohsin's Self-Concept Inventory.* Varanasi : Rupa Psychological Centre.

Pant, S.C. (1935). *The Social Economy of Himalayans.* London.

Piaget, J. (1935a). *The Origin of Intelligence in the Child.* London : Rontledge and Kagan Paul.

Piaget, T. (1954b). *The Construction of Reality in the Child.* New York : Basic Books.

Sandhu, I.S. (1979). The development of formal thought in relation to age : Piaget's formal operational period. *Indian Journal of Psychology.* 54, 133-41.

Singh, J.N. (1982). *Madyavarti Tharu: Ek Parichai,* Uttar Pradesh Information and Public Relations Deptt. U.P.

Srivastava, G.P. (1976). A short form of Maslow security-insecurity inventory, *Manas,* 23, 115-19.

Srivastava, R.P. (1953). Rangbang in the changing Bhotia life *Eastern Anthropologists,* 5, 190-203.

Srivastava, R.P. (1978). Tribe-caste mobility in India and the case of Kumaun Bhotia. In Fuerer Haincuorf (Ed.), *Caste and Kinship in Nepal, India and Ceylon* New Delhi : Sterling Publishers.

Srivastava, S.K. (1958). *The Tharus : A study in culture dynamics.* Agra : Agra University Press.

Verma, R.S. (1983). A study of socio-psychological make-up of adolescents belonging to scheduled tribes, Tharu and Buksa in Nainital district. *Unpublished Ph.D. Thesis,* Nainital: Kumaun University.

Walton, H.G. (1911). *District Gazetteer of the United Provinces.* Vol XXXV, Allahabad.

7

Self-Concept of Shauka and Tharu Tribes

N. Hasnain and *Dipendra Singh Maher*

According to Frederick (1957) self-concept is way one sees oneself. It is the set of characteristics with himself irrespective of particular environment in which he may be at a given time. It is, for the most part, a coherent and internally consistent cognitive system but from time to time new experiences necessitate adjustment and revision of the self-concept. The self-concept varies in one individual from one developmental stage to another. It also varies from individual to individual as a result of differential social learning. Hence one's self-concept differs from other's owing to varied socio-cultural background. It is a product of growth which results from bio-social interaction and in turn influences the course of interaction.

Culture of a society provides readymade sets of values, norms and code of conducts for the development of self-concept. A number of studies showed that Negros significantly surpassed their White counterparts in self-concept (Hodgkins and Stakenas, 1969; Hunt and Hardt, 1969; and Zirket and Moses, 1971). Mc Daniel (1967) found the mean self-concept score of Mexican-American children to be significantly low than that of White but not that of Negro children. Evans (1969) and Hishiki (1969) also found evidences of depressed self-concept for Mexican-American children. Coleman (1966) found that the mean self-concept of Mexican-American children was significantly lower than those of both Negro and White children. Ronald (1987) suggested that the interpsychic development of the self is congruent with the major socio-cultural patterns of a society.

Ameerjan and Thimappa (1982) reported that Scheduled Caste and Tribe students had lower economic values but higher religious values than other caste groups. However, scheduled caste and tribal subjects did not differ from each other in any respect in their perceived self-ideal and self-confidence. Karna and Panjiar (1983) found that Harijans and the most despised groups had the lowest self-esteem. Studies also show that family break-up due to the death or divorce is traumatic for every member of the family. The self-concept of the children are damaged and patterns of life are inevitably upset in such situations (Harmon, 1959; Landis, 1963 and Goode, 1964).

The above quoted researches show cultural differences in self-concept. However, culture itself is not responsible for such differences. Rather, culture through its learning mechanism and transmission of its values, beliefs, rituals, norms and codes of conduct, etc., brings changes in socialization process and child-rearing practices resulting into differences in self-concept. The two tribal cultures of Kumaun Hills, Uttar Pradesh, namely, Shauka (Bhotia) and Tharu are certainly different in values and codes of conduct, learning mechanisms, socialization processes and child-rearing practices from the main or general culture of the region. Therefore, the present study was designed to measure the self-concept of the adolescents of Shauka and Tharu Tribes and to compare them with the self-concept of adolescents of general population.

Methodology

Sample

A total of 600 subjects, 200 each from Shauka, Tharu and non-tribal students studying in class XI were randomly selected from Intermediate colleges. Shauka tribals subjects were taken from Pithoragarh district and Tharu subjects were taken from Nainital district of Kumaun region. 100 non-tribal subjects were taken from Pithoragarh district from where Bhotia subjects were taken and 100 from Nainital district from where Tharu subjects were taken so as to control local variations.

Tools

Mohsin's (1979) 'Self-Concept Inventory' was used to measure the self-concept of the subjects. It is a 48 positively and negatively phrased item inventory and measures abilities and strengths pertaining to the cognitive, affective and conative areas. The positively phrased items affirm a positive quality and negatively phrased items deny negative quality. One mark for each statement is awarded if the subject ticks (✓) it and a zero is given if he crosses (X) it. The minimum and maximum scores on the test are 0 and 48 respectively. Split-half reliability by Spearmen-Brown formula is reported to be 0.73 for its validity its correlation with Maslow's

'Security-Insecurity' short version test were found to be 0.351 and with Mohsin's 'Parents-Child Inventory' it was 0.396. Both were significant at 0.01 level of confidence.

Results

The self-concept scores of subjects of all groups were separately summed up and their means were calculated. Duncan's range test (McGrugan, 1969) was applied to find out significant differences among the means. For this, least significant range (Rp) for comparisons of three groups and two groups were calculated at .05 level of confidence. The results are given in the following table.

Table 1

Mean Self-concept Scores of Shauka, Tharu and non-Tribal Subjects and Results of Duncan's Range Test the Means.

Means	*Tharu*	*Shauka*	*Non-tribal*	*Least Sig. range at .05 level*
	31.82	34.47	37.07	
31.82		2.65	5.25	R_3= 1.06
34.47			2.60	R_2= 1.01

A cursory look over Table 1 reveals that mean self-concept scores of Tharu, Shauka and non-tribal subjects were 31.82, 34.47 and 37.07 respectively. Thus, Tharu tribal subjects obtained the lowest mean score and the non-tribal subjects obtained the highest mean score. Rp for three groups came to be R_3= 1.06. The difference between the means of two extreme groups came to be 5.25 which exceeded the least significance range for three groups. Therefore, the difference between the two extreme groups (Tharu and non-tribal) was taken as significant at .05 level of significance. In the same way the difference between means of Tharu and Shauka tribal subjects came to be 2.65 which exceeded R_2=1.01 value. So the difference between the means of the two said groups was taken as significant at .05 level of confidence. The difference between the means of Shauka tribal and non-tribal subjects came to be 2.60 which also exceeded R_2= 1.01 value. Therefore, this difference was also taken as significant at .05 level of confidence.

Discussions

The results of Duncan's range test revealed that non-tribal subjects obtained significantly greatest mean self-concept score and Tharu tribal subjects scored significantly least mean self-concept score. The Shauka tribal subjects came in between the two groups in terms of their mean self-concept score. The differences between the mean self-concept scores of Shauka and Tharu; and Bhotia and non-tribal subjects also came to be significant.

The results seem to be on expected lines. Tharus as seclusive and lonely group do not interact much with the general population of tarai region of Kumaun. The socio-psychological conditions of Tharus lag far behind those of general or non-tribal group of Kumaun. The observations show that as a tribe they have tried to maintain their tribal customs which is better for customs' sake but is making them suspicious, rigid to change, and backward in accepting the changes taking place as results of fast technical and material advancements. Moreover, they are shy which might be because of their awareness of being different from the general Kumauni population and do not interact frequently with them. All these act as disadvantages for Tharu subjects and bring hinderances to the development of their self-concept.

Table 1 reveals that mean self-concept score of Shauka tribe is significantly lesser than that of non-tribal subjects but significantly greater than that of Tharu subjects. The Shauka tribe of Kumaun, though, a much mobile and moving tribe residing in difficult hilly tracks do face difficulties in movement. Moreover, because of the difficult access to their residential region only limited persons particularly employed in Government and semi-Government services have some chances of movement and interaction with people outside their society. So much so that the Shauka tribe of Kumaun has happened to be one of the restrictive tribe which does not appreciate its people mixing with persons of other cultural (non-tribal) groups. Moreover, some specific traditions like beef-eating and interdining with beef eaters and drinking, particularly with guests inhibit the persons of other castes of Kumaun to interact and mix with Shauka population. Officially they were the members of 'Mangoloid border tribe' and 'dirty beef-eating Bhotias'. As a result, the Kumauni Hindu society has been unwilling to make any concession to accommodate their incompatibilities (Srivastava, 1978). But because of the better level of awareness they have access to education and media of communication, like radio, television, newspapers, magazines, etc. These have made them upto date in modern facilities and knowledge and have increased their level of awareness. As a result they have more chances for interaction with persons outside their world. This enhances their self-concept.

The findings of the present study are in consonance with the findings of Glickman and Whole (1965), Beg (1966), Kakkar and Gorden (1966), and Garsee and Glisman (1967) who obtained significant difference in self-concept of students belonging to different cultures. However, the findings negate the findings of Wylle (1961), Gibby and Gabler (1967), Carpenter and Busse (1969) and DeBlaissie and Healy (1970) who did not obtain significant difference between the self-concept of Negro and White students. The findings of the present study also confirm the findings of Karna and Panjiar (1983) who obtained that Harijans and the most despised group had the lowest self-esteem.

REFERENCES

Ameerjan, M.S. and Thimapha, M.S. (1982). A comparative study of personality dynamics and self-attitudes of the scheduled caste and tribe college students. Abstract of paper accepted for reading at the *Section of Psychology and Educational Sciences of the 69th session of Indian Science Congress,* Mysore.

Beg, M.A. (1966). Values orientation of Indian and American students : a cross-cultural study. *Psychologia,* 3, 111-19.

Carpenter, T.R. and Busse, T.B. (1969). Development of self-concept in Negro and White children. *Child Development,* 40, 935-39.

Coleman, J.S. (1966). *Equality of Educational Opportunity,* Washington : US Government Printing Office.

De Blaissie, R.R. and Healy, G.W. (1970). *Self-concept : A Comparison of Spanish-American Negro and Anglo Adolescents across Ethnic, Sex and Socio-economic Variables.* New York : ERIC Clearinghouse on Rural Education and Small Schools.

Evans, F.B.A. (1970). Study of socio-cultural characteristics of Mexican-American and Angle junior high school students and relation of these characteristics to achievement *Dessertation Abstract,* 30, 4826-A.

Frederick, J.M. (1957). *Educational Psychology.* New York: Overseas Publication.

Garsee, J.W. and Clikman, A.E. (1967). Samoan international values. *Journal of Social Psychology,* 729, 45-60.

Gibby, R.C.S. and Gabler, R. (1967). The self-concept of Negro and White children. *Journal of Clinical Psychology,* 32, 144-48.

Glickman, M. and Whol, J. (1965). Expressed values of Burmese and American university students. *Journal of Social Psychology,* 65, 17-25.

Goode, W.J. (1964). *The Family.* New Jersey : Prentice Hall.

Hishiki, P.C. (1969). Self-concept of sixth grade girls of Mexican descent California. *Journal of Educational Research,* 20, 56-62.

Hodking, B.J. and Stakenes, R.G. (1969). A study of self-concept of Negro and White youths in segregated environment. *Journal of Negro Education,* 38, 370-77.

Hormon, L. (1959). When homes are broken? *Journal of Home Economics,* 51, 332-35.

Hunt, B.B. and Hardt, R.H. (1969). The effect of upward bound programmes on the attitudes, motivation and academic achievement of Negro students. *Journal of Social Issues,* 25, 117-29.

Kakkar, S.B. and Gorden, L.V. (1966). A cross-cultural study of teachers values. *Educational Psychological Review,* 6, 172-77.

Karna, N.L. and Panjiar, I.D. (1983). How they perceive themselves and how others perceive them. Abstracts of papers accepted for reading at the *Section of Psychology and Educational Sciences' of the 70th session of* Indian Science Congress.

Landis, J.T. (1963). Social correlates of divorce and non-divorce among the unhappy married. *Marriage Family Living,* 25, 178.

McDaniel, E.L. (1967). Relationship between self-concept and specific variables in a low income culturally different population. *Final Report on Head Start Evaluation and Research : 1966-67.* Institute for Educational Development. Section VIII.

Mohsin, S.M. (1979). *Mannual for Mohsin self-concept inventory.* Varanasi : Rupa Psychological Centre.

Ronald, A. (1987). The familial self, the individualized self and the transcendent self : psychoanalysis, reflections on India and America. *Psychoanalytic Review,* 74-237-

Wylle, R.C. (1974). *The Self-Concept : A Critical Survey of Pertinent Literature.* Nebraska: University of Nebraska Press.

Ziket, P.A. and Moses, E.G. (1971). Self-concept and ethnic group membership among public school students. *American Educational Research Journal.*

8

Prejudice among High and Low Self-Disclosee SC and ST Females

Qamar Jahan

Indian society has always been in the grip of different types of prejudices. The most prevalent among them are religious, linguistic, regional, cultural and caste prejudices. Prejudice is, however, defined as a composite of stereotypes, myths and legends in which a group label or symbol is used to classify, characterise, and define an individual or group considered as totality. The most consistent point of agreement in various definitions of prejudice is that it is a sort of negative attitudes towards a particular group or its members. Thus, Singh and Khan (1979) have commented "Prejudice is a negative attitude formed in the individual without proper rationality, justice, or tolerance towards a socially defined group and toward any person perceived to be a member of that group".

In the event of increasing tension and social conflict all over the world, social scientists have shown increasingly greater interest in understanding the personality factors which contribute to the development of prejudice. A number of studies (Enayathullah, 1980; Rai, 1980; Singh, 1980; Hassan, 1978; and Chatterjee *et al,* 1972) have explored the association between prejudice and personality variables.

Certain factors predispose individuals towards development of prejudice. For instance, anxiety ridden person tends to develop prejudice by attributing the cause of his anxiety to some person or a group. Rokeach (1960) found that anxiety manifestations were more among close minded or prejudiced person. Siegal (1954) observed that anxious persons were more susceptible to the development of prejudice than non-anxious persons.

On the basis of these findings one may easily infer that psychologically sick personalities are more prone to develop prejudice as compared to healthy personalities. As Jourard (1961) has contended that the expression of 'true-self' in a proper degree and in an approved form is a symptom of healthy personality. In other words, healthy personality is determined by the extent to which an individual expresses his ideas, feelings, desires, aggression, love, hate, etc. to another person in his social environment. Numerous researchers have found a close relationship between self-disclosure and mental health (Jourard, 1959, 1963; Ruesch and Baleson, 1951; Sinha, 1973). It is, therefore, reasonable to assume that there would be a relationship between self-disclosure and prejudice.

Design

A 2X2 factorial design with two different groups (Scheduled Tribes and Scheduled Castes) and two levels of self-disclosure (high and low) was used. Each group consisted of 50 subjects.

Sample

In order to form above mentioned four groups of subjects, Sinha's Self-Disclosure Inventory (1973) was administered on 400 female subjects (200 Scheduled Tribe—Tharus from Distt. Khiri Lakhimpur, U.P. and 200 Scheduled Castes from Moradabad) studying in 9th and 10th standard from various Government schools between the age ranged of 14-20 years.

Tools

Self-Disclosure Inventory

This measure developed by Sinha (1973) was employed to assess the magnitude of self-disclosure. The inventory consists of eight areas of self-disclosure and six target figures.

Prejudice Scale

This scale developed by Qamar Jahan (1986) was used to assess the magnitude of prejudices of the subjects. The scale has different factors of prejudice, like, religion, caste, customs, culture, nationalism, language, society, education, political, economic and general characteristics, etc. This is a Likert-type five-point scale. It has 32 items. The split half reliability of the scale is .86 and retest reliability is .79.

Procedure

Prejudice scale and socio-economic status scale were administered to all the subjects of different groups, namely, high self-disclosee scheduled Tribes, low self-disclosee Scheduled Castes, and low self-disclosee Scheduled Tribes, high self-disclosee Scheduled Castes and low self-disclosee Scheduled Castes subjects.

Results and Discussions

The mean scores obtained by four groups of subjects on prejudiced scale are given in Table 1 and F-ratios in Table 2.

Table 1
Mean Scores Obtained by Four Groups of Subjects on Prejudice Scale.

	Group		
Conditions	*Scheduled Castes*	*Scheduled Tribes*	*Mean*
High	101.84	172.76	137.30
Low	108.92	110.72	109.82
Mean	105.38	141.74	

Table 2
Showing F-ratios

Source of Variation	*Sums of squares*	*df*	*Mean Square*	*F-ratio*
Among the means of groups	2929.68	3	976.56	
Within groups	751444.60	196	3838.90	.26
Total	754374.28	199		

The means for low self-disclosure group is much greater than the mean for high self-disclosure group. It is, therefore, concluded that high self-disclosure subjects are less prejudiced than low self-disclosure group. Table 1 also shows that the mean for Scheduled Caste group is much less than the mean for Scheduled Tribes group. The results demonstrate that Scheduled Tribes are more prejudiced than Scheduled Castes. The interaction of self-disclosure and culture of two different groups was not significant.

The negative relationship between self-disclosure and prejudice is consistent with the findings obtained by Srole (1956) who noted a positive correlation between anomie (the sense of isolation from others) and prejudice. It seems that a person who remains isolated from others is more likely to develop prejudiced attitudes as compared to one who makes frequent social interactions and is likely to communicate his feelings, desires, urges and ideas to another person and consequently there are chances that his psychic energy will be manifested in constructive and creative deals.

In this context it is also important to note that a positive relationship between self-disclosure and interpersonal attraction, self-disclosure and liking, and self-disclosure and the development of interpersonal relationship have been reported (Lefkowitz, 1970; Jourard, 1971; Altman and Taylor, 1973; Rubin, 1974). In short, these investigations have demonstrated that high self-disclosure subjects are more liked by others, are able to develop cordial interpersonal relation with the members of the other groups than the low disclosee subjects as Dozby (1973) has argued that the individual who never discloses may be unable to establish close relationship with others.

The finding that Scheduled Tribes are more prejudiced than Scheduled Castes are consonant with the type of religiosity proposed by Allport (1954). He recognized two types of religiosity namely, 'institutionalized and 'interiorized'. According to him, persons with institutionalized outlook are influenced more by political and social aspect of religion. They adhere to religion because it is a safe, powerful and superior in group. Such type of religiosity tends to be associated with prejudice. Persons with interiorized religious outlook, on the other hand, are personally absorbed in their religion. They adhere to religion because its basic creed of brotherhood expresses the ideal, one sincerely believes in persons with such religious outlook tend to be more tolerant and less prejudice. It appears that Scheduled Tribes are very traditional in order to gain some immediate advantages. They have developed institutionalized religious outlook and therefore, they are more influenced by political and social aspect of religiosity and consequently have developed prejudiced attitudes.

These prejudices may at least be reduced to considerable extent if people are made to disclose their hidden feelings, urges, ideas, love, and hate to others. Further more, prejudices may also be reduced if people of different religions are educated to developed and what Allport (1954) has called interiorized religious outlook.

REFERENCES

Allport, G.W. (1954). *The Nature of Prejudice*. Rading: Addison Wesley.

Altman, I. and Taylor, D.A. (1973). *Social Penetration: The Development of Interpersonal Relationship*. New York: Holt.

Chatterjee, S. *et al.* (1972). Comparison of social prejudices and their correlates for male and female college students. Mimeographed. Indian Statistical Institute. Calcutta.

Cozby, P.C. (1973). Self-disclosure: a literature review. *Psychological Bulletin*, 79, 1-6.

Enayathullah (1980), Religious affiliation and attitude of students in an Indian university. *Ph.D. Thesis*, Ranchi University, Ranchi.

Hassan, M.K. (1978). A study of ethnocentrism, prejudice and related personality factors in Hindu and Muslim college students, *Psychologia*, XXI, 150-54.

Jourard, S.M. (1959). Healthy personality and self-disclosure, *Mental Hygiene*, 43, 499-507.

Jourard, S.M. (1961). Self-disclosure pattern in British and American college females. *Journal of Social Psychology*, 54, 315-20.

Jourard, S.M. (1963). *Personal Adjustment, and Approach through the Study of Healthy Personality*. New York : Macmillan.

Jourard, S.M. (1971). *The Transparent Seif.* New York : Von Nostrand, Rinehart.

Qamar Jahan (1986). *Prejudice Scale.* Department of Psychology, A.M.U.

Rokeach, M. (1960). *The Open and Close Mind.* New York : Basic Bocks.

Rubin, Z. (1974). Lovers and other strangers: the development of intimacy in encounter and relationship. *American Scientist*, 62, 183-90.

Ruesch, J. and Baleson, C. (1951). Communication and neuroticism, *Psychological Reports*, 18, 355.

Rai, I. (1980). Parents of prejudiced Hindu fcmale children : A study of their attitudes and personality traits. *Unpublished Ph.D. Thesis*, Ranchi University, Ranchi.

Siegel, S. (1954). Certain determinations and correlations of authoritarianism. *Genetic Psychological Monograph*, 49, 187-29.

Singh, A.K. (1980). Prejudice: its correlates in school students, ICSSR Project Report. Ranchi University, Ranchi.

Singh. S.N. and Khan, H.R. (1979). *Prejudice in Indian Society*. Varanasi : Rupa Psychological Corporation.

Sinha. V. (1973). Self-disclosure : an index of healthy personality. *Journal of Psychological Researches*, 21, 14-18.

Srole, L. (1956). Social integration and certain correlates : an explanatory study. *American Social Review*, 21, 709-16.

Section II

Minorities

9

Muslim Dilemma in India: A Legacy of the Past

Mujeeb Ashraf

Muslims in India, once a formidable force, are now members of the lower rung of communities. They are largely economically degraded, socially discriminated, politically disorganized and morally depraved. After independence, even the most backward and downtrodden communities have made great strides, but the Muslims have failed to emerge out of the quagmire of indignity and humiliation.

The Muslims, being the largest minority, should have enjoyed a respectable place and made progress after independence so as to walk with honour and dignity along with their non-Muslim brethren. The Indian Constitution guarantees equal opportunities to everyone. The Muslims, however, despite their glorious past and outstanding contributions to the Indian society and culture are far behind in all respects.

The present precarious conditions of the Muslims is largely a result of the legacy of the past. The rot of the Muslim community began with the fall of the Mughal Empire. Since then the Muslims are a bewildered community unable to restore its lost prestige.

A curious mind cannot take rest without understanding this dilemma. In view of emerging consciousness of human rights a thorough understanding of the reasons responsible for the discrimination of a particular community becomes all the more necessary.

The problems of the Muslims, as generally viewed, are not as a result of God's wrath. In fact, whatever is happening is a reaction and sequa to man's own actions in the past. Any religion which treats man inhumanly, arouses aversion and hatred can never be worthy of respect. A person cannot become superior human being merely by following a particular religion unless he proves himself to be noble in his mode of behaviour and good treatment with human beings irrespective of caste and creed. No concept, based on either nationalism, imperialism or ethnic feelings makes any one superior or inferior human being. In fact, through these concepts the vested interests justify their domination over other people.

Hence, the Muslims, when conquered lands and countries posed themselves as chosen people of Allah. The British, when they emerged as the most powerful nation ruling over the greater part of the globe, justified their conquest and perpetuation of their rule on the basis of the superiority of their race and culture. The Hindu revivalists with their feeling of racial superiority and Hindu nationalism assert their right to rule over India at the exclusion of all other non-Hindu Indians from their scheme of life. Though in India, we adhere to the secular way of life, we still continue to entertain an aversion and mistrust against various religious communities. The Muslims, suffering from all types of problems, could come out of this dilemma in two ways: namely, either in the natural course of events or through human efforts. It is always advisable not to wait for a natural course but to understand the basic causes and adopt a right course in solving the problems before it is too late.

The Psychology of the Muslims

The Muslims are proud of the popularity of Islam all over the world. No religion has ever maintained so strong a hold over the people of the world as did Islam. And, in fact, if understood in true spirit, it definitely provides a happy compromise between the spiritual and temporal aspects of man's life. A number of evils did become part of the body of Islamic beliefs. Even then the Muslims continue to consider themselves a class of superior human beings. This vain pride tends to arouse jealousy and enmity among the followers of other religions.

During the eighth, eleventh and twelfth centuries the Muslim rulers from Arabia, Turkey, Afghanistan invaded India and with small armies defeated Indian rulers. None from the powerful Indian rulers could avert their onslaught. This added pride and glory to the Muslim success in India. The early Muslim conquerors, posing themselves a soldiers of Islam took up the mission as deliverers of the enslaved people of India, ridden by caste system and idolaters rites and customs.

Initially, they humiliated their subjects entertaining great aversion for their idolaters practices. They considered them as infidels to be either converted or forced them to work on subordinate positions. They were humiliated and their temples were destroyed, beside appropriating their wealth. This type of behaviour of the Muslim invaders with their subjects was neither commendable nor justified. In fact, it was totally against the sspirit of Islam.

Qasmi (1996) quotes B.N. Pandey substantiating the principle of toleration in Islam. 'Islam can't be aggressive as it stands for brotherhood and fraternity of the entire human race'. Pandey also quotes from Holy Quran (verse No. 7) in support of his observations, 'Allah directs the Muslims. Allah does not forbid you to treat kindly and equitably toward those who have neither fought you in the matter of religion nor driven you out of your homes, indeed loves the just.'

However, when Muslims established their rule over India, they soon understood the realities hence adopted a policy of appeasement, adjustment and tolerance. The policy of toleration became a fundamental principle and hallmark of Muslim polity from the time of Sultan Altutmish.

This delicate fabric of toleration was broken of and on by the successive invaders. The Muslim policy of toleration, thus, in its early stage passed through a checkered course. The policy of toleration became the hallmark of Mughal polity. The founder of Mughal empire, Babar laid down the permanent basis of this policy. Babar left advice to his son, Humanyun and future Mughal emperors "O my son people of different religions inhabit this country... You must... not allow your brain to be affected by religious bigotry and you must do justice to all people without any religious descrimination" (Qasmi, 1996). The policy of toleration, however, got tremendous fillip under the reign of Akbar. In fact, it was a logical culmination of the long association and interaction of the Muslims with the Hindus. By his policy of *Suleh-kul* and novel measures, Akbar, not only created great trust among Hindus, but was responsible for evolving a composite Indian culture which provided a basis for our National Movement. But this fine product of mutual culture got setback for some time as a result of the opportunistic policies of the British rulers.

Muslims under the British Rule

The British, who settled in India, initially for trade and commerce, of course, with the generous patronage of the Muslim rulers, adopted a course of opportunism. With the advancement made in the field of science, the Europeans rose to the great heights of military superiority and material progress. Equipped with latest scientific techniques, the British soon realised their armed supremacy over Indians in various battles . They, thus, justified in advocating the theory of superiority of their race and culture thereby asserting their right to rule over other nations. With a view to establish their paramountcy over whole of India, the political chicanery and the tricks to divide and rule, became the keynote of their polity in India. What did the

Europeans in general and the British in particular view about Muslims is well reflected in the books written on Muslims and is quite evident from their policies. Servier (1924) in his book, *Islam and the psychology of the Musalmans,* thus observed "Islam is the chief obstacle in our mission of modernization and progress of our civilization". The Christian nations, hence undertook the slow work of breaking the Musalmans as a basis of their policy. The British rulers in India adopted a policy to support the weaker sections of the Indian society so as to counter the fanatic Muslims. Hunter (1871) showed his appreciation of this policy when he commended the government of English East India Company for letting the Muslim power die a natural death.

With this attitude, the British, not only usurped the Muslim rule but ousted them from the higher positions in the administration. Even after that the Muslims continued to suffer from a vain pride and complex of their being politically and religiously a superior community in India. However, the failure of the Uprising of 1857 proved to be an eye opener for them.

Since the fall of the Mughal Empire no bold attempt was made by the Muslims to make a re-appraisal of their predicaments. It was only in the second half of the 19th century that Sir Saiyyid Ahmad Khan, realizing the Muslim dilemma attempted to improve the over all position through spreading western learning among Muslims (Ashraf,1982). It was an attempt, which should have been made long before. It, albeit, improved the Muslim conditions, was too late to bear the desired fruits. No sooner did he launch his Aligarh Movement that the English educated Indians began to demand democratic institutions viz. representation in the councils through election and participation in the administration. Though ostensibly, based on nationalism and secularism, it was basically aimed at improving the lot of Hindu elite. Hence, the movement, in its early phase, never aimed at achieving freedom but to improve the economic lot of those who had learnt English education and aspired for higher jobs (Sarkar, 1983). The Muslims, who had just begun in this direction, could not afford to compete with their Hindu brethren and being in minority, they could not hope to be elected to the councils without reservation. Hence the little success which the Congress movement made served the economic interests of English educated Indians, mostly Bengalis and south Indian Hindus who were well versed in western learning. Sir Saiyyid's movement, although made a faint beginning towards progress, however, by then the Hindus had forged ahead in worldly progress, this legacy continues even today.

The Crisis of Leadership among Muslims

The Muslims, at first, took pride for having ruled over India for about eight hundred years. In fact, the Muslim rulers had long before forfeited their right to be the leaders of the Muslim community let alone Indians, after succumbing to British power. The political leadership of the Indian Muslims then fell in the hands of Ulema. They adopted religious approach to the political and secular problems of the Muslims. Prior to 1857, the Muslims had two alternatives : one, attempting to restore India under Muslims based on *Shariah* which they did try but failed. Besides under new circumstances such a move would have not been acceptable to non-Muslims. The other course could have been to restore the rule of Muslim kings which would have proved a retrograde step unacceptable to those who got acquainted with democratic trends. Till the beginning of the 20th century no effort was made to find out any other alternative course. Different groups of Muslims adopted different approaches. As a result, the Muslim leadership failed to cope with the new conditions.

Unfortunately the Muslim religious reformers also failed to devise a practical way out. In fact the various Muslim Religious Reform Movements further divided the community on religious platform, each adhering to their rigid principles. The renowned Muslim thinker Shah Waliullah made a vigorous attempt to bring about an integration and unity among different schools of thought. However, his movement was rendered in vain, when his basic principles of unity and *ijtihad* were overlooked by his own successor Ulema viz., Shah Abdul Aziz, Shah Ismail, Syed Ahmad Barelvi *et al.* Instead, rose another school, so called Wahhabis, who proved to be more rigid and uncompromising, (Ashraf, 1982). Hence, with the beginning of the 20th century the Muslims were a divided house from even the religious point of view. The staunch religious groups could be identified as Sunnis, Shias, Wahhabis, Deobandis, Barelvis, adding to it Tablighi Jamat and Jamait-i-Islami, each having their different approaches to Muslim problems.

Education and Muslims

Prior to the introduction of western education in India, which ensured better prospects of career, Muslims could be considered to be a highly educated community. Because most of the Muslims, even from amongst the poor family, learnt *Quran,* Persian and other religious disciplines in *Maktabas* and *Madrasas.* However, when the question of English education was posed to the Muslims, Ulema adopted an ambivalent attitude, almost prohibiting them to learn English. They also advised the Muslims to avoid to enter English services. for, they were suspicious of the British intentions and designs. They feared adverse effects on Muslim life. When they began to learn English it was already very late. They had been lagged far behind from their co-religionists in the progress of education. Hence, all these problems, which still continue, are in a way the legacy of the past.

Causes of Failure and the Solution

Why did the Muslims of India fail to ameliorate their problems and cope with the new conditions? The answer is self-evident from the factors discussed above. Briefly speaking the vain pride of the Muslims, their attitude towards their Hindu brethren, inveterate aversion of revivalist Hindus against Muslims as a reaction, half-hearted attempt of Ulema, lack of political and secular leadership among Muslims and lastly too much dependence upon governments are the main factors responsible for Muslim failure to improve their deplorable conditions. However, if the Muslims are eager to come out of the quagmire of indignity, they have to make concerted efforts to unite Muslims on one political platform irrespective of their religious differences. They have to strengthen secularism in India as a way of life. It does not pose any danger to their creed if followed in true spirit. They have to join secular forces unitedly to solve their problems. They should no more allow themselves to be swayed by hollow sloganism of any political party.

The Muslims still continue to be educationally backward. Following the example of Sir Saiyyid Ahmad Khan. They have to establish their independent institutions of modern learning. modern education, as was rightly understood by him, is the only panacea of all the ills of Muslims. In addition to that for achieving economic prosperity the Muslims have to give up dependence upon the government and they have to engage in trade and other independent professions. They have to establish their own industries so as to become self-reliant. The sooner the Muslims realize their predicarnent the better.

On social level, it is sure that Muslims' broadmindedness and their urge to co-exist with the majority community would ultimately ensure them respectable place in India.

REFERENCES

Ashraf, Mujeeb (1982). *Muslim Attitudes Towards British Rule and Western Culture in India.* Delhi : Idara-e-Adabiat. 1-28.

Hunter. W.W. (1871). *The Indian Musalmans* (London. 1871). Lahore : Sheik Mohd. Khalil Premier Book House. 1964 (Reprint).

Qasmi. M. Saud Alam (1996). In reply of letter to "Islam not Bigotry". *The Times of India,* January 12. 10.

Sarkar. S. (1983). *Modern India* (N.B.T.). Delhi : Macmillan India.

Servier. A. (1924). *Islam and the Psychology of the Musalmans,* (As Moss Blundel Trans.). London : Chacman & Hall. VIII-IX and 12. 76.

10

Religious Fanaticism and Communalism: A Socio-Economic Analysis

Asghar Ali Engineer

Religious fanaticism and communalism are two different things yet they have many similarities. Sometimes it becomes difficult to draw a line between the two. These two words are often used interchangeably though not justifiably. We have to understand their proper connotations. It is always not possible to define every concept correctly and precisely. Each living concept is rooted in human life and, like it, tends to be very complex hiding within it various dimensions. Yet we cannot do without definitions. We shall try to define both fanaticism and communalism to convey some of their relevant aspects, if not all.

Before we go on to define fanaticism and communalism we would like to say a few words about religion as it is a common denominator for both. Religion is also not easy to define. However, we would like to throw some light on its main characteristics. The word religion is of Latin origin and its Latin form *religio* carries the sense of binding together. Religion not only binds its followers together but also provides them with a system of beliefs, rituals, institutions, traditions and a sense of sacred. It also gives meaning to their life and a way of relating themselves to the universe and its creator. In other words, it gives them a sense of divine.

Thus *The New Webster's Dictionary and Thesaurus* defines religion as 'man's expression of his acknowledgement of the divine, a system of beliefs and practices relating to the sacred and uniting its adherents in a community, e.g., Judaism, Christianity etc. ...'

As pointed out above, definitions and dictionary meanings do not convey the complexities of real life. For the people religion is much more than this in practice. Many of them claim religion is a whole way of life and in reality compasses all aspects of their lives. Also, all religions are not God-centred. In Asia from these God-centred religions, there have been other religions which are either atheistic or indifferent to God like Jainism and Buddhism. For these religions, God is irrelevant yet they have rich content of spiritualism and holiness. They also evolved a complex constellation of ritual, traditions and institutions. Also, fanaticism, may not be quite alien to them.

Fanaticism

We would now like to define fanaticism and communalism. Let us tackle fanaticism first. Fanaticism can be defined as over enthusiasm and zealousness. This over enthusiasm may cross all bounds of reason and may tend to become wild and dangerous. Fanatics always act overzealously. Such overzealousness may result in severe problems for humanity at large. It must be pointed out here that unlike common understanding, fanaticism is not related to religion, it is related to human psychological type. In other words, fanaticism is not religious but a psychological category. A believer in religion may be open and liberal and another one may be fanatical and overzealous about his/her beliefs. Unfortunately these two distinct categories are often mixed up both by believers and non-believers. Many people tend to think that religion means fanaticism and closed-mindedness. It is far from true. In fact religion *per se* is neither fanatical or liberal. It is what its follower makes it out to be. Also, fanaticism may not be a permanent characteristic of a person. He or she may be fanatic in certain phase of life and may become more open in another phase. Fanaticism has partly to do with lack of knowledge too. One may hold fast to a belief simply on account of ignorance. Acquisition of knowledge may bring about radical change of belief. But again there are different character types. Some people may refuse to acknowledge new frontiers of knowledge and may stick fast to their own age-old beliefs.

Also, at times it becomes difficult to distinguish among firmness, zealousness and fanaticism. In certain situation firmness in ones beliefs may become socially and politically necessary and yet it may border on fanaticism. Such situations arise during the periods of radical social changes and political upheavals. The role of Ulema after the British take over in India is a good example of this. They firmly adhered to their religious beliefs and traditions. They considered the British rule as not only alien but also an invasion on their religion. Though the Christianity (which was formally the religion of the British rulers) was not alien to them as the *Quran* considers it a revealed religion and categorizes the

Christians as *Ahl al-Kitab* (people of the book) yet the 'Ulema developed a strong prejudice against them and even described them as *kafirs* which was not technically correct.

Such a behaviour was not quite unexpected in the context of the radical socio-political changes which were occurring then in the country India was witnessing a great socio-political upheaval. Indian people in general, and Indian Muslims, in particular, had developed a great sense of insecurity which any social or political upheaval naturally brings. In such insecure situations one wants to conserve all beliefs, traditions and institutions. One wants to raise walls of separation from the one perceived as 'the other'. And those who show excessive zeal in such conservation in times of upheaval, become totally blind to the newly emerging reality and display the characteristics of fanaticism.

Going further back into Islamic history one notices that the sack of Baghdad in 1258 by the Mongols similarly induced great sense of insecurity among the Muslims in general and the 'Ulema in particular that the gates of *ijtihad* (creative interpretation) were closed thereafter and the Islamic spirit of dynamism began to stagnate. Imam Ghazali's *Ihya al-'Ulum* Revivification of Knowledge) is representative of this sense of conservation. Thus the firmness of beliefs in a period of social upheavals and radical changes can push one to the boundaries of fanaticism.

Also, one cannot ignore the role of interests in determining ones attitude towards religion or any system of beliefs, for that matter. No doubt one may tend to be fanatic due mainly to ones sincere zeal for a particular religion or political ideology. But, more often than not, ones interests hooked upto that religion or ideology may also make a person 'fanatic'. In this connection it is interesting to note that during the phase of modernization in Afghanistan during the 1930s some highly orthodox 'Ulema issued a *fatwa* that it is un-Islamic to construct roads mainly for the fear that if these roads are constructed modern medicines and judicial system will enter the remote villages and they will loose hold over people's minds and hearts and may probably starve. Many who take religion as their profession (being ordained as priests or earning ones livelihood through leading prayers in mosques or temples etc. or by selling amulets) would more likely resist change than others since their interests lie in maintaining *status quo.*

The Indian 'Ulema also resisted change in the post-mutiny period because they feared that they will have absolutely no place in the British judicial system. The Britishers were ushering in radical changes all around. During the Moghul period the 'Ulema wielded great influence in several spheres, including the political (though not always as far as the political sphere was concerned). They feared, and rightly so, that under the British, they would be great losers. The Muslim feudal as well as the religious elites were great losers as they lost political and religious power to the new rulers. Of course a section of the feudal elite could politically collaborate with the British but the 'Ulema had no such avenues available. They thus remained vehemently opposed to everything British, be it social, legal or political. That partly explains the total refusal of the 'Ulema to collaborate with the alien rulers. It is also to be noted that the 'Ulema generally came from the poorer classes (either from the lower middle or the artisan classes in the urban areas and the poor or marginalised peasantry in the rural areas) they not only had narrow social vision but also felt threatened by the modern changes and hence opposed them. It is a well-known fact that the Muslim artisanry was totally ruined by the introduction of British modern industrial products and thus they remained the greatest opponents of the British rule in India. Many children of these artisans subsequently joined the ranks of the 'Ulema. Thus these sections of Indian society completely lost out when modern changes were introduced in the society.

As opposed to the 'Ulema a section of the scions of feudal families began to enthusiastically welcome British rule and modernization and change as it could benefit them if they collaborated with the British rulers. They thus welcomed change and legitimised the changes by invoking relevant religious traditions. Sir Saiyyid Ahmad Khan, a man of great vision provided leadership to this section. It is interesting to note that both, those opposing change, and those welcoming it, invoked religion to justify their respective positions. It clearly shows that orthodoxy or fanaticism are not integral part of religion. Religion can be made to respond to different human interests and situations.

There was not much resistance to change on the part of Muslims in western India as they benefited by it. North India was the real seat of Muslim power but Muslims in western India faced entirely different situation. Unlike the north, Muslims in western India were led by trading communities who benefited by the new prospects of trade and the new educational system was thought to be beneficial for promoting it. While Sir Saiyyid faced stiff resistance when he founded MAO College in Aligarh, Badruddin Tyebji received full cooperation from Muslims of Bombay when he founded the Anjuman-e-Islam High School. Such an educational institution was thought to be beneficial by the trading classes.

Thus it will be seen that fanaticism and resistance to change is often dictated by the interests which are served by the old system. Moreover, as pointed out before, fanaticism cannot be associated with religion alone. It can be true of any system of belief and ideology, social, cultural or political. When socio-cultural systems are under attack or invaded by foreign socio-cultural system, dogged and fanatical resistance can be built against it. Today we are passing through very critical phase ushered in through television and ever faster means of communication. It has become much easier now than the nineteenth century, for western culture to invade us. Afro-Asian cultures have common elements but western culture—though it also differs from one western country to the other, have striking commonalities and is seen as totally alien by the peoples of Afro-Asian countries. No wonder that we often talk of "cultural invasion" from the west. It is producing strong reaction in the Afro-Asian countries and various fundamentalist movements are partly the result of this invasion which is perceived with hostility.

We would like to throw some light on the fundamentalist movements which are considered as fanatical and rightly so. Fundamentalist movements, particularly the Islamic fundamentalist movements are partly the result of westernization, secularisation and modernization. All these processes are seen as totally alien by those who lost out and could not gain anything from them. The entire Muslim society is deeply divided due to modernisation and secularisation. The economic and political elites who have benefited support it and religious elite and those strata of the society which were left out, oppose it (i.e., modernization and secularisation). Be it in Algeria or Iran in the Middle East, or Indonesia in the Far East, causes are almost similar though regional and local specificities cannot be ignored.

In Iran before the Islamic revolution the Shah's modernization campaign though enthusiastically supported by the higher classes, was a disaster for the lower classes, specially the small peasantry and the slum dwellers of south Tehran. Shah's so-called land reforms also brought unmitigated disaster for the small holders as the big landsharks took over their land and they ended up in slums in big cities. The increased oil prices also led to high rate of inflation hitting the poorer sections much harder. Unemployment also greatly increased as there was not much scope for industrialisation in Shah's economic policies.

It is these deprived sections of society in Iran who basically stood with Ayatullah Khomeini. These deprived sections of society perceived modernisation and secularisation as nothing less than unmitigated disaster.

Their economic plight worsened as fast as the upper class elite's plight improved. Their only refuge was traditional religion. It gave them emotional and mental comfort. For them what Khomeini called 'the great Satan' was an evil embodied, responsible for bringing change which harmed their lives. How could change *per se* be welcome to them? Moreover the change eroded all their cultural values. Women's modesty was destroyed and they were seen sporting mini-skirts exposing parts of the body considered sin in a traditional culture. All traditions were hated by the westernised elite.

The religious elite either came from these lower classes or was in close touch with them. Also Iran had long history of confrontation between the clergy and the rulers. When the rulers trampled upon all traditions thoughtlessly and supported westernisation project totally ignoring the prevailing social ethos, it produced strong reaction calling upon people to fight western imperialism and go back to Islam which is complete way of life. Such movements tend to be fanatical as they have to fight against the system and need much greater verve and energy. Moreover the movement was perceived to be the liberator of the poor and the oppressed. It is interesting to note that Khomeini used a Qur'anic concept which stressed the inevitable struggle between the oppressed *(mustad'ifin)* and the oppressors *(mustakbirin)*. In the given conditions in Iran this Qur'anic concept was highly appealing and people responded enthusiastically. Thus the battle between the western neo-imperialism and Iran also became a battle between the western *kufr* and Iranian Islam. Being the battle of liberation, the oppressed people of Iran fought it with unprecedented zealotry and vigour. Call it fanaticism or fundamentalism.

The traditional Asian societies in general, and the Islamic societies in particular, have a strong sense of sacred and are inspired by intuitional or revealed truth. The concept of sacred and values derived from revealed truth plays central role in the lives of the Asian people. Westernization and modernization, on the other hand, have no place for the sacred, not even for values. Being secular in nature, the western civilization is achievement oriented—achievement through any means. The Asian and Islamic civilizations, on the other hand emphasise values, as opposed to achievements. The former leads to more competition and dynamism while the latter induces an attitude of contentment and stasis. For the former market is the greatest arena of achievement, for the latter it is only a means to fulfil the genuine—as opposed to the artificial—basic needs of life.

But while the West does not believe in reigning in or tempering its limitless desire for change and achievement with a sense of values, the orthodox and conservatives among Muslims do not accept any desirability for change at all. They tend to accept new science and technology if it benefits them (many of them are jet-sets like business elite and they are also using computers, television, etc. for spreading Islamic orthodoxy) but reject any idea of change when it comes to religious dogmas, traditions and ideas. This duality is giving rise to serious social and spiritual malaise. Several contradictions have arisen which cannot be resolved easily.

The question of status of women is foremost among these contradictions. When the Taliban captured power recently in Afghanistan, they declared that all girls schools will be closed down and that women cannot go out of their homes unaccompanied by close male relatives. In Saudi Arabia also, women cannot go out unaccompanied by male relatives nor can they drive. This is not Qur'anic requirement at all. There is no such divine injunction in the Qur'an. It was a convention which developed in early history of Islam—much after the death of the Prophet of Islam—when Islam was medievalized. The Islamic jurisprudence came under the influence of medieval feudal values. The liberative impact of Islam was completely lost.

It is this medieval Islam which is sought to be perpetrated by Taliban and others. The Taliban—*madrasa* students—themselves are product of conservative tribal society and their understanding of Islam is deeply influenced by their own tribal social ethos. They refuse to admit any change. For them change is *bid'ah*—innovation and hence sin. Product of a stagnant society, the transcendent and liberative aspects of religion are totally lost on them. To refuse to admit any change, and excessive zeal for inherited religion, is fanaticism. Such fanaticism is harmful for deeper religious truth and its liberative potential.

Fanaticism, an irrational zeal for the given, not only refuses to admit liberative and spiritual potential of religion, also refuses to see the sociological impact on religious traditions. While the founder of a religion deeply influences social ethos, is also influenced by social traditions and practices. The religion cannot be frozen in a given spacio-temporal frame. Social dynamics brings about profound changes and one has to continuously endeavour to apply the core-values of religion to the newly developing situations. This is what the fanatics refuse to do. In the Islamic societies the women have suffered most by this fanatical refusal to admit change. And such fanaticism has brought only ridicule. These fanatics are trying to preserve their own traditional social values in the garb of Islam.

In fact no society escapes this fanaticism, not even western societies. The concept of 'fundamentalism' is in fact the product of modern American society. Some Christians believed during the thirties of twentieth century, in the literal truth of Bible and they were described as 'fundamentalists'. It is this borrowed western concept which is being applied to some religious movements in Asia. Even today there are evangelists in America who vigorously preach fundamentalism and have bought special T.V. channels for the purpose. Some, known as pro-life, kill those doctors and nurses performing abortion and burn down their dispensaries. New sects are born who preach violence and end of the world. The Shinrikhyo (the Supreme Truth) movement used poisonous gas in a Tokyo subway system to kill several people.

Hinduism, religion of amorphous nature, quite unlike Islam or Christianity, supposedly much more tolerant, also could not escape this fate. It produced fanatics who considered it their religious duty to demolish Babri Mosque. Their tolerance was at its lowest ebb and their behaviour totally irrational. In fact their fanaticism brought great shame to India. Of course such high degree of fanaticism was induced through high pitched political propaganda to achieve a political goal. Nevertheless the fact is that those hordes who demolished Babri Masjid behaved as most excited zealots out to destroy the place of worship of others. Also, a large number of trishul wielding *sadhus* joined in the despicable act. A *sadhu* is supposed to be highly restrained and capable of self-control because he achieves sadhuhood through years of *sadhna* (spiritual exercise). Unfortunately they also behaved like an agitated mob showing high degree of fanaticism like common man. The educated Hindu middle classes (with honourable exceptions of those who were committed to secularism and fought religious fanaticism) also showed similar traits. At certain junctures in history entire community comes under the influence of either religious or political fanaticism. The sense of being different and unique from others grips the mind. This so happens at a time of crisis and social upheaval.

Similarly the Buddhist monks in Sri Lanka showed strong trait of fanaticism and put pressure on the government not to give concessions to the Tamil community. Like Hinduism, Buddhism also apparently has no traits of rigidity and dogmatism. In fact, if one goes by the Buddha's teachings it is most rational, open and tolerant. There are no theological dogmas of any kind as far as Buddhism is concerned. Yet the Buddhist monks, who are also supposed to be self-restrained behaved like fanatics and zealots and contributed to ethnic crisis in Sri Lanka.

These examples clearly show that religious fanaticism exists in all religious or national communities which exhibits itself at crucial junctures. No community can boast of being free from it. However, what is necessary to understand the underlying causes.

Communalism

As pointed out at the outset of this essay, there is much in common between religious fanaticism and communalism and yet there are important differences. Religious fanaticism leads to strong feeling of self-righteousness and feeling of 'otherness' towards followers of other faiths. Also, it leads to the feeling of truth being the monopoly of ones own religion. In other words, it leads to the feeling of theological superiority. The communal feeling is distinct in this respect from fanatical attitude. Communalism is more about conflict of interests between two communities. Before we discuss communalism, let us define communalism as best as we can.

Communalism has been defined in different manners by different scholars. In fact in English language, it is considered a positive rather than a pejorative term. For example, *The New Webster's Dictionary* defines it as something "belonging to a community" or a "system of decentralized government by which large powers are delegated to small communities". However, in Indian context, it is used in a negative and condemnatory sense. In Indian context we can define communalism as 'secular conflict between two religious communities'. Or, it can also be defined as 'an attempt to achieve secular goal through religious means'.

Communalism in this sense is a modern and not a medieval phenomenon. We do not hear of communal conflict between Hindus and Muslims in the Sultanate or Mughal period. This conflict came into being during the British period, specially after the failure of war of independence in 1857. There were two important factors contributing to the genesis of communalism : one, the British policy of divide and rule; and second, competition for political power between the Hindu and Muslim elites.

When the Britishers introduced, under pressure of public opinion, certain democratic measures and agreed to give some elective seats to Indians, the question arose in what proportions it should be distributed between the Hindus and Muslims. In other words, it was competition between the power elites which threw up the problem of communalism. It should be understood that religion *per se* is not responsible for genesis of communalism, as commonly misunderstood. Religion, at best, is an instrumental and not the fundamental cause. Since religion has a strong appeal, it is used as an instrument by the power elites for achieving their secular objectives. The whole history of communalism is a witness to this.

In communal conflict, as distinct from religious conflict, no theological controversies are involved and no disputes about superiority or falsehood of this or that religion. The question is always about some secular objective. We will give few examples to show the real nature of communalism in India.

The biggest communal controversy during the freedom movement was about the share in power between the Hindu and Muslim elite. Pakistan came into being on this question, not on any question of religious nature. It is interesting to note that the Pakistan movement was led by Jinnah who was highly westernized and secularized person. He paid only lip service to Islam and was never a practitioner of his nominal faith. He was a political Muslim rather than a follower of Islam. He fought, not to uphold any Islamic doctrine, but to get larger share of power for the Muslim elite in independent India. A section of Muslim elite was demanding 33 per cent share in seats in Parliament as against the 25 per cent population of Muslims. It was not acceptable to the Hindu elite.

The orthodox 'Ulema, on the other hand, stood for composite nationalism and vehemently opposed the creation of Pakistan. The Jami'at-e-Ulema-i-Hind, the organization of the Deobandi 'Ulema, which was highly prominent organization of the Indian 'Ulema, always remained an ally of Indian National Congress. In fact Jinnah was hard put to find support of any such prominent Muslim theologians. It clearly shows that the basis of Pakistan was not religion but a purely secular goal of share in power. Had that question been resolved to the satisfaction of both sides, Pakistan would not have come into existence.

Similarly in the post-partition period, all communal controversies were secular in nature: either seeking the votes of this or that community or economic competition. Many scholars in this field, including this writer have been theorising that communal riots in the post-partition India have taken place in those regions where political or economic competition between the Hindus and Muslims was quite intense. Certain districts of the western UP which have more than 20 per cent Muslim population and which also have newly emerging Muslim entrepreneur class, saw much more communal violence than other districts. The first major riot after independence in Jabalpur in 1962, was caused, among other things, by intense competition between a Hindu and a Muslim beedi manufacturers. Another major riot in Ahmedabad in 1969 was a result of polarization of secular and communal forces in the country after Mrs. Indira Gandhi split the Congress and appealed to the minorities for support.

The decade of eighties saw the highest degree of communalisation of Indian politics. There were several reasons for this and all these reasons were quite secular in nature. Firstly, Mrs Gandhi leaned towards the Hindu vote after being unsure of the minority votes, particularly of Muslim votes. She, in a very subtle—and at times in an open manner tried to mobilize upper and middle caste Hindu votes and ended up communalizing the political scene. She even lent subtle support to the Vishwa Hindu Parishad (VHP) and used the controversy about conversion of few *Dalits* to Islam in the Meenakshipuram district of Tamil Nadu to win the Hindu sympathy. She also tried to manoeuvre the militant Sikh politics in Punjab to her advantage. She lent support to the militant Sikh like Bhindranwale.

Mrs. Gandhi's attempt to mobilize the Hindu vote in her favour led to intense competition with the BJP as the BJP considered the upper caste and middle caste Hindus as its own constituency. The BJP was further marginalised in the 1984 parliamentary elections after the assassination of Mrs. Gandhi and could win only two seats. The BJP then began searching for a powerful issue which would politically rehabilitate it. The unfortunate Shah Bano controversy, which the orthodox Muslim leadership—both religious as well as non-religious—tried to exploit to the hilt for its political windfall, led to another controversy, i.e., about the Ramjanambhoomi-Babri Masjid. Rajiv Gandhi, a politically inexperienced person and ineptly advised by his friends, while on one hand, agreed to change the secular law and enacted the Muslim Women's Bill (depriving them of the benefit of maintenance under the secular law), agreed, on the other, to throw open the doors of Babri Masjid for Hindus to worship the idols of Ram and Sita which were smuggled into the mosque in 1948.

These controversies, i.e., the Shah Bano and Ramjanambhoomi, apparently religious in nature, were, in fact political controversies and led to intense communalization of Indian politics. The communal fanatics at last demolished Babri Masjid leading to a communal disaster. The decade of eighties thus witnessed several major communal riots which shook the whole country. Beginning with the Moradabad riot in 1980 this decade witnessed major riots in Biharsharif (1981), Meerut and Baroda (1982), Anti-Sikh riots (1984), Bhivandi-Bombay riots (1984), Ahmedabad riots (1985-86), Meerut riots (1987), Bhagalpur riots (1989), Hyderabad and several other riots in Karnataka, Gujarat, UP (1990). These riots were of course followed by Mumbai, Surat, Ahmedabad, Kanpur, Delhi riots after demolition of Babri Masjid in December 1992-93. Several thousands of people, specially Muslims, died in these riots and their properties worth several crores destroyed.

However, there has been a general respite in communal situation thereafter and in last couple of years there have been no major communal riots. The year 1995 witnessed only two minor unplanned riots in February in Moradabad and in March in Aligarh. However, 1996 was almost riot-free year except three very minor skirmishes in Pen and Junnar in Maharashtra and in Lucknow in UP, all at the end of September. This again shows that communalism and communal violence gets intensified during the period of political crisis or economic downturn generating high rates of unemployment or intense economic competition. Any religious controversy could be seized by the vested interests as a powerful instrument to promote their political or socio-economic interests.

It will be seen from the above analysis that in almost all the countries ethnic and communal conflicts have emerged due to democratic competition for controlling political or economic power. In all such conflicts, it is a universal rule that minorities suffer more than the majority.

11

Muslim Minority: Their Quest for Survival against Communalism

Sheema Aleem

There has been steep rise in communal violence in recent years. In India, the politics of division, separation and communalism are ruining the age-old traditions of the unity and fraternity by hampering the psycho-social and economic development of the minorities on some pretext or other. As a result their overall development is affected, on occasions their identity is challenged.

Due to this incidence of communal violence since independence minorities are in constant fear of their existence and they find it difficult to face such situations from time to time. Thus it is needed to suggest and extend devices to alter world so that they can overcome the situation and maintain the psycho-social well-being.

Communalism is perhaps one of the most serious problems which Indian society faces. There is no instant or manipulative solution to this problem nor can any short-term compromises solve the problem.

The Nature of Communal Conflicts

The communal conflict, manifested in the form of communal disturbance is primarily a result of social disharmony, disequilibrium and demagogy.

In a communal disturbance, layers of agitated emotions permeate the atmosphere. Revenge, enemity and hatred are symptoms of the fury of one group against the other. The violence exercised by the people can be described as violence of confrontation emerging from the wrath of one community against the other due to either injured status, prestige or feelings, it can also be described as a release of hostile tendencies of the masses.

What is Communalism?

Communalism is 'above all an ideology', 'a false consciousness', 'a struggle for scarce resources', 'competition for jobs', 'an instrument of ruling class politics' and so on. At a general level, W.C. Smith has defined it as 'the ideology which has emphasised as the social, political and economic unit the group of adherents of each religion and has emphasised the distinction, even the antagonism between such groups' (Smith, 1979).

Communalism operates at different levels ranging from individual relations and interests at the local, institutional and national level and to communal politics and riots. There is a whole range of social relations and politics over which communalism prevails. This spread of communalism involves two inter-related central issues. First is the state of consciousness in society. The second is communalism as an instrument of power, not purely for capturing state power, but political, social and economic power at almost all levels of social organization (Panikkar, 1991).

Communalism involves conflict among caste, ethnic and religious groups. It involves social conditioning and the forces of history alongwith the psyche of the individual.

Communalism as an Expression of Class Conflict

Asghar Ali Engineer (1986) links 'communalism' to conflicts of the elite of community and to their class interest.

Communalism is described as a tool to mobilize people for or against, by raising appeal on communal lines. According to him the threat to the privileges of the elite is expressed through communal channels what he calls the 'ideologisation of interest'.

Explaining the 'why and how' of a communal riot, Asghar Ali (1980) writes 'it is the product of transformation of socio-economic censation into a religious one'.

Gulam Rabbani Taban holds that communalism of every hue and variety is a social problem. To him the 'process of communalisation is a part of the imperialist intrigue carried on through imperialist agents'.

Communalism as an Expression of Religious Hostility

Bipan Chandra (1986) describes communalism as the product of a certain social situation as understood in terms of society, economy and politics which creates problems. For Chandra it is something to be set right by transforming the social situation.

Communalism as a Political Phenomenon

Prabha Dixit (1974) explains 'Communalism as a political doctrine, which makes use of religious-cultural differences to achieve political ends.' She expounds that communalism was not the result of religious hostility between the Muslims and Hindus but was evolved as a political doctrine and was closely linked with the struggle for power.

One way of looking at the phenomenon of communalism is to consider it as the urge for differentiation and autonomy of a community and its resistance to the so-called integrationist attempts of the forces of uniformity. It is the consequence of the failure of nationalism to represent and accommodate urges of all communities (Puri, 1985).

Communalism in India is essentially a political phenomenon. The outcome of communalism in the form of group prejudices, communal contradictions, tensions and riots is due to struggle for control over the scarce resources. Its roots are economic power and political dominations. Individuals struggle to gain control over these through various devices. A common device adopted in developing countries is the exploitation of the illiterate and tradition bound masses. The masses in these countries belonging to different ethnic or plural groups even today remain unorganized. They have a strong bias for traditions. Religiosity is one of the strong-holds of traditionalism. The power seekers, therefore, do their best to influence the masses. Communalism, therefore, needs to be analyzed from the perspective of power relations and control over the means of production in the local or national markets (Banu, 1985).

Ethnic Identity

The affiliation with any group or organization is strengthened only if one derives strength or power in any form as a result of his affiliation. This inferred power is termed as 'identity'. The evolution of identity is based upon the inherent need of human beings to feel that he/she belongs to a particular community.

Tajfel (1972) has tried to explain that it can be assumed that an individual will tend to *reamer rotating as a member or seek membership* of new groups. These groups have some contributions to make towards the positive aspect of his social identity, i.e., aspects from which he derives some satisfaction. An individual's identity is mixture of social and personal factors.

Minorities are far more sensitive on the question of identity for understandable reasons they as are more apprehensive of their religion and culture. This is precisely where the danger of identity becoming aggressive and status quoist lies. Those who wish to perpetuate status quo take advantage of this sensitivity and bring about communal polarization to oppose any change.

When the individual finds himself belonging to a particular group, at that time the processes of social comparison occurs at the intergroup level and to a great extent belongingness with a group contributes to his or her sense of positive social identity and an individual will remain a member of that group. If the group fails to satisfy these requirements, the individuals may (i) try to change the structure of the group, (ii) seek a new dimension of comparison to enhance a sense of positive social identity, and (iii) leave the group and distance himself from it. However, individuals who are members of a group that suffer inferior social status or caste develop weaker identity. Racial and ethnic minorities are the best examples of this. Members of ethnic minorities usually find themselves in complex network of social relationship, within which they try to define their social identity (Tajfel, 1984).

The minorities in any society develop a number of negative feelings towards majority because of many reasons demand new system of maintaining itself and over a period of time it takes place. The minorities are aware of their cultural, social, political or historical differences, and claim at the same time for the right to shed some of the most of these differences. The term 'minority' has generally been described as a diversity of group and social categories. Majority-minority relations do not appear until one group successfully imposes its will upon the other.

Communalism is a disease, which warps the mind. It is a way of thinking, the result of the perversion of religion and the distortions of history. Those who have lived for decades with communalism as their creed are beyond redemption.

The tragedy is that as they think, so do their children grow to think. Indians have classed to think of themselves as Indians, but look upon themselves only in terms of their religion, state or region. Article 25 of our Constitution provides for freedom of conscience, and the free profession, practice and propagation of religion. The ringing sovereignty of this article of the Constitution has, however, fallen on deaf ears and may who so glibly prattle about "Secularism", and "National Integration" are themselves communalists at heart. In order to root out this cancer from our country, it is necessary to re-orient the thinking of the youth of our country and thus save them from communal brain-washing by their parents" (Justice Madan, 1984).

Communalism and its disastrous effect are matters of life and death for our society. Therefore, all of us need planning effect of the active of the thinking about the problem, thinking about the planning effect problem that communalism gives birth.

The Muslims owe a responsibility to themselves their leadership is too poor in ideas and imagination and is backward looking, perhaps even incompetent to guide them. What then need in their own interest and for a better future is education and not only in Madrasas (Aloo Dastur).

Communalism can best be combated by providing non-communal forums for meeting the legitimate needs of the people and a sense of belonging to a community and cultural and political urges. Unless alternative basis of identity are made available mere appeal to shed communalist basis of identity would have marginal effect.

Without damaging the roots of the society, any attempt to inform its natural and traditional identities with universal and human values would certainly be useful.

Communalism is manifestation of frustration, expression of anger, weakness and overcoming of failure. It is a mean to achieve goals through foul means. Moreover, communal riots and its continuity for a larger period of time brings the victims at the point of revolt, aggression, alienation and withdrawals because of their sufferings. The minorities and poor have been the worst sufferers of the communal carnage. The need of the hour is to stop these monstrous and barbaric practices in society. For this the basic principles of discouraging the exploitation of emotion, stoping the division of society, giving fair treatment to all and bringing the minorities and downtrodden to the mainstream will be a step in the direction of achieving the goal. Moreover, politics of opportunism appeasement, communalism and discrimination have to be tackled with honesty and justice. State terrorism, stubborness of the governments and concentration of power in particular group must stop for the integrity, prosperity and strength of the nation.

REFERENCES

Chandra Bipin (1984). Communalism—The way out. *Many Forces of Communalism*. Publication Centre for Research in Rural and Industrial Development.

Dastur (1985). Communalism as viewed by a political scientist. *Communalism in India*. In Asghar Ali (Ed.). Delhi : Ajanta Publishers.

Engineer, A.A. (1980). Why and how off communal riots. *Mainstream*, XIX. 7:18.

Engineer, A.A. (1986). Communalism, its facts and roots. *Mainstream*. XXIV, 43:16.

Justice Madan (1984). *View on Communalism*. Seminar on Multidimensional approaches to communalism. Organized by the Institute of Islamic Studies, Bombay.

Panikkar, K.N. (1991). *Communalism in India : History, Politics and Culture,* New Delhi : Manohar Publications.

Puri Balraj (1985). Understanding and Transcending Communalism. In Asghar Ali Eng. (Ed.). *Communalism in India.* Delhi : Ajanta Publishers.

Smith, W.C. (1979). *Modern Islam in India : A Social Analysis.*

Taban, G.R. (1981). New Dimensions of Communalism. *Mainstream,* XIX, 48:7.

Tajfel, H. (1982). Social identity and intergroup relations. *P. Maison desk society de L'Homme,* Cambridge : Paris and Cambridge University Press.

Zainab, B. (1985). A political scientists. *View of Communalism : Communalism in India,* edited by Asghar Ali Eng. Delhi : Ajanta Publishers.

12

Intra-Societal Tension and Feeling of Insecurity as Factors Related to Prejudice in Hindus and Muslims

Mohammad Ghufran

The problem of intergroup relations and tension is of vital importance. Prejudice is one of the factors determining the inter-group behaviour. Because of its importance social psychologists have long been engaged in analyzing the various factors which are responsible in increasing or reducing the prejudice. Authoritarianism, dogmatism, alienation, anxiety, and religiosity are some of the most studied factors that are found to be positively related with prejudice, while education is considered to be negatively related with it. In the present investigation, the roles of the feeling of insecurity, social tension and religion of the subjects in the development and/or maintenance of prejudice have been explored.

Feeling of insecurity has been regarded as a factor contributing to the development of prejudice. Two well known publication, *Nature of Conflict* (UNESCO, 1957) and *Nature of Prejudice* by Allport (1955) provide penetrating analysis of factors which ultimately lead to group violence and prejudice. Feeling of insecurity is one of the important factors. Murphy *et al.* (1953) considered feeling of insecurity prevailing among Muslims as one of the most important causes of Hindu-Muslim tension in India. On the other hand, Chatterjee *et al.* (1967) in their ex-post-facto research in Rourkela did not find any permanent social insecurity or deep rooted communal mistrust among Muslims for non-Muslims.

Mohsin (1976), in his study of attitude formation and change, observed a high correlation between feeling of insecurity and ethnic prejudice. He also found a strong negative attitude of the two major ethnic groups towards each other, which was consistent with the realistic group conflict theory developed by Campbell. It may be pointed out that Campbell (1966) had maintained that a real threat causes hostility towards source of the threat. Thus real threat increases ethnocentrism and prejudice. Conflicts among members of different castes and religious groups are important force in the development of prejudice. Dodd (1935) mentioned on the basis of his findings that amount of hostility shown by different groups towards each other was closely related to the amount of recent group conflict. Dudycha (1942), Seago (1947) and Buchanan (1951) also obtained the same results. The experimental studies carried out by Sherif *et al.* (1961) also showed that intergroup competition and conflict led to the development of hostile-feelings and tensions between the groups. Not only the social distance between the groups increased but in addition the members of one group developed and applied highly negative stereotypes to the members of other group.

Keeping in view the above discussion, the present study was conducted to investigate the prejudice among Muslim and Hindu subjects in relation to the feeling of insecurity and social tension.

Methodology

Sample

Social tension is one of the variables of the present study, so the first step of sampling was to identity cities with high and low social tension, where the study was to be conducted. The two cities from where the sample was drawn were Azamgarh—a city free from communal riots and regarded as low tension city, and Mau Nath Bhanja—a city where several communal riots have occurred and regarded a high tension prevailing city.

Initially 130 male adult subjects were selected from Azamgarh and 130 from Mau Nath Bhanjan in such a manner that half of the subjects from both cities were Muslims and remaining half were Hindus. The short form of Maslow Security-Insecurity Inventory developed by Srivastava, (1976) was administered to identify subjects for high and low insecurity groups. These groups were identified on the basis of median. The value of median was computed separately for each group of subjects. In the process of identifying subjects of high and low insecurity feeling subjects falling at median point were dropped. In order to equate the groups in terms of the size, some cases were further dropped. so the final sample comprised of 240 subjects.

Tools

1. Srivastava's 'Short Form of Maslow Security-Insecurity Inventory' (Srivastava, 1976) was used to identify the low and high insecure subjects.

2. Mohsin's (1976) 'Measure of Ethnic Attitude' was used to measure prejudice. It is comprised of 50 trait descriptive adjectives; 50 per cent desirable and 50 per cent undesirable. A score of one is given for each adjective ticked by the subjects. Prejudice score of the subjects is obtained by totalling the bad qualities ticked by the subjects to the outgroup and substracting from it the total good qualities assigned to the outgroup and adding to it 10, a constant.

Results

The present investigation consisted of three variables, viz., religion, insecurity feeling and social tension and each variable was varied in two ways. Thus using a 2×2×2 factorial design, the scores obtained by eight groups of subjects were analyzed with a view to studying separate, as well as interactional effects of religion, insecurity feeling and social tension on prejudice. The three-way analysis of variance was used for this purpose.

Table 1

Mean Prejudice Scores Obtained by Eight Groups of Subjects and Mean of Means for Religion

	High Tension		*Low Tension*		
Religion	*High insecurity feeling*	*Low insecurity feeling*	*High insecurity feeling*	*Low insecurity feeling*	*Mean of Means*
Hindu	17.47	10.23	12.98	08.50	12.30
Muslim	16.93	11.74	13.86	09.86	12.95

Table 2

Mean of Means of Low and High Insecurity Feeling

	High Tension		*Low Tension*		*Mean of*
	Hindu	*Muslum*	*Hindu*	*Muslim*	*Means*
Low insecurity feeling	10.23	11.74	08.50	09.26	09.93
High insecurity feeling	17.47	16.93	12.98	13.86	15.31

Table 3

Mean of Means for Social Tension

Social Tension	*High insecurity feeling*		*Low insecurity feeling*		*Mean of Means*
	Hindu	*Muslim*	*Hindu*	*Muslim*	
High Tension	17.47	16.93	10.23	11.74	14.09
Low Tension	12.98	13.86	08.50	09.26	11.15

Table 4

Summary of Analysis of Variance

Source of Variation	*Sum of Squares*	*df*	*Mean Squares*	*F*
Religion (A)	122	1	122	02.98
Insecurity feeling (B)	681.20	1	681.20	16.65*
Social tension (C)	1651.71	1	1651.71	40.37*
Interaction :				
Religion × Insecurity feeling (AxB)	103.42	1	103.42	02.53
Religion × Social tension (AxC)	65.34	1	65.34	01.60
Social tension × insecurity × feeling (BxC)	318.68	1	318.68	07.79*
Religion × insecurity feeling × Social × tension (AXBXC)	163.14	1	163.14	03.99**
Within treatment or Error	9491.99	232	40.91	--

** Significant at .01 level*

*** Significant at .05 level.*

Discussion

A perusal of Table 4 reveals that the F-ratio for the main effect of religion is not significant, indicating that Hindu and Muslim subjects do not differ significantly in their prejudice scores. This result does not support the earlier findings of Adinarayana (1953), Hassan(1975, 1978), and Enayatullah (1980) who found Muslim subjects to have more religious prejudice than Hindu subjects. While the studies conducted by Natraj (1965), Chatterjee *et al.* (1967), and Sarkar and Hasan (1973) support this finding. These investigators also did not obtain any significant difference between the mean prejudice scores of Hindu and Muslim subjects. It seems that religions being advocate of moral and humanitarian values do not generate prejudice in their followers towards the followers of other religion.

F-ratio B or the main effect of insecurity feeling is 16.65, which is significant at 0.01 level of confidence. Table 2 for mean of means of low and high insecurity feeling shows that high insecure subjects have obtained 15.31 mean prejudice score and the mean prejudice score of low insecure subjects is 9.93. Since F-ratio for feeling of insecurity has come out to be significant the subjects having high insecurity feeling are more prejudiced than the subjects having low insecurity feeling. This finding suggests that feeling of insecurity is the important factor in the development of prejudice. Feeling of insecurity generates sectarian tendencies and leads the subjects to interact negatively with members of other communities. Allport (1955), Murphy *et al.* (1953) and Mohsin (1976) also observed that the feeling of insecurity is one of major contributing factors in developing the negative attitudes.

The results presented in Table 4 also show that the F-ratio for the main effect of social tension is 40.37, which is significant at .01 level to confidence. The higher mean prejudice score of subjects belonging to high social tension prevailing area than the subjects of low tension prevailing area (vide Table 3) indicates the social tension is very important factor in the formation of prejudice. Social tension limits the contacts between intergroups, which, in turn, accentuates a more negative attitude towards members of outgroups. The communal riots and conflicts compel the members of both Hindu and Muslm communities to take shelter into their own shell and do not interact with the members of other communities. Although, there are no specific study on the effect of social tension on prejudice, yet, studies conducted by Dodd (1935), Dudycha (1942), Seago (1947) and Buchanan (1951) show that open conflicts between the nations led to develop an unfavourable attitude for the other nation.

The interactional effects of religion and insecurity feeling is not significant. In the same way the interactional effect of religion and social tension is also not significant. These results indicate that neither religion and insecurity feeling nor religion and social tension interact to influence the prejudice of the subjects. The F-ratio for the interactional effect of insecurity feeling and social tension is 7.79, which is significant at .01 level, indicating that insecurity feeling and social tension interact in a significant way to influence the prejudice of the subjects. This finding suggests that the feeling of insecurity among the subjects residing in high social tension prevailing area may add to the increment of their prejudice. The F-ratio for the interactional effect of all three independent variables is 3.99, which is significant at .05 level of confidence, indicating that religion, insecurity feeling and social tension interact to influence the prejudice significantly. This finding lead us to explain that the feeling of insecurity among Hindus and/or Muslims of high social tension prevailing area may further add to the increment of prejudice.

REFERENCES

Adinarayan, S.P., (1953). Before and after independence : A study of racial and communal attitudes in India. *British J. of Psychology*, 44, 108-15.

Allport, G.W. (1955). *The Nature of Prejudice, Boston, Massachusetts* : Harvard University.

Buchanan,W. (1951). Stereotypes and tensions as revealed by the UNESCO International Poll. *International Social Bulletin*, 3, 315-28

Campbell, D.T. (1966). Ethnocentrism and other altruistic values, In D. Levine (Ed), *Nebraska Symposium on Motivation*. Nebraska : University of Nebraska Press, 1966, 238-311.

Chatterjee, B.B. Singh, P.N. and Rao, G.R.S. (1967). *Riots in Rourkela : A Psychological Study*. Bombay : Popular Book Services.

Dodd, S.C. (1935). A social distance test in Near East. *American Journal of Psychology*. 41. 194-204.

Dudycha. G.K. (1942). The attitude of college students towards war and the Germans before and during the Second World War. *Journal of Social Psychology*. 15. 317-324.

Enayatullah (1980). Religious affiliation and attitude of students in an Indian University. *Unpublished Ph.D. Thesis*. Ranchi : Ranchi University.

Hasan. M.K. (1975). Religious prejudice among college students : A Socio-Psychological investigation. *Journal of Social and Economic Studies*, 3, 101-107.

Hasan, M.K. (1978). A study of prejudice, ethnocentrism and related personality factors in Hindu and Muslim College students. *Psychologia*, XXI, 150-154.

Mohsin. S.M. (1976). Reinterpretations of the dynamics of attitude formation and change. *Indian Journal of Psychology*. 51. 1-60.

Murphy. G. (1953). *In the Minds of Men : The study of Human behaviour and social tensions in India*. Basic Books. Inc.

Natraj, P. (1965). Social distance within and between caste and religious groups of college girls. *Journal of Social Psychology*. 65. 135-140.

Sarkar, S.H. and Hasan, M.K. (1973). Economic conservation as related to religion. caste. political affiliation and authoritarianism. *Indian Journal of Psychology* 48. 64-70

Seago, D.W. (1947). Stereotypes : Before Pearl Harbour and after, *Journal of Psychology,* 48, 83, 55-63.

Sherif M. et al. (1961). Intergroup conflict and cooperation : The Robbers care experiment. Norman, Oklahoma : *University of Oklahoma : Institute of group Relations.*

Srivastava G.P. (1976). A short form of the Maslow Security-Insecurity Inventory, *Manas,* 23, 2, 115-120.

13

Perceived Reactions of Minorities Towards Police

Md. Intekhabur Rahman

In India police system has existed since the time of the Mauryas, Guptas and Mughals. The Imperial Governments maintained a more elaborate system in the cities and towns with a kotwal as head of the police administration. The clearest description of police activities is available in Mughal sources, like *Ain-i-Akbari.* The kotwal was to raise and maintain a police force for night patrolling, arrest of criminals, guarding the prisoners and elimination of prostitution and control of consumption of alcoholic beverages. The kotwal was usually perceived as being ruthless, cruel, arbitrary and effective (Bailey, 1969). But this was not unusual as the police in India had always been attributed with such qualities. In the medieval era police were the official gatekeepers of the justice system and most commonly in contact with the citizenry. Police were charged with a multitude of different tasks, (existed in a wide variety of organizations), and operated within the community in ways that highlighted special problems of law enforcement. In the modern world, the term "Police" generally refers to persons employed by Government who are authorized to enforce and maintain law and order in society. The ideal purpose of police in a community can best be described in the words which spellout the duties of law enforcement officers laid down in the *International Code of Enforcement Ethics* : "As a law enforcement officer, my fundamental duty is to serve mankind; to safeguard lives and property; to protect the innocent against deception, the weak against oppression or intimidation, and the peaceful against violence and disorder; and to respect Constitutional rights of all men to liberty, equality and justice".

The modern police have to face the challenges posed by the society and learn to live and grow under the given set of circumstances by arriving at a balance. The police have to perform a much more delicate and dangerous task while dealing with riots and public disturbances compared to what they have to do in dealing with the problem of ordinary crime. It is in \this area of police activity that the risk of public criticism and condemnation is maximum. In India, the variety of public disturbances are exceptionally unique and wide. Riots take place due to the exploitation of religious, communal, regional and political issues. The police stand to gain unpopularity, if the force used is considered "excessive" and also if they do not use adequate forces. Frankly speaking, pliant and uninspiring leadership is a hindrance to the police-minorities relations. Many police officers often recklessly indulge in display of power and authority. Apart from this they seem to serve the interests of politicians. The subordinates readily follow the murky example, serve the interest of the persons in power. In such pursuits the spirit of impartial and legitimate public services assume secondary importance and languish. Under such circumstances, image on the police is despised and tarnished (Saha, 1987).

Police-Minorities Relationship

The police-minorities relationship in India has always been far from pleasant and antagonistic to each other. It has also been observed that police force, as represented by villainous darogha, was known for its wanton atrocities and unabashed corruption in the medieval period. The British rule did not make much difference except that the darogha was replaced by the sub-inspector. Consequently the police and minorities relationship continued to be rather, uneasy. The Uttar Pradesh Police Commission (1960-61) examined police behaviour towards minorities in detail and it adversely commented on the lack of politeness and courtesy towards minorities. It is reported by the commission that "we have no doubt in our minds that if the police take strong attitudes towards turbulent and anti-social elements and deal them with firmness it will win approbation of public instead of incurring its displeasure". Contact with police, either personally or through personal acquaintance, make people to view the police less favourably than otherwise (Bailey, 1969).

The refusal and negligence of registration of cases, rudeness in interaction, demanding bribe, implication in false cases and misbehaviour are closely related to each other. The usual method of attending to complaints is so rude that the complainants avoid visiting the police station.

The relationship between police and minorities based on religion, race or language, presents some peculiar problems. It is obvious that the police being in the hands of the politically dominant majority group, the minorities are bound to have some real or imaginary grievances against them. Minority and weaker groups perceive that the police do not act impartially and they are not properly protected. The National Police Commission in its sixth report of March, 1981, found several instances where "police officers and men appear to have shown unmistakable bias against a particular community while dealing with communal situations." Similarly many people of the Muslim Community express a feeling that they are the worst victims of police action in the wake of communal riots. A perusal of press reports after various communal flares would show that such a feeling against the police is fairly widespread. One of the problems tragically highlighted by the demolition of Babri Masjid and its aftermath is the partisan attitude of the police. The police personnel posted at Ayodhya did not offer any resistance to the Karsevaks indulging in the demolition. Even CRPF Jawans paid homage to the idols placed on the demolition site (Mukhopadhyay, 1992). The riots that erupted in the wake of the demolition provided other instances of the antiminorities attitudes which surfaced in Bombay, Bhopal, Gujarat and U.P. on a large scale. The affected Muslims usually believed that it was not a clash between Hindus and Muslims but between Muslims and the police. In fact the general Muslim opinion against the PAC has never been more bitter. Consequently the demand to abolish the force gained impetus. The Madan Commission enquiring into Bhivandi riots concluded that "the policemen have disgraced their uniforms". Perhaps the worstever police carnage occurred, during the 1987 riots in and around Meerut. In its report, the Amnesty International found strong evidence to suggest that members of the Provincial Armed Constabulary (PAC) had been responsible for dozens of extrajudicial "killings" and "disappearances".

Causes of bad Image of Police

One of the obvious causes of bad image of police is the lack of effective minority relation management or image building activity of the police. Another contributory factor is the relative lack of constructive contact with the community. There are no fora where the police can exchange information, opinion and views with the local community. The paramilitary nature of the organization is the root cause of all this. The hierarchical and the militaristic nature of the organization, and the massive denial of rights even of communication with the press contribute to this negative and mischievous state of affairs.

Refurbishing Police Image

The first and foremost pre-requisite would be a change in the attitude of police. There is a need for broadening their mental horizons so that police can sincerely believe in the essential dignity of every human being irrespective of his religion, caste and status. The police need re-orientation in their training, in moral education and ethics and psychology of humane heartedness so that they can contribute to the social justice. Secondly, the police must develop a sound system of police-community relations so that a better understanding of police activity develops among the people. Thirdly the police must regularly devote times to self-assessment and initiate corrective steps on their own. Fourthly, inservice training programmes on police science, forensic science, Law, Human Behaviour and Criminology should be prepared. Workshops and refresher courses should be designed specially to bring about a change in the attitude of the police towards minorities. India choses to be a secular democratic country where the state shall ensure security, freedom and equality of opportunity to all citizens irrespective of caste and creed. These ideals should be reinforced through proper training. Butter and *et al.* (1993) found in their study that the use of mental health professionals in a law enforcement negotiating team may decrease risk of hostage injury and death. In India, too, plans and programmes of a wing of mental health professionals in police organization should be seriously chalked out and implemented.

Conclusion

While analyzing the discussions and suggestions regarding refurbishing the police image, the immaturity on the part of minority groups can also be not denied. Mostly political leaders or religious leaders create such an environments of suspicion and distrust which psychologically ensure the minorities with a kind of horror. Sometimes, the police take such an erroneous step that it causes perdition of the minority community and leading to development of a kind of negative image of police amongst people. Plans and programmes should seriously be chalked out in order to develop mutual trust and understanding in both police and the minorities.

REFERENCES

Balley, D.H. (1969). *The Police and Political Department in India,* Princeton: Princeton University Press.

Butter. W.M.; Leitenberg & Fuselier. G.D. (1993). The use of mental health professional consultants to police hostage negotiation teams. *Behavioural Science & The Law.* 11.

Mukhopadhyay, N. (1992). *Economic Times,* 28th December.

Police Commission Report (1902). *Report of the Indian Police Commission.* Government of India.

Saha, B.P. (1987). Police-Public Relations. *The Indian Police Journal*, July-December, XXXIV.

U.P. Police Commission (1960-61). Lucknow : Government of Uttar Pradesh.

14

The Role of Religion and Locale in Altruistic Behaviour

Sanwat Singh

Altruism has been defined by Rushton (1980) as a 'social behaviour carried out to achieve positive outcomes for another rather than for the self'. Since reviews by Bryan and London (1970) and Krebs (1970), researches have been increasingly involved in studying the determinants of altruistic behaviour. In recent years, altruistic behaviour has become one of the central concerns of social psychology. The study of altruism is particularly important for understanding the socialization process (Rushton 1976).

Locale and culture are considered to be important variables for altruistic behaviour. Milgram (1970) and Merrens (1973) found that city dwellers were less helpful compared to town dwellers. Korte and Kerr (1975) conducted a field experiment to test the generality of the urban incivility hypothesis. The experiment revealed that interaction between strangers was less civil, less helpful and less cooperative in urban environments than in non-urban environments. They concluded that the likelihood of receiving help was greater in non-urban than in urban locales. Evidence for the greater helping rates in rural and small towns vicinities is available in many empirical studies (see Amato, 1981; House and Wolf, 1978; Rushton 1978). However, the opposite outcome has at times also been documented; i.e., some researches have shown urban dwellers to be the more helpful (see Hansson and Slade, 1977; Hansson, Slade and Slade 1978; Wiener 1976).

In a review of sixty-five researches Stabley (1987) examined and found forty-six studies in support of greater rural helpfulness, nine in support of greater urban helpfulness and ten studies reporting no significant differences. Thus, there is a great deal of ambivalence regarding the effect of locale (i.e., city, towns and villages) on altruistic behaviour.

Cross cultural differences in altruism has also been recorded. Feldman (1968) investigated differences in reactions among Bostonians, Parisians, and Athenians to request for aid. Bostonians were generally more helpful than Parisians or Athenians. L'Armand and Papetone (1975) found that Indians were less altruistic than Americans. Indian subjects were found to be less generous than Canadians (Krishnan 1980). Quoting her subsequent study, Krishnan concluded that Indian subjects accepted less help than Canadian subjects. Huang and Harris (1974) explored differences in altruistic behaviour among Chinese and Americans. Wispe and Freshley (1971) studied differences in helping behaviour among Germans and south Europeans. These studies reveal cross cultural differences in altruistic behaviour. In India, different religions may have an important effect on altruistic and helping behaviour. However, since Hindus and Muslims constitute the major part of Indian society, a comparison of their altruism may be meaningful. It seems, therefore, worthwhile to study the effect of locale and religion on altruism.

Methodology

Design

A 3X2 factorial design was used. The first independent variable, i.e., locale was studied at three levels—city, town and village. The second independent variable was religion with two levels—Hindus and Muslims.

Sample

From Meerut district of Uttar Pradesh 360 subjects were selected from different schools and colleges. Out of the total sample, 120 subjects were from city, 120 from town and 120 subjects from villages. In each locale there were 60 Hindus and 60 Muslims of both sexes ranging from the age of 10 to 19 years.

Tool

For measuring altruistic behaviour an 'Altruism Scale' constructed and standardized by Rai and Singh (1988) was used. The scale has been prepared for the age group of 10 to 19 years in the Hindi language with thirty items. The reliability and validity coefficients are .84 and .63 respectively.

Results

To find out the significance of difference of the two independent variables in the dependent variable of altruism, the data were analyzed with the help of Analysis of Variance Technique (ANOVA) followed by

Duncon's Range Test. The mean scores on the independent variables have been detailed in Table 1.

Table 1

Mean Scores of the Two Independent Variables (Locale and Religion)

Levels	*Independent Variables*	
	(A) Locale	*(B)* Religion
1.	39.825	41.722
2.	42.067	39.306
3.	39.650	

Locale is designated as A and its three levels as A1 (City), A2 (Town) and A3 (Village). Religion is designated as B and its two levels as B1 (Hindu) and B2 (Muslim).

The results of ANOVA are given in the following table.

Table 2

Results of Analysis of Variance

Source of Variation	*Sum of Squares*	*df*	*Mean Squares*	*F*
Locale : A	435.83	02	217.915	3.42*
Religion : B	525.61	01	525.61	8.24**
Interaction : AxB	221.54	02	110.77	1.74
Within Treatment or Error	22648.95	355	63.8	-
Total	23831.93	359	-	-

** *p<.01*   * *p<.05.*

The results of Duncan's range test are presented in Table 3.

Table 3

Significance of Difference among Locales

		A3 (Village)	*A1 (City)*	*A2 (Town)*
	Means	*39.650*	*39.825*	*42.06*
A3	39.650	--	.175	2.417*
A1	--	--	--	2.422*

**denotes p <.05.*

Table 2 indicates that F-value for locale is significant at .05 level of confidence (F = 3.42 ; <.05). It means that locale is an influential factor in altruism. Table 1 reveals a greater tendency of altruism for the subjects residing in the town locality vis-a-vis those residing in city and village locales. To compute the inter-group mean significant differences Duncan's Range Test was applied. Table 3 reveals that A1 and A2, and A2 and A3 are significantly different in their mean altruistic scores. The greatest mean score of town indicates that altruism is greater in semi-urban-town localities than in urban and rural localities.

Table 2 shows that F-ratio for the second variable of religion was highly significant (F = 8.24, <.01). Indicating that religion was an important factor in influencing altruistic behaviour. Table 1 shows that the mean altruism scores of Hindus (Mean B1 = 41.722) is greater than that of Muslims (Mean B2 = 39.306). This would indicate that Hindus are more significantly altruistic than Muslims. Table 2 indicates that the interactional effect of locale and culture was found to be insignificant (F = 1.74; >.05). It suggests that the two independent variables, i.e., locale and religion have significant effect on altruism independently but in combination their effect becomes marginal.

Discussion

It was found that main effects of both independent variables locale and religion were significant factors in influencing altruistic behaviour.

The subjects residing in towns achieved greater mean altruistic score than those from the city or village. Milgram's (1970) explanation stresses that the characteristics of a city, particularly the stressful environmental input produces a general indifference to the needs of strangers. A city dweller's adoptive response to old types of outside stimulation is to ignore what is non-essential to personal goals. Fischer's (1976) explanation of urban impact stresses the diversity of behaviour and appearance which is likely to occur in a large city of heterogeneous population. Because an individual is less likely to feel secure in the midst of many dissimilar others, the expectation is that social interactions will be inhibited. Rural subjects were found to be less altruistic than semi-urban subjects. This differential in tendencies of altruism may be due to 'diffusion of responsibility' (Darley and Latane, 1968). Piliavin *et al.* (1981) suggested that in an emergency situation the potential helper chooses a response after quick appraisal of perceived costs and benefits. If the costs of providing help are greater than the reward of such behaviours, the bystander is likely to pass personal responsibility to others, to attempt escape from the unpleasant situation or to distort perception of the actual need involved. That is why altruism has been found highest in the subjects of town and almost at par with that in the subjects of villages and the city. It is interesting that this psychological finding puts the village and city in the same altruism bracket despite being on the extreme poles in terms of size.

The finding of this study that Hindus are significantly more altruistic than Muslims indicates the cultural differences. Altruistic behaviour can be developed through socio-cultural evolution which is carried out through cultural adaptation (Campbell 1972). Cohen (1972) concludes that altruism develops only through a socio-cultural reality in which the individual finds himself. Both Campbell and Cohen agree that altruism is developed in human groups as a result of certain cultural conditions.

REFERENCES

Amato, P.R. (1981). Urban rural differences in helping: Behaviour in Australia and United States. *Journal of Social Psychology,* 114, 289-290.

Bayan, J.H. and London, P. (1970). Altruistic Behaviour by Children. *Psychological Bulletin,* 73, 200-211.

Campbell, D.T. (1978). On the genetics of altruism and the counter hedonic components in human culture. In L. Wispe (Ed.): *Altruism. Sympathy and Helping : Psychological and Sociological Principles.* New York: Academic Press. 39-55.

Cohan, R. (1972). Altruism, Human Cultural or What? *Journal of Social Issues.* 28(3), 39-57.

Darley, J.H. and Latane, B. (1968). Bystender intervention in emergencies: Diffusion of responsibility. *Journal of Personality and Social Psychology,* 8, 377-383.

Feldman, R.E. (1968). Response to Compatriot and Foreigner who seek assistance. *Journal of Personality and Social Psychology.* 10. 202-214.

Fischer, C.S. (1976). *The Urban Experience:* New York: Harcourt Brace Jovanovich.

Hansson, R.D. and Slade, K.M. (1977). Altruism toward a decient in city and small town. *Journal of Applied Social Psychology,* 7, 272-279.

Hansson, R.A., Slade, K.M. and Slade, P.S. (1978). Urban-rural differences in responsiveness to an altruistic model. *Journal of Social Psychology.* 105, 99-105.

House, J.S. and Wolf, S. (1978). Effect of urban residence on interpersonal trust and helping behaviour. *Journal of Personality and Social Psychology,* 36, 1029-1043.

Huang, L.C. and Harris, E. (1974). Altruism and imitation in Chinese and Americans; A cross cultural experiment. *Journal of Social Psychology,* 93.

Korte, V. and Kerr, N. (1975). Response to altruistic opportunities in urban and non-urban settings. *Journal of Social Psychology,* 95. 183-184.

Krebs, D.L. (1970). Altruism—An examination of concept and review of the literature. *Psychological Bulletin,* 73, 258-302.

Krishnan, L. (1980). Behavioural and personal correlates of helping behaviour : Some question in the cross cultural context. Vth ACCP Conf. 1980, Utkal Univ. Bhuvaneshwar, Orissa.

L'Armand, K. and Papeton, A. (1975). A helping to reward another person : A cross cultural analysis. *Journal of Personality and Social Psychology.* 31, 189-198.

Merrens, M.R. (1973). Non-emergency helping behaviour in various sized communities, *Journal of Social Psychology,* 90, 327-338.

Milgram, S. (1970). The experience of living in cities, *Science,* 167, 1461-1468.

Pilvian, J.A., Dovidio, J.F. , Caertner, S.L. and Clark, R.D., III (1981). *Emergency Interventions.* New York : Academic Press.

Rai, S.N. and Singh, S. (1988). *Altruism Scale,* Agra : National Psychological Corpn.

Rushton, J.P. (1976). Socialization and Altruistic Behaviour of the Children. Psychological Bulletin, 83, 898-913.

Rushton, J.P. (1980). Altruism, Socialization and Society, New Jercy : Prentice Hall.

Rushton, J.P. (1978). Urban density and altruism: Helping stranger in a Canadian city, Suburb and small town, *Psychological Bulletin,* 43(3pt.1). 987-990.

Stebley, N.M. (1987). Helping behaviour in rural and urban environments : A meta-analysis, *Psychological Bulletin,* 102, 346-356.

Weiner, F.H. Altruism, Ambiance and action : The effect of rural and urban on helping behaviour. *Journal of Personality and Social Psychology,* 34, 112-124.

Wispe, L.G. and Freshley (1971). Race, sex and sympathetic helping behaviour. *Journal of Personality and Social Psychology,* 17, 59-65.

SECTION III

Women

15

Are Women Inferior in Achievement?

N. Hasnain

The layman's view that men are better than women in terms of various abilities and personality factors led to the psychologists to undertake researches to measure and find out differences if they exist in the abilities and personality make-up of men and women.

There seem to be four main strands of research findings regarding sex differences: (i) women as superior vis-á-vis men (ii) men as superior vis-á-vis women, (iii) mixed findings, and (iv) no differences.

Women as Superior vis-á-vis Men

Tyler (1969) while reviewing the literature on sex differences in achievement has pointed out that all studies of school achievement indicate that girls consistently make better school records than boys. Differences of this sort have been reported from a vide variety of investigations. Using various criteria of school success, it is recognized that girls are less frequently retarded and more frequently accelerated than boys and more of them receive high marks and fewer of them receive unsatisfactory marks. Donna (1974) reported that women tended to achieve a higher level in academic achievement than men. He also predicted that grade-point averages would be higher for women. In another study Singh (1986) obtained the mean school achievement scores of girls significantly better than those of boys.

In a survey of 12,826 students who graduated in 1956 from 83 Connecticut high schools, Northy (1956) found the predominance of girls in high categories and boys in the lower ones. Clark (1959) reported that girls were better in all three grades (third, fifth and eighth) in spelling than boys. Girls also scored significantly better than boys in mechanics of English in the fifth and eighth grades and in arithmetic fundamentals in the eighth grade. Terman and Tyler (1954) found that girls were better than boys in English, spelling, writing and art but boys were better than girls in reasoning, history, geography and science. Ames and Ilg (1964) reported that in kindergarten, first and second grade girls scored significantly higher than boys on tests of aptitute for learning. Herzberg and Lepkin (1954) found that senior high school girls were significantly better than boys on verbal fluency for 16,17 and 18 years of ages. Havighurst and Breese (1949) obtained females better than boys in rote memory.

In clerical works also women have been found superior to men. Summarizing the data from several sources in this direction Schneidler and Paterson (1942) came to the conclusion that at all ages and grades only 20 per cent of the males exceeded the median for females. Females were found to be better on clerical aptitude sub-test of "Differential Aptitude Test" (Wesman, 1949: McGuire, 1961). Females had also been found better in perceptual speed coding and digit symbol tests (Gainer, 1962; Miele, 1958; Norman, 1953). Thus these studies demonstrate supremacy of women over men in certain abilities and achievements.

Men as Superior vis-à-vis Women

In the studies that follow men have been reported to be superior to women in other abilities and achievements. Miele (1958) reported that in amount and range of general information males were usually superior to females. Hobson (1947), Havighurst and Breese (1947) obtained that in solving problems with numbers, boys manage more successfully than girls. D'Halloran (1983) while giving a report on 1982 mathematical competition in New Zealand involving 5156 males and 4424 females from grades 2 through 7 mentioned that at each grade males attained higher mean scores than females. They found sex differences to be greatest in the performance of three-dimensional geometric problems. Bennet and Cruikshank (1942) used mechanical comprehension test in which the scrutiny of pictures representing mechanical relationships in order to answer questions about them was used. They found that not a single one of 60 items on which women averaged higher than men. Terman and Tyler (1954) reported that males scored significantly higher on space factor of "Mechanical Aptiture Test" than females. Tyler (1969) summarized the finding of studies on the judgement and manipulation of spatial relationships and concluded that a consistent male superiority has been obtained in these studies.

Sweeney (1953) found that males were significantly superior to females on all problems requiring restructuring. Duggan (1950) and Sommer (1958) reported that where the material to be remembered was more familiar or interesting to males or where it was of a quantitative nature males were better than females.

The above quoted studies show that men are superior to women in problems related to numbers, mathematical competitions, space relationship and restructuring of problems, etc.

Mixed Findings

There are some studies which show that men are superior in some community functions while they are inferiors in others.

A study conducted by Scottish Council for "Research in Education" (1949) reported that girls were about 2 points higher on the group tests, while boys were 4 points higher on the individual tests. In the same way Miele (1958) obtained that on some of the sub-tests of Stanford-Binet and Wechsler intelligence scales boys excelled to girls, while on certain other sub-tests the girls excelled to boys.

Hobson (1947) and Havighurst, and Breese (1947) found that girls of junior high school age were significantly higher on verbal fluency but not on the grasp of verbal meaning. Terman and Tyler (1954) obtained that 17 year-old girls scored better on speed but not on vocabulary or Comprehension. Duggn (1950) and Sommer (1958) found that where the material to be remembered was more familiar or interesting to males or where it was of a quantitative nature males were better than females. Terman and Tyler (1954) reported boys to be better in arithmetic tests requiring reasoning at the lower age level while poorer in number tests involving simple counting or identification, the differences disappeared in the tests for all age levels where only mechanical arithmetic was involved. In this way these findings show that in certain arena males excel to females but in others females excel to males.

No Differences

There is another line of evidences which does not demonstrate any significant differences in achievements of males and females.

Clark's (1959) study on girls and boys of third to fifth and eighth grade levels did not show any difference in the scores on reading vocabulary. Similarly Fraser (1978) found insignificant difference between males and females on vocabulary. Bennett *et.al.* (1959) found very little difference between males and females on verbal and numerical aptitude. McAndrew's (1943) study on primary and pre-school children did not demonstrate any significant sex difference in science achievement.

Sex has also been found to be an insignificant determinant of reminiscence (Mohan, Sehgal and Bhandari, 1981; Mohan and Dhodi,

1969; and Mohan and Neelam, 1969). However, results obtained by Horn (1976) and Payna and Huang (1977) show definite sex-difference in reminiscence.

Fennema and Sherman (1977) obtained a complex result on the relationship of mathematics achievement and sex. They reported few sex related cognitive differences but many attitudinal differences. The results also showed important relationship between socio-cultural factors and sex related cognitive differences. Parsons, Adler and Meece (1984) employed 200 students of grades eighth to tenth and obtained that subjective task value emerged as the strongest mediator of sex differences in achievement related behaviours and plans. There was little support for helplessness models of sex differences in achievement. However, there was some evidence of sex differences in ability attributions but the difference occurred only among low expectancy subjects. Verbal and behavioural indices of achievement-believes were often inconsistent.

While reviewing the researches upto 1969 Tyler opined that in any discussion of average differences reference should be made to the importance of noting variability as well as averages. To him in most of the abilities difference between the sexes are so small and differences between individuals of the same sex are so large that it is possible to an individual who regardless of his or her sex will show almost any specified degree of difference in any special ability. So the differences are not due to sex, but rather due to individual differences.

Explanations of Sex Differences

Different explanations have been given by psychologists to explain sex differences in achievement. In the following paragraphs critical reviews of these explanations will be given and an amicable explanation of the same put forth by the author will also be presented.

The sex differences have often been explained in terms of differential rate of maturing the males and females. According to this view since girls reach puberty on the average about two years earlier than the boys and during the period preceding this change the girls are taller, heavier and more mature in their interest than boys, so girls are better than boys in achievement. But this explanation has never appeared to be very convincing, for mental and physical characteristics related to it accelerate physical growth very slightly, if at all. So much so that the earlier quoted studies very apparently show that boys excel to girls in many abilities and aehievements (refer to male supremacy over female) and in some of the achievements no difference between males and females (refer to no differences) have been found. Had the differential rate to maturing been responsible for sex differences, the girls should have demonstrated always a superiority in each and every ability and achievement.

Following the above explanation another explanation of sex differences in achievement has been given in terms of general intellectual inferiority or superiority. Actually, this is a layman's view that women are generally inferior to men in abilities and hence in achievement. But this can be proved false on the same lines on which the earlier explanation has been proved false. So much so that Northy's (1956) findings show the predominance of girls in high categories and boys in the lower ones. Parsons *et. al.* (1984) have also refuted the helplessness model of sex-differences in achievement. Tyler (1969) has noted that the differences are not due to sex but due to individual differences. He has advocated that it would be difficult to account for both kinds of achievement differences to account by any general intellectual inferiority or superiority. If women are on average less intelligent why do they consistently do better at school and in certain other intellectual works? If, on the other hand, they are brighter than men why do they not do better always in each and every work including arithmetical works?

Thompson (1975) has explained the sex difference in reading in terms of faminine bases of school environment, of differential exposure of the printed words. But as we know and see that there are exclusive separate schools for the students of two sexes and schools of males do provide masculine basis of school environment. Moreover, it has been seen that the girls in predominantly male schools often do better than boys. In the same way, explanation of differential exposure of words also seem to be incorrect on two lines. First, so far as our country is concerned if there is any difference in the exposure of words, certainly it is the female child who is always at disadvantageous position. So she should show inferior performance in reading and writing. But this is not the case. Rather, the fact is opposite to this assumption. Second, the females are not better in all abilities and performances. On the contrary, the members of two sexes excel each other in one ability but recede in others.

After reviewing the researches on sex differences in academic achievement, ability and attainment of higher education, Levine and Ornstein (1983) have pointed out that many studies indicate that women in U.S. have higher verbal achievement, while men have higher achievement in mathematics and science. So, to them functional and biological differences are insufficient and inconclusive for the explanation of sex differences in achievement. Moreover, experiences depress female achivement in mathematics and the interaction between socialization practices, behaviour and classroom outcomes are complex and cannot be explained in terms of functional and biological differences. So they have given an explanation in terms of differences in pay and occupational status, experience, marital status, work commitment, differential expectations and discrimination to be important in sex differences of achievement.

But to the author even this explanation cannot be accepted, for this and other above mentioned explanations are contingent upon socio-cultural factors adhering to the differential roles of two sexes in a culture. Due to different socio-cultural factors the roles of the same sex in different cultures and those of two sexes in the same culture differ. The different roles and expectations for two sexes adhering to the cultural and social factors start to be inculcated from the very beginning of life of the children of two sexes. To Oakley (1972) a new born baby is classified immediately after birth by sex and treated accordingly. Oakley has also reported studies revealing differential parental expectations for male and female children. To Chappell (1978) the parents expect relatively outward directed and aggressive behaviour for males (boys will be boys) and relatively passive and inward directed behaviours for females (girls don't do that). Ambert (1976), and Goffman (1977) are of the opinion that differential clothing, punishment, toys and activities as well as the interaction between children and parents and the roles of models provided by each parent and other siblings all contribute to sex role socialization within the family. Needless to say here is that the matrix of these interactional and socialization processes are provided by the social and cultural values, customs, assumptions and style of works of the society.

In western countries in general and in India in particular, the girls are supposed to be engaged in household activities and the boys are expected to do outward activities. Because of this, the roles for girls and boys are supposed to be different. The socio-cultural factors resulting into different role expectations give rise to different types of child-rearing practices for the children of two sexes, which bring differences in their abilities and capacities.

However, the facts reveal that university results and the results of competitive examinations frequently show women at the top of the list. The empirical findings of psychological researches seem to negate the monopoly of men in achievements. Though, the Indian Constitution vehementally negates the discrimination on the basis of sex, caste and creed, but the fact remains that girls from the very beginning of their life are not treated at par the boys in Indian society. Many a times, they are deprived of the socio-psychological, educational and political stimulations. A sharp drop-out in the schools and meagre literacy rate of girls show the general apathy of parents and the society for females. A girl child even when she is grown up is often discriminated. The conditions of women in many underprivileged and deprived religious and caste groups entangled with the miseries of poverty is much more deplorable. However, as discussed above, psychologically they do not seem to have lesser potentials than men.

REFERENCES

Ambert. A.M. (1976) *Sex Structure.* Don Mills : Longman Canada.

Ames, L.B. and Ilg, F.L. (1964). Sex-differences in test performance of matched girl-boy pairs in the five to nine year-old range. *Journal of Genetic Psychology* 104, 25-34.

Bennett, G.K. and Gruikshank, R.M. (1942). Sex differences in the understanding of mechanical problems. *Journal of Applied Psychology,* 26, 121-127.

Bennett, G.K. *et al.* (1959). *Differential aptitude tests manual.* New York : Psychological Corporation.

Bobson, J.R. (1947). Sex-differences in primary mental abilities. *Journal of Educational Research,* 41, 126-132.

Chappell, N.L. (1978). The social process of learning sex roles: A sociological viewpoint. In H.M. Lips and N. Colwill (Eds). *The Psychology of Sex Differences.* New Jersey: Prentice Hall.

Clark, W.W. (1958). Boys and girls are there significant ability and achievement differences. *Phi Data Kappan,* 41, 73-76.

Donna. C. (1974). Library skills, study habits and attitudes and sex as related to academic achievement. *Educational and Psychological Measurement.* 34, 967-969.

Duggan. L. (1950). An experiment on immediate recall in secondary school children. *British Journal of Psychology,* 40. 149-154.

Fennema, E. and Sherman. J. (1977). Sex related differences in mathematics achievement, spatial visualization and affective factors. *American Educational Research Journal,* 14. 51-71.

Fraser. N.K. (1978). Relationship between personality factors and performance in academic achievement; school adaptation and physical fitness in elementary and junior high school children : A cross cultural study. *Dissertation Abstract,* 3386-3389.

Gainer. W.L. (1962). The ability of WISC subtests to discriminate between boys and girls of average intelligence. *California Journal of Educational Research,* 13, 6-16.

Goffman. E. (1977). The arrangement between the sexes. *Theory and Society* 4. 301-331.

Havighurst. R.J. and Breese. F.H. (1949). Relation between ability and social status in a Mid-Western community in primary mental abilities. *Journal of Educational Psychology,* 38, 241-247.

Herzberg, F. and Lepkin, M.A. (1954). Study of sex differences on the primary mental abilities test. *Educational and Psychological Measurement,* 14, 687-689.

Horn (1976). Quoted by J. Mohan, M. Sehgal and A. Bhandari. Personality, age and sex as determinants of reminiscence in children. *Asian Journal of Psychology and Education.* 1981, 7, 1-7.

Levine, D.U. and Ornstein, A. (1983). Sex differences in ability and achievement. *Journal of Research and Development in Education,* 16, 67-72.

McAndrews, M.B. (1943). An experimental investigation of young children's ideas of causality. *Stu. Psychol. Psychiat. Cathol.* Univ. Amer, 6.

McGuire, E. (1963). Sex role and community variability in test performance. *Journal of Educational Psychology,* 103, 185-194.

Meile, J.A. (1958). Sex differences in intelligence: The relationship of sex to intelligence as measured by Wechsler intelligence scale for children. *Dissertation Abstract,* 18, 2213.

Mohan, J. and Dhody, P. (1968). Performance, sex and drive. *Journal of Education and Psychology,* 26, 108-112.

Mohan, J. and Neelam (1969). Reminiscence as a function of personality and motivation. *Journal of Psychological Researches,* 13, 90-93.

Mohan, J. Sehgal, M. and Bhandari, A. (1981). Personality, age and sex as determinants of reminiscence in children. *Asian Journal of Psychology and Education,* 7-17.

Norman, R.D. (1953). Sex differences and other aspects of young superior adult performance on the Wechsler - Bellevue scale. *Journal of Consulting Psychology,* 17, 411-418.

Northy, A.S. (1958). Sex differences in high school scholarship. *School and society,* 86, 63-64.

Oakley, A. (1972). *Sex, gender and society.* New York : Harpe and Row.

O'Halloran (1983). Sex-differences in mathematics. *Newzealand Journal of Educational Studies,* 18, 188.

Parsons, J.E., Adler, T. and Meece, J.L. (1984). Sex-differences in achievement: A test of alternate theories. *Journal of Personality and Social Psychology,* 46, 26-43.

Payne, R.B. and Huang, K.L. (1977). Interaction of sex and task differences in reminiscence. *Journal of Motor Behaviour.* 9, 29-32.

Scheneidler, G.G. and Paterson, D.G. (1942). Sex-differences in clerical aptitude. *Journal of Educational Psychology,* 33, 303-309.

Scottish Council for Research in Education (1949). *The trend of Scottish Intelligence.* London: University of London Press.

Singh, I.R. (1986). A study of sex on school achievement of high school children. *Perspective in Psychological Researches,* 9, 67-68.

Sommer, R. (1958). Sex differences in the retention of quantitative information. *Journal of Educational Psychology,* 49, 187-192.

Sweeney, E.J. (1953). Sex differences in problem solving. *Technical Reports.* 1.

Terman, L.M. and Tyler, L.E. (1954). Psychological sex differences. In L. Carmichael (Ed). Manual of Child Psychology. New York : Wiley.

Thompson, G.B. (1975). Sex-differences in reading attainments. *Educational Research.* 18, 16-23.

Tyler. L.E. (1969). *The Psychology of Human Differences.* Bombay : Vakils, Feffer and Simons.

Wesman, A.G. (1949). Separation of sex groups in test reporting. *Journal of Educational Psychology*, 40. 223-229.

16

Sources, Effects and Behaviours of Stress in Working and Non-Working Women

Navita Daga and *Akbar Husain*

The problem of stress has acquired considerable importance in recent years. It is not only a clinical or organizational problem but has family and social ramifications also. More and more people are now recognizing its negative effects in terms of physical and psychological disorders. Recent researches demonstrate that the stress may also have beneficial effect (Mathew, 1985; Pestonjee, 1987).

Meaning of Stress

Both the terms 'stress' and 'strain' are used synonymously in a non-scientific manner. Cannon (1929) introduced the concept of stress in life sciences. This concept has been popularised in the field of physiology and it has been widespread to almost in every field of physical and life sciences, social sciences, medical sciences, and engineering. Stress is difficult to define partly because it means different things to different people.

Mason (1975) reviewed literature on stress and concluded that there was confusion and a lack of consensus regarding its definition. The term stress has been used variously to refer to (a) stimulus — external force acting on the organism, (b) response — changes in the physiological functions, (c) interaction — interaction between an external force and the resistance opposed to it, as in biology, and (d) more comprehensive combinations of the above factors (Selye, 1979). Most definitions tend to emphasize one aspect of stress more than the other.

Selye (1956, 1973) has defined stress as a non-specific response of the body to any demand made upon it. Cannon (1929) considered it as a pattern of physiological reactions that prepare an organism for action, "either fight or flight." He explained the stress phenomenon on the basis of this "fight" or "flight" theory. The fight or flight response used by stone ancestors is no longer appropriate. It is dangerous also. In later years, the concept of stress has been substantially modified by Selye (1979) himself from "non-specific response of the body" to "general adaptation syndrome".

Psychologists of different branches have explained and defined the concept of stress in four different perspectives :

Stimulus Oriented Approach

This approach describes stress in terms of stressors — the variety of external and internal stimuli that evoke stress such as surgical trauma, burns emotional arousal, mental or physical effort, fatigue, pain, fear, loss of blood, intoxication by drugs, etc., (Cannon, 1929). According to Selye, any external event or any internal drive which threatens to upset the organismic equilibrium is stress.

Response Oriented Approach

The response oriented approach emphasizes the importance of our perception and response to such events. Stress is the systematic biological response of an individual to a variety of provocative situations. Further, stress response consists of a sequence of physiological changes involving almost all body parts and systems, and such a response is characterized by extensive and intensive changes of autonomic effectors including heart rate, rate of stomach and duodenal movements, and the gastric and adrenal gland secretion (Misra and Pandey, 1993). Kagan (1971) defines stress as a pattern of adaptive physiological reactions. Zimbardo (1988) defines stress as "the pattern of specific and non-specific responses an organism makes to stimulus events that disturb its equilibrium and tax or exceed its ability to cope". Note that it is when events disrupt our usual level of functioning and require us to make an effort to re-establish our equilibrium that we experience stress.

Selye's General Adaptation Syndrome (GAS) consists of three progressive stages: the alarm reaction, the stage of resistance, and the stage of exhaustion.

Alarm Stage

This involves "fight or flight" reactions, and therefore, the activation of the sympathetic division of the A.N.S.

Resistance Stage

In this stage the stress continues, the body attempts to revert to normal functioning, while at the same time coping with the additional adrenaline in the bloodstream and the effects which it produces.

Exhaustion Stage

In this phase, the GAS is characterized by a return to apparently normal levels of heart rate, blood pressue, and the like, but is identifiable by an excessively high level of adrenaline remaining in the bloodstream. This produces immediate and strong — sometimes excessive reactions to even mild source of additional stress.

Interaction Approach

This approach takes into account individual differences in cognitive and social variables and views stress as an interaction between the individual and the environment. Lazarus (1980) sees stress as a result of a transaction between person and environment. The way people appraise or construe their relationship with the environment is a function of cognition, or thought. These thoughts influence the way people feel.

The Psychodynamic Approach

This approach describes external or internal events which pose a threat to the integrity of the organism leading to the disorganization of personality as stress. Stress may be induced by interpersonal (external) or intrapsychic (between own impulses and ego) factors resulting in anxiety.

Asthana (1983) advocates that the concept of stress has been studied by most of the disciplines, there is a sad neglect of a phenomenological analysis of the concept which appears crucial to an understanding of the stress phenomena. In phenomenological psychology, man is perceived as existing. All experiences are related to existing human beings and the world. Consciousness is always being aware of something else. Psychologists use the language of physics, physiology or biology. Asthana preferred the use of psychological terms to describe experience and situation.

All positive and negative situations that require adjustment are stressful. According to Selye (1980), the notion of stress can be divided into four basic variations : distress, eustress, hyperstress, and hypostress. When events have a harmful effect, stress is correctly labelled distress. Stress which has a beneficial effect, Selye suggests it as eustress or good stress. Hyperstress, or excessive stress, usually occurs when events included positive ones, pile up and stretch the limits of our adaptability. Hypostress, or insufficient stress, is apt to occur when we are lacking stimulation.

Research on stress in India is extremely limited and confined to organizational, occupational or job stress and clinical case studies. A strong need for identifying the stress sources, effects, and behaviours among working and non-working women is being felt. It is expected that stress sources, effects, and behaviours will be more pronounced among working women as compared to non-working women. Working women in comparison to non-working women experience an extra organizational stress which in turn increases the sources and effects.

Methodology

Sample

A sample of 100 women (50 working and 50 non-working) were taken from Aligarh city. Working women were married ones engaged in teaching profession in different schools. Non-working women were the housewives. The mean ages of working and non-working subjects were 33.36 and 36.22 respectively.

Tools

Personal Stress Source Inventory (PSSI)

PSSI developed by Farmer *et al.* (1984) was used in the present study. It is comprised of 30 items and is consisted of a brief listing of items that relate to the categories of personal, financial, and relational sources. There were four alternative response categories: "seldom", "sometimes", "frequently" and "does not apply''. Scoring was done by summing up the total number of checks for seldom, sometimes and frequently. There was no numerical score associated with "does not apply" category.

Stress Effects Inventory (SEI)

SEI developed by Farmer *et al.* (1984) consisted of 26 stress effects. Item numbers 1 to 10 represent physical effects and 11 to 26 emotional effects. Subjects response were obtained on a 4-point rating scale: "never" "seldom", "sometimes", and "frequently".

Personal Behaviour Analysis (PBA)

PBA developed by Farmer *et al* (1984) included some of the more common ways in which people behave when under stress. The PBA is consisted of 15 behaviours with the 4 alternative response categories:

"never", "seldom", "sometimes", and "frequently". Scoring was done by counting the number of times "sometimes" or "frequently" checked.

Procedure

The data were collected individually either from subjects residences or schools. Prior to administering three inventories, subjects were assured that their responses will be kept strictly confidential and data will be used only for research purposes. All the three inventories were administered in one session. Subjects generally took 30 to 45 minutes time in completing all the inventories.

Results and Discussion

Data were analyzed by means of t-test. The results are given in Tables 1 to 4.

Table 1

Comparison between the Mean Scores of Working and Non-Working Women on Stress Sources, Effects and Behaviours.

Subjects	*N*	*Mean*	*S.D.*	*t-Value*	*P*
		Stress Sources			
Working	50	58.62	19.29	1.68	>.05
Non-Working	50	52.08	19.42		
		Stress Effects			
Working	50	51.10	20.13	1.94	>.05
Non-Working	50	43.38	19.52		
		Stress Behaviours			
Working	50	17.26	9.76	0.86	>.05
Non-Working	50	16.00	3.39		

Table 2

Comparison between the Mean Scores of Working and Non-Working Women in Numerical Scores Range 80 or Higher 48 to 79, 31 to 47, and 0 to 30.

Subjects	*N*	*Mean*	*S.D.*	*t-Value*	*P*
		Numerical score range 80 or higher			
Working	7	88.71	7.99	0.44	>.05
Non-Working	3	91.33	9.87		

		Numerical score range 48 to 79			
Working	29	62.44	8.30	0.07	>.05
Non-Working	26	62.26	9.26		
		Numerical score range 31 to 47			
Working	9	43.77	3.42	1.99	<.05
Non-Working	14	39.92	5.09		
		Numerical score range 0 to 30			
Working	5	21.00	6.78	0.22	>.05
Non-Working	7	21.71	4.36		

Table 3

Comparison between the Mean Scores of Working and Non-Working Women on Physical Effects and Emotional Effects.

Subjects	*N*	*Mean*	*S.D.*	*t-Value*	*P*
		Physical Effects			
Working	50	18.48	8.33	1.48	>.05
Non-Working	50	16.18	7.23		
		Emotional Effects			
Working	50	32.62	13.52	1.96	>.05
Non-Working	50	27.20	14.13		

Table 4

Comparison between the Mean Scores of Working and Non-Working Women in Categories A, B, and C of Stress

Subjects	*N*	*Mean*	*S.D.*	*t-Value*	*P*
		Category - A			
Working	50	3.54	3.20	0.70	>.05
Non-Working	50	3.08	3.39		
		Category - B			
Working	50	4.90	4.29	1.53	>.05
Non-Working	50	3.72	3.46		
		Category - C			
Working	50	8.76	5.83	0.53	>.05
Non-Working	50	9.20	6.62		

There were no significant differences between working and non-working women on Personal Stress Sources Inventory scores ($t=1.68$, $p>.05$). This finding suggests that the personal sources of stress are equally important in the lives of working and non-working women. Further analysis was also done on the basis of numerical score obtained on Personal Stress Source Inventory. Findings revealed that there were no significant differences between working and non-working women in terms of numerical score range of 80 or higher ($t=.044$, $p>.05$), 48 to 79 ($t=0.07$, $p>.05$) and 0 to 30 ($t=0.22$, $p>.05$). Working and non-working women whose scores fall 80 or higher possess high levels of stress. Women whose scores fall between 48 to 79 may be called moderate. This finding may be interpreted in terms of the interpretation advanced by Farmer *et al.* (1984). That is, women "whose scores fall in this category should be concerned about their level of stress, and should attempt to be somewhat cautious and avoid those issues that may place them in a higher category". Working and non-working women whose scores fall between 0 to 30 represent the lowest possible numerical score. It could represent a form of denial. That is, working and non-working women may possibly be ignoring or denying that they had concerns over stressors in their personal life. Working women scored significantly higher than the non-working women in the category of scores lie between 31 to 47 on Personal Stress Source Inventory ($t=1.99$, $p<.05$). This finding indicates that working women are more aware of sources of personal stress. Working women as compared to non-working women appear to be relatively free from concerns over life events.

Significant difference was not found between working and non-working women on physical effects of stress. Since the physical effects are highly individualistic, i.e., everyone of us may experience headaches, stomach upsets, skin rashes, or high blood pressure, etc. Perhaps this is the reason that both the groups did not differ significantly on physical effects of stress. The mean score of working women was higher than that of the non-working women, though not significantly on emotional effects ($t=1.96$, $p>.05$). The emotional effects of stress seem to revolve around related feeling categories: depression and anxiety among working women. The feelings and emotions cause stress to the working women rather than to the non-working women to a greater extent, to get sick or have trouble of falling asleep. Working women as compared to non-working women may experience both physical and emotional effects to a greater extent.

Working and non-working women did not differ significantly on stress behaviours ($t=0.86$, $p>.05$). Category-wise Personal Behaviour

Analysis revealed that there were no significant differences between working and non-working women in category A ($t=.70, p>.05$), category B ($t=1.53, p>.05$) and category C ($t=0.35, p>.05$).

Working and non-working women whose scores fall in category A indicate that their behaviours are maladaptive stress related. Furthermore, this finding suggests that working as well as non-working women frequently behave in ways that are not good for them in the long run physically, emotionally, or both. Working and non-working women whose behaviours fall in category B suggest that their behaviours are less obviously self-destructive. In addition, their behaviours do nothing to change or reduce the stress. Subjects whose scores fall in category C indicate that their behaviours are adaptive that generally encourage physical and emotional health because they do not directly change stress sources.

Putting it all together, the present study gives some ideas concerning the sources of stress, the effects of stress, and the resulting behaviour of working and non-working women. In the present study we have found that working and non-working women view stress in similar way. The women of the present study very often hit the stress and use it positively.

REFERENCES

Asthana, H.S. (1983). *The concept of stress: A phenomenological approach.* Paper presented at the seminar on Stress, Anxiety and Mental Health, University of Allahabad.

Cannon, W.B. (1929). *Bodily changes in pain. hunger. fear and rage.* New York : Appleton.

Farmer, R.E., Monahan, L.H. and Hekeler, R.W. (1984). *Stress management for human services.* (A sage human services guide 37). London: Sage Publications.

Kagan. A. (1971). *Society stress and disease* (Vol.1) New York : Oxford University Press.

Mason, J.W. (1975). A historical view of stress field. *Journal of Human Stress.* March 6-12.

Mathew, V.J. (1985). Job stress of a creative manager. F.P.M. written comprehensive examination paper. O.B. Area. *Indian Institute of Management.* Ahmedabad.

Misra, K.K. & Pandey, H.P. (1993). Stress disorders : A growing challenge. *Everyman's Science,* XXVIII, (April-May), 45-47.

Pestonjee, D.M. (1987). Executive stress: Should it always be avoided. *Vikalpa,* 12, 23-30.

Selye, H. (1956). *The stress of life.* New York: McGraw Hill.

Selye, H. (1973). Stress. *Forces,* 24, 50.

Selye, H. (1979). *The stress of life* (Rev. Ed.) New York : Van Nostrand Reinholt.

Selye, H. (1980). The stress concept today. In I.L. Kutash et al. (Eds.). *Handbook on stress and anxiety.* San Francisco: Jossey-Bass.

Zimbardo, P.G. (1988). *Psychology and life* (12th Ed.). Glenview, I.L. : Scott, Foresman.

17

Gender and Caste Differences in Adjustment

S.K. Srivastava

Adjustment is the outcome of human attempts to deal with stress and meet the needs. It is a continuous process to maintain harmonious relationship with the environment. Thus adjustment is a process of interaction between oneself and one's surrounding environment, and so it is inseparably bound up with the nature of human personality. Adjustment is the process by which a living organism maintains a balance between its needs and the circumstances that influence the satisfaction of these needs. In short it can be said that an organism's behaviours is governed by his wishes and desires and that different forms of behaviour are outcome of different forms of wishes as well as needs. If an organism is able to cope with his wishes, desires and the circumstances and maintains equilibrium, he is said to be well adjusted whereas his failure results in maladjustment. The following are the main areas of adjustment.

Home Adjustment

Home is the source of greatest satisfaction and security to its members. The relationships among the family members and their ways of behaviours play a leading role in the adjustment of an individual. All problematic and delinquent behaviours are the results of maladjustment which is caused on account of faulty rearing and uncongenial atmosphere at home.

Health Adjustment

One is said to be adjusted to one's physical health if the physical abilities are in conformity with those of others of the same age and sex. And there is no difficulty in progressing due to defects or incapabilities of physical organs.

Social Adjustment

How far one is adjusted can be ascertained by one's social development and adaptability to the social environment. Social adjustment requires the development of social qualities and virtues in an individual. It also requires that one should be social enough to live in harmony with others and feel responsibility and obligations towards his fellow beings and society.

Emotional Adjustment

Emotions play an important part in one's adjustment to self and environment. An individual is said to be emotionally adjusted if he is able to express his emotions in the socially approved ways at a proper time. It requires one's balanced emotional development and proper training in the outlet of emotions.

School/Educational Adjustment

The school/college environment casts its influence over the adjustment of the students. How far a student is satisfied with other students in the school, building, discipline level of the school, time-table, curricular activities, methods of teaching, teachers and head of the institution contribute significantly towards his total adjustment.

Adjustment is an important state of the person which influences the relationships to others. The adjusted person is said to be mentally sound who seems to be happy in every walk of life. On the other hand, a maladjusted person is disturbed with marked failures in life and unsatisfactory relations with others. Several studies have been conducted by Agrawal (1970), Gohrepade (1979), Mukherjee and Upadhyay (1980), Krishna (1982), Mehta (1982), Saxena and Sharma (1982), Shah (1986), Tripathy (1986), Mohan and Gulati (1988), Vasishtha (1989), Jones and Reznikoff (1989), Leong, Mallinchrodt and Kralj (1990) and Khan (1991). These studies deal with the relationships of adjustment and other related variables, but none of the studies is concerned with the adjustment of male and female students of Scheduled and non-Scheduled Castes. The present study attempts to explore sex and caste differences in some of the areas of adjustment among students. It is hypothesized that: (i) there would be significant difference in the adjustment of male and female students, and (ii) there would be significant difference in the adjustment of Scheduled and non-Scheduled Caste students.

Methodology

Sample

This study was conducted on 100 male students (40 belonged to Scheduled Caste and 60 to non-Scheduled Caste), and 100 female students (35 belonged to Scheduled Caste and 65 to non-Scheduled Caste) randomly selected from two Intermediate Colleges of Hardwar. The age of the students ranged from 17 to 20 years. The students taken for the sample were of the same socio-economic status.

Test Used

Sinha and Singh (1971) adjustment inventory was used for data collection. This inventory measures adjustment in five areas, viz. home, health, social, emotional, and educational. The inventory consists of 102 items (home 16, health 15, social 19, emotional 31 and educational 21). The responses are recorded in terms of 'Yes' or 'No'. The scoring was done on the basis of scoring keys and instructions prescribed in the manual. In this inventory, high score indicates unsatisfactory adjustment while low score indicates better adjustment.

Results and Discussion

Total scores of each subject in all the five areas were obtained separately. (i) Home adjustment - (a), (ii) Health adjustment - (b), (iii) Social adjustment - (c), (iv) Emotional adjustment - (d), and (v) Educational adjustment - (e). Finally the total adjustment score of each subject was obtained by summing up the total scores of all the five areas.

Means and standard deviations of the five areas of adjustment as well as total adjustment for all groups were calculated. Means and standard deviations of male and female students are presented in Table1.

Table 1

Means, S.Ds. and t-value of Male and Female Students in Various Areas of Adjustment and Total Adjustment.

Areas of Adjustment	*Male students (N=100)*		*Female students (N=100)*		*t-value*
	Means	*S.Ds.*	*Means*	*S.Ds.*	
(1)	*(2)*	*(3)*	*(4)*	*(5)*	*(6)*
(a) Home	5.49	2.89	7.13	3.12	3.90**
(b) Health	5.14	2.67	6.89	2.97	4.37**

(1)	(2)	(3)	(4)	(5)	(6)
(c) Social	7.62	2.15	9.25	2.91	4.53**
(d) Emotional	12.32	5.49	14.56	4.78	3.07**
(e) Educational	6.05	3.17	7.34	3.69	2.63**
Total Adjustment	36.62	12.19	45.17	13.05	4.80**

****Significant at 0.01 level.*

The above table reveals that significant differences exist between male and female students with respect to home, health, social, emotional and educational adjustment as the calculated t-values for these five areas of adjustment are highly significant at .01 level. As the mean values of male students are low in these five areas, their adjustment in all the areas are definitely better than the female students. Table 1 also reveals that there is a significant difference between the male and female students with respect to the total adjustment. It means that first hypothesis has been accepted in this study. Sex was found to be a significant determiners of all the five areas of adjustment as well as total adjustment at .01 level of significance. These results are in the line with the results of Bhavsar (1975), Gohrepade (1979), and Mohan and Gulati (1988) who reported that males are better adjusted than females.

Table 2

Means, S.Ds. and t-values of Scheduled Caste and Non-Scheduled Caste Students in Various Areas of Adjustment and Total Adjustment.

Areas of Adjustment	*Scheduled Caste Students (N=100)*		*Non-Scheduled Caste Students (N=100)*		*t-value*
	Means	*S.Ds.*	*Means*	*S.Ds.*	
(a) Home	6.239	2.73	4.96	2.57	3.26**
(b) Health	7.13	3.06	5.32	2.39	4.52**
(c) Social	8.98	2.69	7.12	2.64	4.77**
(d) Emotional	13.35	3.76	11.15	3.06	4.31**
(e) Educational	9.81	3.43	7.46	2.96	4.89**
Total Adjustment	45.50	12.96	36.01	12.16	5.13**

****Significant at 0.01 level*

Table 2 reveals that the adjustment of non-Scheduled Caste students in home, health, social, emotional, and educational areas of adjustment are significantly better than the Scheduled Caste students. Bansal (1973) and Rangari (1987) reported that adjustment was found to be better for non-Scheduled Caste than for Scheduled Caste students. Table 2 also indicates that significant difference exist between the mean total adjustment scores of Scheduled and non-Scheduled Caste students ($t=5.13, p<0.01$). It is concluded that second hypothesis has been accepted in this study and caste factors significantly influence the adjustment. Singh and Sinha (1982) found that the Santhal students are inferior in their home, health, and educational adjustment but superior in their social adjustment to the non-Santal students. However, the difference in the emotional adjustment level of both Santhal and non-Santhal students has been found to be significant. In this way, the findings of the study reveal males are significantly better adjusted than females, and non-Scheduled Castes subjects than Scheduled Caste subjects.

REFERENCES

Agrawal, M.C. (1970). Adjustment among the college students. *Indian Psychological Review*, 6, 85.

Bansal, J.P. (1973). A study of the adjustment differences among the Scheduled Caste and high caste Hindu adolescents. *Educational and Psychological Research Journal*, 1, 39-41.

Bhavsar. D.M. (1975). A study of social adjustment among high school students. *Journal of Education and Psychology*, 1, 7-10.

Gohrepade, M.B. (1979). The extent of maladjustment among Bombay University students. *Bombay Psychologists*, 1. 60-62.

Jones. D.N. and Reznikoff. M. (1989). Psychological adjustment to a mastectomy. *Journal of Nervous and Mental Disease*. 177. 624-631.

Khan. Razia (1991). Study of adjustment in relation to some personality and personal background factors among college students. *Indian Psychological Review*. 36, 38-39.

Krishna. K.P. (1982). Differential adjustment in adolescents and youths. *Indian Journal of Clinical Psychology*. 9. 169-170.

Leong. F.T., Mallinckrodt. B. and Kralj. M.M. (1990). Cross-cultural variations in stress and adjustment among Asian and Cavcasian graduate students. *Journal of Multicultural Counselling and Development*, 18. 19-28.

Mehta. C.S. (1982). Caste and adjustment differences among the obedient and disobedient students. *Indian Psychological Review*. 22. 1-5.

Mohan. J. and Gulati. Anita (1988). A study of academic achievement in relation to personality and adjustment. *Asian Journal of Psychology and Education*. 21. 3-15.

Mukherjee. M. and Upadhyay. S.N. (1980). Adjustment. anxiety and health. *Indian Psychological Review*, 19. 11-13.

Rangari. Ashok (1987). Differences in adjustment of scheduled caste and non-scheduled caste students. *Indian Psychologist*, 4, 59-64.

Saxena, M. and Sharma, V.K. (1982). An Empirical Investigation of Adjustment Patterns of high and low creative adolescents. Mysore : *Paper presented in 69th Session of the Indian Science Congress.*

Shah, Beena (1986). Study of social adjustment of graduated students in relation to caste and educational development. *Journal of Psychological Researches,* 30, 34-39.

Singh, L.B. and Sinha, V. (1982). Level of Adjustment in the Santal Undergraduate Students. Mysore : *Paper presented in 69th Session of the Indian Science Congress.*

Sinha, A.K.P. and Singh, R.P. (1971). *Adjustment Inventory for College Students.* Agra: National Psychological Corporation.

Tripathy, S.L. (1986). Adjustment problems of college students. *Asian Journal of Psychology and Education,* 17,11-14.

Vasishtha, K.K.(1989). A study of relationship among achievement motivation, adjustment, self concept and academic achievement at +2 level. *Journal of Education and Psychology,* 47, 72-75.

18

Self-Disclosure of Maritally Adjusted and Unadjusted Scheduled Caste Women

P.N. Arora and *Dileep Kapoor*

The Scheduled Caste who accounts for 14.6 per cent of Indian population have long suffered from extreme social and economic backwardness. With a few exception, all of them have also been for centuries the victims of 'untouchability'. Though attempts have been made to improve their conditions but much remains to be seriously taken up. Females on the other hand, constitute near about 45 per cent of the total population and in spite of their equal participation and active role in the family life, they have not been treated equal to men. The conditions of females belonging to Scheduled Caste are much more deplorable.

Women of this weaker section of society face multiple difficulties. She has to adjust with all the odds of life. An extraburden is put on her shoulders of taking the role of wife and adjusting with the marital responsibilities. The magnitude of woman's marital adjustment provides the basis for the adjustment of entire family and society ultimately. Therefore, a lady with well marital adjustment leads a well adjusted family, while a lady as a maladjusted wife or mother is supposed to be responsible for maladjusted husband, children and society ultimately (Saxena, 1983).

Marital adjustment may be defined as the process of modifying, adopting or alerting individual and couple patterns of behaviour and interaction in order to achieve satisfaction. Self-disclosure, on the other hand, is also an important personality factor. It may be considered as a very prominent factor that interacts with the adjustment. The term 'Self-Disclosure', may be defined as the capacity of the individual to express his inner feelings, ideas, deeds and reactions in the outer world by receiving some inner or outer stimulus. Various researchers have tried to correlate these two factors of the personality. Kinney (1963) on the basis of his study inferred that maladjusted women show a greater amount of self-disclosure. Pachauri (1994), on the other hand concluded an insignificant difference in the home adjustment of high and low disclosee females, while in case of social adjustment, she found a significant relationship between the self-disclosure and adjustment. Sinha (1980) is of the opinion that adjustment affects the magnitude of the self-disclosure in a significant way. These studies are confined to the general adjustment of women only. And also there seems a controversy in findings. Moreover, the difference between marital adjustment of high and low self-disclosee Scheduled Caste women has not been ascertained. The present study is an attempt in this direction.

Methodology

Sample

Two groups of 400 urban literate married Scheduled Caste Females (ranging in age from 22 to 45 years) were randomly selected from the Scheduled Caste families residing in district Rampur (U.P.). The entire sample was classified into two groups, well adjusted and maladjusted on the basis of Q1and Q3.

Each group comprised of 90 urban literate females. The two groups, thus obtained, were from same socio-economic status, religion, educational qualification and age.

Tools

The 'Marital Adjustment Test' devised by Burgees and Cattell was administered for the measurement of marital status of the subjects. The test consists of 26 items based on 5 variables. The reliability and validity of the tool was found to be high and applicable. To measure the extent of self-disclosure, Sinha's Self-Disclosure Inventory: Adult Form (1982) was used. This inventory has been designed to measure the extent of self-disclosure of Indian adults of both the sexes. It measures self-disclosure in 8 areas of self and towards 8 larger figures. It includes 80 items and takes 60 minutes on the average for its completion. This is a highly reliable and valid tool.

Result and Discussion

Critical Ratio (CR) test was applied to find out the significance of the difference in mean self-disclosure scores of well adjusted and unadjusted married literate Scheduled Caste adult urban females. Means, S.Ds. and result of CR have been shown in Table 1 below:

Table 1

Difference between Mean Self-disclosure Scores of Maritally Adjusted and Unadjusted Scheduled Caste Women.

Groups	*N*	*Category on SSDI Manual*	*Mean Scores*	*S.D.*	*Mean Differ-ence*	*SEd*	*C.R.*	*P*
Well Adjusted	90	High Disclosee	402.45	8.78	12.53	1.1605	10.88	.01
Maladjusted	90	Average Disclosee	392.82	6.65				

CR Value to be significant at .01 level of confidence and with 178 df is 2.60.

Table 1 shows that there is a significant difference in the mean self-disclosure scores of two groups. The calculated CR value is 10.88 which is much greater than CR value needed to be significant at .01 level of confidence. It means that the extent of marital adjustment affects significantly the extent and magnitude of the self-disclosure of females belonging to Scheduled Caste. The adjusted females seem to be high disclosee (M=402.45) than unadjusted females (M=392.82). The result of the present study is in accordance with the findings of Sinha (1980), while on the other hand, the findings of present study are in contrast to the findings of Robert (1979) and Pachauri (1994). The results are also contrary to the findings of Kinney (1963) who found that maladjusted females are high disclosee. It is quite evident that in modern set-up of Indian society, increasing literacy rate and better job opportunities as well as the facilities provided by Indian Government altogether have made a lady quite bold and daring to express herself. An adjusted women can disclose herself frankly and freely in her family as well as in society. So it may be suggested that by providing them more facilities, better job avenues as per their talent and qualifications and a respectable position in the family, we can enhance the disclosure among the Scheduled Caste females which will further be helpful in the development of their creative talents and ultimately this will be a real, pious and genuine creative and healthy contribution of society to this weaker section of Indian population.

REFERENCES

Kinney, F.M. (1963), *Psychology of Personal Adjustment.* N.Y.: Norton.

Pachauri, M.L. (1994). A psychological study of family adjustment in relation to self-disclosure among the educated females of Rohilkhand region of U.P. *Unpublished Ph.D. Thesis,* Rohilkhand University, Bareilly.

Robert, D. Mood (1979). Satisfaction with interpersonal relations as a function of love and self-disclosure. *Journal of Psychology,* 102, 21-26.

Saxena, S. (1963). Personality traits of primary school children in relation to their mothers marital adjustment and child rearing practices. *Unpublished Ph.D. Thesis.* Rohilkhand University, Bareilly.

Sinha, V. (1980), Family adjustment in relation to self-disclosure among urban adult females. *Indian Psychological Review,* 16, 58.

Sinha, V. (1982). *Manual for Self-disclosure Inventory for Adults.* Agra : National Psychological Corporation.

19

Gain and Retention of Nutrition Knowledge in Santhal Tribal Women

Meera Singh and *N.C. Verma*

Knowledge is one of the components of human behaviour and as such plays an important role in the covert as well as overt behaviours of an individual. Further, a person gains knowledge about facts and phenomena through certain stimulus and tries to retain such knowledge gained for use in future. In doing so, the person is influenced by many socio-personal and economic characteristics.

This study aimed at determining the association and nature of effects of selected characteristics of 'Santhal tribe' women on their gain and retention of knowledge of nutrition training programmes. The socio-personal characteristics taken in the study were education of the husband, education of the respondents, type of family, size of family, size of land holding, family income, number of animals, number of birds, number of meal per day, social participation and cosmopoliteness. In the light of such findings the characteristics may be modified to the extent possible by the individual themselves and the extension workers as well for more and more effectiveness of their effects and strategy.

Methodology

The study was conducted in Dumka block of Santhal Pargana division in Bihar, following pre-and post-experimental research design. A sample of 25 'Santhal tribe' pre-and post-married women in the age group of 18 to 50 years, having at least one child with initial readiness for participation in a 12-day nutrition training programme, were selected.

In all, 12 socio-personal characteristics (variables) were selected for the study and appropriate measurement technique was employed. The gain in nutrition knowledge was measured by using the nutrition knowledge test developed for the purpose, which was administered to the participants before and after the training. The retention of knowledge was assessed employing the same instrument after 15 days of training. The data were subjected to path analysis.

Results and Discussion

With a view to know the relationship between a set of selected socio-personal variables and direct and indirect effects on gain and retention of knowledge as a result of participation in nutrition training programme, correlation co-efficient and path analysis were computed. The results are presented below :

Table 1

Correlation Co-efficient and Direct and Indirect Effects of Independent Variables on Gain in Knowledge.

Variables	*r-value*	*Direct effect*	*Rank*	*Total indirect effect*	*Rank*	*Largest indirect effect through*	*(XI)*
Age (X1)	—0.4369**	—0.1926	XII	—0.2443	XI	0.0669	(X2)
Education(X2) of the husband	0.9723**	—0.1614	X	0.6337	I	0.1201	(X6)
Education(X3) of the respondents	0.5431**	0.7445	I	—0.2014	X	0.7850	(X1)
Type of (X4) family	—0.0643	0.2261	III	—0.2904	XII	0.0319	(X2)
Size of (X5) family	0.1909	0.1381	IV	0.0528	XI	0.2452	(X3)
Size of (X6) land holding	0.2776**	0.2658	II	0.0118	XII	0.0644	(X5)
Family (X7) Income	0.3069**	—0.0606	IX	0.3675	III	0.1563	(X6)
No. of (X8) animals	—0.0880	—0.0229	VII	—0.0657	IX	0.0295	(X12)
No. of (X9) birds	0.0545	—0.0172	VI	—0.0373	VIII	0.0566	(X6)
No. of (X10) meal per day	0.2443*	—0.0461	VIII	0.2904	V	0.3687	(X3)
Social (XII) Participation	0.3965**	0.604	V	0.3361	IV	0.5039	(X3)
Cosmo - (X12) politeness	0.2725**	—0.2066	XI	0.4791	II	0.1294	(X6)

Residual effect = 0.6249

* Significant at .05 level

** Significant at .01 level

The table under discussion indicated that variables such as age, education of husband, education of the respondents, size of land holding, family income, social participation and cosmopoliteness were highly and significantly correlated with gain in nutrition knowledge. However, age was negatively correlated, which means older participants of the training programme could gain less knowledge as compared to the younger participants.

The table further revealed that there was maximum direct effect of education of respondents on gain in nutrition knowledge which was followed by size of land holding and type of family. Thus on the basis of value of path coefficient a few dominant variables that emerged were education of the respondents, size of land holding and type and size of family.

The last column of the table indicated that the largest indirect effect on gain in knowledge of the variables was education of the respondents which is channeled through age of the respondent. It is justified because formal education plays definite role in the development of one's personality. It provides a base for specialised learning among individuals. A person who has some schooling, understand and comprehend the message more sharply than those who are illiterate and have little education. Probably these facts are adhered to in gain in knowledge.

An observation of the value of the residual effects obtained through path analysis indicated that only 38 per cent variability in knowledge gained was explained due to these independent variables. Relationship between knowledge retained and a set of selected independent variables are presented in Table 2.

Table 2

Correlation Co-efficient and Direct and Indirect Effects of Independent Variables on of Knowledge.

Variables	*r-value*	*Direct effect*	*Rank*	*Total indirect effect*	*Rank*	*Largest indirect effect through*	*(XI)*
Age (X1)	–0.5385**	—0.3748	XII	—0.1637	XI	0.1028	(X2)
Education (X2) of the husband	0.4472**	0.2483	XI	0.6955	I	0.6625	(X3)
Education (X3) of the respondents	0.5499**	0.7674	I	—0.2175	XII	0.1528	(X1)
Type of (X4) family	–0.0923	0.0219	V	—0.1142	IX	0.0556	(X2)

Size of (X5) family	0.1163	—0.0086	VI	0.1249	VII	0.2528	(X3)
Size of (X6) land holding	0.1969*	0.0283	IV	0.1686	VI	0.3292	(X3)
Family (X7) Income	0.3081**	—0.0896	III	0.2185	V	0.4883	(X3)
No. of (X8) animals	–0.1953**	—0.1217	IX	—0.0736	VIII	0.0355	(X2)
No. of (X9) birds	0.0230	—0.1408	II	—0.1178	X	0.0060	(X6)
No. of (X10) meal per day	0.2354*	—0.0457	VIII	0.2811	IV	0.3000	(X3)
Social (XII) Participation	0.3663**	0.0220	VII	0.3883	III	0.5194	(X3)
Cosmo- (X12) politeness	0.2556**	—0.1649	X	0.4205	II	0.5036	(X3)

Residual effect = 0.6723

* Significant at .05 level

** Significant at .01 level

The variables such as education of the husband, education of respondents, family income, social participation and cosmopoliteness were highly and positively correlated, whereas, age and number of animals are such variables which are highly correlated but in negative direction with retention of nutrition knowledge.

On the basis of value of path co-efficient under the direct effect column, there is maximum direct effect of education of the respondents on retention of nutrition knowledge.

Age has negative influence on both direct and indirect effect on retention of knowledge. It indicated that as the age increases, the retention power decreases. The finding is also supported by the study of Menon and Prema (1982). On the basis of analysis, it could also be inferred that as the self-education, size of land holding, social participation and cosmopoliteness increase the retention power of participants of nutrition training programme also increases.

An observation of the values as indicated in the column of indirect effect indicated that education of husband had maximum indirect effect on retention of knowledge which is channeled through the education of the respondents.

The overall picture that emerged from the path analysis is that the education of respondents has a maximum direct effect on both gain and retention of knowledge. An individual who has formal schooling has a changed outlook than those who had not undergone formal education. The education of the respondents facilitates them in comprehending the message and remember the same for a longer period.

Table 2 also revealed that the residual effect obtained through path analysis was 0.67, which indicated that only 33 per cent variability in retention of knowledge as a result of participation in nutrition training programme was explained by selected independent variables.

Conclusion

The study leads to conclude that education is such a variable of the respondents which exerted maximum direct effect on gain and retention of nutrition knowledge. This variable can be manipulated for best results of any educational programm designed for 'Santhal tribal' women.

REFERENCES

Menon, A.G. and Prema, L. (1982). Retention of knowledge on human nutrition by rural women as related with their socio-economic status. *Indian Journal of Home Science*. 12, 107.

Murthy. V. and Ramadas (1991). Nutritional information communication. *Nutrition*, 25, 4-10

20

Personal Space Orientation among Women

S.P. Sinha and *Neelima Mukherjee*

Personal space refers to the interpersonal distance chosen during social interactions. Hall (1963, 1966) conceptualizes personal space primarily as a form of non-verbal communication. According to him, the distance between individuals determines the quality of stimulation that is exchanged, information about the type of relationship between individuals, and about the type of activities that can be engaged in. Personal space informs both the participants and the outside observers about the very nature of participants relationship. It has been emphasized that not only the size of the personal space is important but also the angle of orientation between the interactants (Cook 1970; Hayduk 1994; Sommer 1969). Studies on personal space orientation show attraction-proximity relationship, i.e., increased attraction is associated with closer physical distance (Allgeier and Byrne 1973; Edwards 1972). Dyads interact at closer distances as their relationship become more intimate (Heshka and Nelson, 1972; Rustemili, 1992). It has been found that one's interactions with spouse, friends, co-workers and neighbours differ (Jost, Schatzle, Schenk and Wagner, 1985). Personal space is culturally acquired (Hall 1959; Mazur 1977) and affected by socio-economic status (Saxena, 1987). In each culture, children gradually learn the rules. Sex differences in personal space reflect differences in socialization of males and females. Indian women are still conservative and follow traditional value and traditional family ideology (Chauhan, 1986). Depending on their upbringing and other social influences they are expected to have largest personal space for other sex dyads (wife-male and husband-Female) and least personal space for wife-husband dyad. Thus, the present study intended to test the prediction that personal space requirements of Indian women differ for different dyads (WH, HM, HF, WF and WM).

Subjects

From Dholpur City (Rajasthan), 100 conventional Hindu wives age ranging from 22 years to 30 years (mean age 26 years 2 months), belonging to educated middle socio-economic status families (where husband was the only bread winner), living with their spouse, were randomly selected.

Tools

Comfortable Interpersonal Distance Test : This test was developed by Desor (1972) in which grey dolls of height 14.8 cms, were used, mounted on circular bases of diameter 3 cm. They were modelled to show as distinct features, only head and shoulders and directions in which they were facing. Both the dolls were placed on a sheet of graph of 21×29.5 cm.

Procedure

For the doll placement task the subjects were asked to think of one doll as one of the members of dyad and to place the other doll representing the other member of the dyad at the distance that they would like to have between themselves when the other member of the dyad appears to be a stranger of their own age and status.

Results

Table 1

Summary : Analysis of Variance

Source of Variation	*SS*	*df*	*MS*	*F*
Rows	8089.038	99	81.70	
Columns	3841.078	4	960.27	28.85
Interaction	13181.322	396	33.28	

The results of the repeated measures single factor ANOVA (Winer, 1971) revealed that there was significant effect of the dyad condition, (F=28.85, $p < .01$ Table 1)

The mean personal space for different dyad conditions show that the lowest mean personal space was for WH dyad (M=2.29 cms.) followed by WF, HM, HF and WM dyads (M= 5.71, 8.93, 13.49, 15.09 cms. respectively). The critical value of mean differences on post-hoc test (Tukey's) was 0.99 (5.396) = 2.75 which revealed that all the mean differences (except between HF and WM dyads) were significant.

Table 2

Mean Personal Space (in cms.) for Different Dyads

Dyads	*WH*	*HM*	*HF*	*WM*	*WF*
Personal Space	2.29	8.93	13.49	15.09	5.71

Discussion

The findings of the present study confirmed the results obtained by Hill, Blackham and Crane (1982) that the personal space requirements differ for different dyad conditions. The subjects required for personal space for other sex dyads i.e., HF and WM whereas the WH combination required the least personal space. Indian middle class women have traditional values, they are still conservative and they do not want intimate interaction with other sex dyads (Sinha and Mukherjee, 1990). From the very childhood the girls are brought up under strict control and parents do not like to give much freedom for mixing with the opposite sex. The most intimate interactions were found for the WH dyad. Spouse plays a unique role for the subjects. Indian women are mainly dependent on their husbands for the economic and social security. In close interaction with their husbands (close personal space) they feel more comfortable. These findings support the results obtained by Albas and Albas (1989) that in situations perceived to be potentially threatening, people react by standing farther back and using personal space as a buffer zone. The attraction proximity relationship depends on the socialization differences. Females are socialized to be more dependent, to be less afraid of intimacy with others of the same sex and generally to be more comfortable in affiliative situations (Crawford, 1994; Maccoby, 1966).

The other finding of the present study is that out of the two same sex dyads i.e., WF and HM, the lesser personal space was required for WF dyad as compared to HM dyad. Thus it is evident from the results that female-female pairs position themselves closer together than male-male pairs. For females close distances may evoke concerns about dependency, whereas, for males far distance may reflect their independence and self-reliance.

REFERENCES

Albas, D.C., and Albas, C.A. (1989). Meaning in context: The impact of eye contact and perception of threat on proximity. *Journal of Social Psychology*. 129, 525-531.

Allgeir, A.R., and Byrne, D. (1973). Attraction toward the opposite sex as a determinant of physical proximity. *Journal of Social Psychology*, 90, 213-219.

Chauhan, R. (1986). Conservatism and radicalism among females as related to traditional family ideology, freedom of children, *Dissertation*, Agra University, Agra.

Cook, M. (1970). Experiments on orientation and proxemics. *Human Relations*, 23, 61-76.

Crawford, C.B. (1994). Effects of sex, and sex roles on avoidance of same and opposite sex touch. *Perceptual and Motor Skills*, 79, 107-112.

Desor, J.A. (1972). Towards a psychological theory of crowding. *Journal of Personality and Social Psychology*, 21, 79-83.

Edwards, D.J.A. (1972). Approaching the unfamiliar: A study of human interaction distances. *Journal of Behavioural Sciences*, 1, 249-250.

Hall, E.T. (1959). *The Silent Language*. New York : Doubleday.

Hall, E.T. (1963). A system for the notation of proxemic behaviour. *American Anthropologist*, 65, 1003-1026.

Hall, E.T. (1966). *The hidden dimension*. New York : Doubleday.

Hayduk, L.A. (1994). Personal Space : Understanding the simplex model. *Journal of Non-verbal Behaviour*. 18, 245-260.

Hashka, S. and Nelson, Y. (1972). Interpersonal speaking distance as a function of age, sex and relationship. *Sociometry*. 35, 491-498 .

Hill, R.D. : Blackham, R.E. and Crane, D.R. (1982). The effect of marital relationship on personal space orientation in married couples. *Journal of Social Psychology*, 118, 23-28.

Jost, G.: Schatzle, E.: Schenk, J. and Wagner, F. (1985). Interaction with spouse compared to that with friends, co-workers and neighbours. *Zeitschrift fur Experimentelle und Angewandte Psychologia*. 32, 471-483.

Maccoby, E. (1966). The *Development of Sex Differences*. Standford : Standford University Press.

Mazur, A. (1977). Interpersonal spacing on public benches in 'contact' and 'non-contact' cultures. *Journal of Social Psychology*. 101, 53-58.

Rustemli, A. (1992). Crowding effects of density and interpersonal distance. *Journal of Social Psychology*, 132, 51-58.

Saxena, P. (1987). Role relationship, socio-economic status, sex and interacting situations as related to territoriality. Unpublished master's dissertation. H.S. Gour University, Sagar, India.

Sinha, S.P. and Mukherjee, N. (1990). Marital adjustment and personal space orientation. *The Journal of Social Psychology*. 130, 633-639.

Sommer, R. (1969). Personal space. Englewood Cliffs, NJ. : Prentice Hall.

Winer, B.J. (1971). Statistical principles in experimental design. New York : McGraw-Hill.

Section IV

Children

21
Equality of Educational Opportunity and Children

M. Akhtar Siddiqui

India is a country of diversities in many senses of the term. From socio-economic standpoint, there are privileged and underprivileged classes, forward and backward castes, majority community and minority communities, etc. Diversities among individuals and groups also exist due to regional variations in development of different kinds. These diversities and inequalities, however, are not a typical feature of the Indian society alone, rather, these may be found in almost all the societies of the world. In a developing Country particularly, these inequalities are mostly the result of prolonged discriminatory and inequitous treatment meted out to different individuals and groups by various power apparatus of society ignoring their genuine needs and aspirations by not accepting them as equally respectable and rightful human beings, and in the process, also relegating the need of optimum development of society as a whole. Obviously, the primary objective of such a treatment has been to perpetuate the hegemony of certain groups and individuals in the cultural and politico-economic arenas of society.

In the post-Industrial Revolution era, for various reasons, societies began to slowly realise that the approach of treating different groups of human beings co-existing in same society as unequals and restricting opportunities for their full development is unjust. It is often said that these were the western societies which first raised the issue of extending equal opportunity to all individuals and social groups within a society for their best development and considered this a symbol of a humane and civilised society. However, much before what had dawned on the west in the direction of giving equal opportunity and treatment to all human beings, Islam, in as early as seventh century A.D., had propounded and, eversince, has also vigorously practised the proposition of equality of all human beings and of extending social justice and equal treatment to all, irrespective of caste, colour, race or region, one may belong to. The west might have been inspired to implement the idea of equality and social justice due to the exigencies arising out of the fast industrialising societies, but Islam had introduced the principle of equality purely on human and rational considerations and strived to restore the honour of all human beings and groups and build a just and humane society. To bring such a lasting change, Islam stressed change in attitude of the people and inculcated positive attitude for equality. Today, most of the societies of the world advocate equal opportunity to all for their best socio-economic and cultural development but the societies which follow the cherished ideal of democracy are in the forefront of this campaign. These societies have framed legislations and laws guaranteeing various rights of individuals and groups and often the State machinery is used to give affect to these provisions of law for equality and social justice.

Constitution of India accepted democracy as the core principle of the future development of the Indian people and while considering the inequalities existing among them due to the indiscriminate and unjust curbs imposed on many of them by vested groups in the past, conferred equality on all individuals and social groups in the country. However, this equality as envisaged in the democratic principles remains a de-jure equality until sincere and perseverent efforts are made by the society and the State to implement such measures as would bring in true equality of opportunity for socio-economic development of all members of the populace.

In today's world, education is considered as the primary means that equips individuals to take advantage of the development opportunities arising in and outside a society, provided that the society enables all individuals to acquire it without any restraints. To make the ideal of equality a reality, it is incumbent on the democratic state to first provide equal opportunity to all to acquire education so as to affect full development of human resources of society. Once educated, the weaker individuals and sections of society will particularly be able to use education as a lever to improve their socio-economic condition.

In order to effectively equalise educational opportunity one will have to understand in what ways and forms inequality in opportunity may arise and what measures would be needed to remove them to the extent possible. When we talk of educational opportunity we certainly include both, quantitative as well as qualitative aspects of education and equalisation has to be done on both the fronts. This will only help education in achieving its social objective, besides others. While surveying the state and problems of education in the country, Kothari Education Commission (1964-66) had identified various ways in which inequalities in educational opportunities seem to arise in our society.

In places where no primary, secondary or collegiate institutions exist, children do not have the same opportunity as those who have these facilities in the neighbourhood. No educational facility in certain areas is the result of unbalanced educational development in different parts of the country and even in different districts of a State. There are about seven States and a large number of districts spread in many States where provision of education is below the national averages. In spite of manifold expansion in school education after independence, imbalance in provision still persists. To equalise the availability of educational facilities across the districts and States, expansion of educational facilities have to be done in a more regulated and planned fashion through a detailed perspective plan for expansion based on the need for different levels and types of education in each area and, where this is not feasible due to economic or technical reasons, arrangements have to be made to take children to the facility by making available transport and hostel facilities. In this regard, Government of India has decided to provide a primary school within a radius of one kilometre and a middle and secondary school within a radius of three kilometres of the habitation. According to Fourth All India Educational Survey in 1978-79 there were 1,90,000 habitations in the country without a primary school. Since then many new schools have been opened, but, at the same time, many new habitations have also come into existence. For example, in 1986 there were about 32,000 habitations with population of 300 or more and after opening many primary school since 1986, in 1992 number of these habitations still stood at 35,000. In the Programme of Action (PoA) for the National Policy on Education (NPE) 1986 it was envisaged that, besides providing a primary school in each habitation with a population of 300 (200 in the case of tribal, hilly and desert areas), a detailed mapping exercise will be initiated in order to prepare a Master Plan of Universal Provision of Facilities for providing elementary education wherein each habitation which can potentially have 50 children in the primary school, will be provided one primary school. An upper primary school,would be provided on primary school. catchment basis. For deprived sections, including SC/ST, residential schools and hostels will be provided on a large scale; the programme of Ashram schools will be improved and enlarged; inexpensive systems of hostels using the school building and providing kitchen room where local villagers will be engaged on part time basis to assist cooking and supervision, will be created; and possibility of providing free foodgrains to the students in those hostels out of the accumulated stocks in the country will be explored. In order to improve provision of schools in neglected, hilly, tribal and difficult areas in the Revised Policy Formulations 1992 and its PoA 1992 envisage a scheme of Voluntary Schools. These schools will be run by voluntary organisations who will receive aid from the Government and operate under the supervision of Village Education Committee and will be expected to complete primary/elementary education of the required level in a specific period which is adequate for the pupils to master the curriculum. Learners involved in the Voluntary Schools may appear as external students for entry into any class of full time formal school. As for the secondary stage, in the pre-NPE survey, as was reported in the document, Challenge of Education—A Policy Perspective (1984) it was found that there were a good number of tribal, hilly or desert areas where there was no secondary school for 10 to 20 kilometres due to low density of population in these areas. To provide secondary school facility in all areas, the PoA-1986 suggested for carrying out the school mapping exercise in each State and it also proposed that by 2000 AD all the unserved areas will be fully served. It is hoped that the State Governments will be able to make necessary finances available for these programmes. Until the successful implementation of the above mentioned provisions for elementary and secondary stages, obviously, the inequality in opportunity for education for this reason will persist.

Inequality of educational opportunity also arises due to the reason of a large section of the population being substantially poor. One can easily vouch the fact that in spite of a school being there in the neighbourhood, the children from poor families do not have the same chance of joining education as those who come from richer families. The situation becomes more complex in view of the fact that about 37 per cent of the population of the country, according to a recent survey conducted in 1996, still lives below poverty line. The problem arises due heavy private cost of education and also due to the unbearable opportunity cost of education for the poors. Despite education being free, and books, stationery, uniform, food, etc. also being free which brings down the private cost to a nominal level, below poverty line families cannot afford to withdraw their children from work and send them for education as this would mean loss of opportunity for subsistence earning necessary for their survival. For such families and their children educational opportunity remains grossly unequal. Even the programme of scholarships, as envisaged in the National Policy on Education 1986, and in the revised PoA, 1992, is going to serve very little egalitarian purpose. To meet this situation the economic condition of the poor families will also have to be improved by way of creating and providing livelihood and employment opportunities through various schemes, besides offering merit-cum-means scholarships, so that poor parents can afford to spare their children for education. In this regard, some schemes like IRDP, RLEGP, Jawahar Rozgar Yojna, etc. have already been launched during the last few years, yet, a large section of population continues to live below poverty line. In the last fifty years of independence we have been able to bring down the percentage of people living below poverty line from 50 to 37 only. It seems that it is a long drawn battle and a pretty long period of time will be required to solve this problem and, until then, the non-egalitarian trend in education is going to stay.

Home environment of the learners also causes inequality in educational opportunity as a child from a slum, or a rural household or from a family doing a petty job, or having illiterate parents does not have the same opportunity of learning and education which a child from an upper class educated parents has. These inequalities are most difficult to overcome. To same extent, the problem may be overcome by introducing day-study centres, supervised study programmes, remedial teaching programme in the school, etc., after school hours. Initially, these, programmes may have complications. Teachers attitude towards the whole problem, their willingness to devote extra time for the needy children and their intrinsic motivation to help these children come up near the level of other students in studies are some of the basic issues associated with these programmes which have to be handled intelligently. As far as possible, these programmes should avoid monetary incentives to the teachers. To partly compensate the educational deprivation caused to children coming from these underprivileged families, particularly in SC/ST and educationally backward minorities, a scheme of remedial teaching and coaching in important secondary school subjects was launched under the NPE-1986 for SC/ST students. In the revised PoA 1992 this was decided that the remedial coaching scheme for SC/ST students will be extended to students belonging to educationally backward minorities also and the same has to be implemented by the Departments of Education in the States and Union Territories. The remedial coaching scheme which is being implemented through voluntary organisations for its success, needs proper publicity and also demands sincere efforts on the part of voluntary agencies to take it to the needy groups of learners. But more importantly, such strategies have to be evolved through which children with weak home environment can preferably be helped to acquire reasonable standard of learning during the course of school routine itself.

The educational opportunity has also been perenially unequal between the two sexes. This inequality cuts across all classes, sections, castes and religions of the country. For various socio-economic and historical reasons girls are worse off in all kinds of education. The problem exists in its compounded form in rural and backward areas and among the SC/ST and educationally and economically backward classes. To quote an example, in 1991, female literacy rate was 39.29 per cent compared to 64.13 per cent for male, the national rate being 52.21 per cent. Similarly, at the primary and upper primary stages in 1994-95 the girls accounted for 42.8 per cent and 38.9 per cent of the total enrollment, respectively. Their drop out rates are also higher compared with the dropout rates of boys. The situation is worse in the cases of rural areas, SC/ST and educationally backward minorities. Right from the First Five Year Plan efforts are on to bridge the gap in education between the two sexes. The impact of various Central and State, as also voluntary, initiatives, was reflected in the decenial literacy growth rates which were 7.76 per cent for men and 9.54 per cent for women in the 80s. The NPE-86 is committed to ensure a well conceived edge in favour of women. The unequal education between the two sexes is the result of a particular role expectation of girl child and a consequent bias at home and in the community towards education of male child. Parental desire to send their daughters to a segregated and not a co-educational institution right from upper primary stage also limits opportunities for girls education. The Government, in association with NGOs, has launched various schemes and programmes to make the community understand the role of girl child in a right perspective and make arrangements for girls education according to the sensitivity of the community. A programme of Mahila Samakhya is operational in 17 districts spread over the four States of Andhra Pradesh, Gujarat, Karnataka and U.P. and their Mahila Shikshan Kendras basically meant for achieving adult literacy are emerging as centres of mainstream education for women. Many States have now switched over to the scheme of bifurcated boys and girls upper primary and secondary schools to bring more girls to the fold of education.

A typical inequality in educational opportunity arises when two groups of children having been educated in educational institutions with varying degrees of educational facilities, environment and achievement standards are treated at par for granting entry into next level educational institution in the name of treating all of them equally without discrimination. In the process, the students coming from rural or slum schools which are poorly equipped for quality education fail to compete with the students coming from urban and better equipped schools and thus they get eliminated at the entry point and lose the opportunity for higher education. To handle this problem more rational admission procedures need to be evolved. On the other hand, to improve competitive ability of these students for higher education as also for various employment opportunities they need to be provided additional coaching and guidance and their learning standards need to be improved before they go for any next level education or examination. The Ministry of Welfare had launched during 1990-91 a scheme of pre-examination coaching/training to prepare candidates belonging to educationally backward minorities for entrance examinations/professional courses/ competitive examinations. Similarly, University Grants Commission had also launched a coaching scheme in 1984 for educationally backward minorities with a particular emphasis on preparing candidates for competitive examinations for recruitment in services and for admission to professional courses including Engineering, Medical, etc. To improve opportunity for good quality school education for children from rural areas and thus to provide them equal opportunity for higher education, scheme of Navodaya Vidyalayas was incorporated in the NPE-1986 which was basically meant to provide quality education upto class XII free of charge to rural children. Besides these programmes more egalitarian and extensive measures including those for selection for admissions to higher and professional courses need to be taken up in this direction for rural children.

This is evident from the foregoing discussion that while many programmes and measures to bridge the gap in educational opportunities and attainments between various individuals and groups have been initiated, still these opportunities are at variance when seen from different angles and the task seems to be too huge to be fulfilled within a short foreseeable future. However, complete *de facto* equality of educational opportunity, like all ideals in life, is perhaps unattainable and so what is more important in the context of this problem is our continuous, sincere and concerted striving towards reducing this inequality to a minimum level with an unshaken faith in and commitment to the egalitarian principles.

REFERENCES

Government of India (1984). *Challenge of Education—A Policy Perspective,* New Delhi.

Government of India (1986). *National Policy on Education-1986,* New Delhi

Government of India (1986). *Programme of Action to the NPE-86,* New Delhi

Government of India (1992). *Programme of Action-1992,* New Delhi

Government of India (1996). *Annual Report, 1995-96,* New Delhi.

NCERT (1966). *Education and National Development—A Report of the Education Commission 1964-66,* New Delhi.

22

Trends in the Education of Girls

Ataur Rahman Khan

In most developing countries, the astounding rate at which new luxury goods are being introduced in spite of the ever increasing poverty betrays the extent to which the development process is benefiting only some privileged classes. India is no exception to it. Despite growth in the number of urban poor all over the world, the rural poor still account for over 80 per cent of the total number of poor in the world. The largest number of the poor live in Asia (Some 633 million) and ultimately the poverty translates into hunger and malnutrition. In fact, formal acknowledgement of the importance of women's roles for achieving economic development and social well-being came with the 1973 - Percy Amendment to the U.S. Nonetheless it was Foreign Assistance Act which called for their full integration into all subsequent development projects. It took the United Nation "Decades for Women" to begin to make women's, productive, as well as their productive roles visible to the world. As a result of this, global consciousness raising attempts to reformulate measures of economic output to include what women do and can do began to appear. The present order of address of the social scientists in general, in this area, is to focus on the issues of enabling women to be productive, to control their own labour, their means of production, their earnings and their educational and overall social well-being. It also has indirect effects, buffering women from oppressive conditions that place them at risk for overall development and allowing them to escape situations of violence and abuse.

In fact, women's poverty can be addressed better through educational and economic activities that increase the productivity of women through access to technology and knowhow, providing equitable opportunities for wage earnings. For this, it is imperative to ensure access to a continued enrollment of all girls in schools. Though many societies face similar educational and social concerns, however, diversities across nations also must be taken into account to set priorities in policy from work, as the programmes that do not consider these sources of diversity are likely to be less successful; for the sources of diversity are natural, material, cultural, political as well as historical. In view of this background the study attempts to address to the issue of female education in some of the regions facing almost the similar conditions.

There is a considerable variation in educational attainment within Asia. Typically poor countries have lower literacy rates and levels of educational attainment. Post primary coverage has increased considerably in Asia in the last 20 years. Significant variations, however, still exist in the secondary and post secondary levels. Evidence does show wide disparities in enrollment pattern as presented in Table 1.

Table 1

Percentage of Females in Total Enrollment in Selected Countries upto Early Mid-1980s at Secondary Level.

Country	*Secondary*
Bangladesh	28
Bhutan	18
People's Rep. of China	40
India	34
Indonesia	43
Rep. of Korea	47
Malaysia	49
Nepal	23
Philippines	50
Singapore	50
Sri Lanka	53
Thailand	48
Regional Average	40

Source: Hob Craft J. 1985. "In the Collection and Analysis of Community Data". Edited by J. Casterline Voorburg. Netherlands: International Statistical Institute. Cited in *Urban Poverty in Asia: A survey of critical issues,* New York: Oxford University Press. 1994.

One finds in the above table that Malaysia has substantially higher secondary coverage among the poor, possibly, because of the residential secondary school programme which targeted lower income children for more intensive academic preparation.

In India the key issue remains making secondary education more relevant to the needs of the individual and society. Stress is on the need to vocationalize secondary education; owing to this pressures of vocationalization, secondary education here in India too, is likely to receive attention in the years to come.

Some Common Issues

Before considering the secondary schools in India, however the features which are rather common in some other countries are to be noted, as it is difficult to generalize about secondary education, not only because of diversities but also because of the socio-cultural make-up of society and the changes that take place at this stage rapidly.

New Zealand

During the 1980 there has been a substantial increase in unemployment in New Zealand and young people with low academic qualifications have been generally victims to this unemployment. Secondary schools responded to this issue by introducing transition programmes for such students, through the in-school courses and community based work—experience aimed to provide young people with relevant knowledge understanding and skills to assist them to move confidently into the adult world. At present, about one-third of all secondary students here leave school without a certificate. Ministerial committees of inquiry keep on reviewing the curriculum, assessment procedures for the transition from schools to adult-life.

Philippines

In Philippines, high school students are exposed to both academic and generalized vocational training and to ensure that the linkage between education and culture and education for work is forged, a subject called work-experience has been added to the curriculum.

Australia

Secondary education in Australia provides more open role to schools; linking their work with the community, seeking deliberately to foster and develop continuity, meaning and responsibility for the students. The idea is that when schools cannot solve social problems they should prepare people to play an intelligent and informed role in society. Secondary education in Australia has become a cooperative effort involving participation of Government, the professionals, and the public.

Republic of Korea

Secondary school system is composed of three-year middle schools and three-year high schools. High schools are further divided into "general" "vocational" and "specialised" high schools. Generally all applicants are accepted and allocated on a random basis to schools within the district of residence.

China and Thailand

In China high schools academic-courses are complemented with work labour and technical education programmes. The rationale is to introduce a productivity labour-education programme. The aim is to produce manpower developed in all-round way. Therefore, high schools in China are successfully changed into agricultural and vocational schools. This has helped the country to eliminate the issues of mismatch of knowledge and application; theory and practice, and of course, study and employment.

Similarly, Thailand includes the work-experience and values-education as new subjects in curriculum of secondary education. Work-experience is aimed at developing in the youth desirable work-habits, and self-sufficiency. Values education on the other hand is intended to provide students a cognitive based "value-pattern" of the society.

Malaysia

Similar to India, Malaysia is a multiracial country. It is moving from an agricultural to an industrial society. The system of education here is being reviewed along the objectives of national unity and a balance between individual development and expected contribution from him to the national development. Educational goals centre on the development of individual potentials relevant to social needs, practical living-skills, respect for others rights, needs, creative and innovative talents. The social relevance provides them with socio-cultural orientation, political maturity and international understanding.

In view of the aforesaid order in secondary education in different countries world over, India has to re-submit the issues of education for analyses — as secondary education throughout the world is more variable than elementary and higher education. Elementary schools have similar curricula and do not provide accessibility to all. Secondary schools vary in purposes, control, curricula, number of years (in division), democratic features and also in names at times.

Overview

The countries like Japan, Australia, Republic of Korea and New Zealand are well developed and have an advanced technology, a literate and skilled population as well as highly developed and effective educational systems. On the other, there are countries with underdeveloped educational systems like that of India, China, Bangladesh, Bhutan, Myanmar, Nepal, Pakistan, etc. These countries are characterised by a widespread poverty and a large illiterate population and are in marked contrast to those which have highly developed systems of education like that of Japan, Republic of Korea and New Zealand.

Most of the underdeveloped countries face shortage of resources as well as of teachers and schools. Therefore, these countries are designing better school system in solving their educational issues. They have consultants through the U.N. and to some extent directly with the developed countries. Also because, they have to confront the traditional attitudes as well, like : "Education was for a few only" and that "the upper-class elite scholars should not dirty their hands with ordinary labour" and also for the least-value attached to the 'female-education' in these countries. In view of this perspective, attempt has been made in the present study to determine the direction of movement of girls in the secondary school education in India as compared to the boys within the same specific age groups over the last three decades, irrespective of the race, socio-economic status or the place of residence, as secondary school education is considered to be key point from where the students either enter the world of higher education or the world of work.

Objective

The main objective of the present study, therefore, was to determine whether there is a definite trend in the enrollment of girls in secondary schools education in India over the last three decades.

Method of Data-Collection

Data on secondary school enrollment of girls were collected from 1951 to 1986 recorded from the different sources of the Ministry of Education and Culture, Government. of India, and "Urban Poverty" in Asia on 'selected educational statistics' and 'the education and Allied Statistics' of the Ministry. Enrollments in secondary and higher secondary levels were clubbed together as 'secondary education'.

Analysis and Results

Enrollment growth rates for the girls, boys and the total enrollment were computed separately for the different lengths of time period ranging from 12 to 35 years viz, 1951 to 1983, 1951 to 1986,1961 to 1983, 1961 to 1986, 1971 to 1983 and 1971 to 1986.

Table 2

Growth Rates : Secondary Education in India in Terms of Total Enrollments (1951-1986).

Period	*Boys*	*Girls*	*Total*
1951-83	6.87	10.29	7.05
1951-86*	7.05	10.97	7.89
1961-83	5.89	8.73	6.04
1961-86	6.92	9.02	6.98
1971-83	3.89	5.87	4.52
1971-86	6.53	7.05	6.01

Source : The Ministry of Education and Culture, Government of India (1951-84).

* : On extrapolation

Break-up of the enrollment growth rates in the above table shows a higher growth rate of enrollment during the period 1951-1986 in the total enrollment of girls, wherein 7.05 per cent boys and 10.97 per cent girls were enrolled. Analysis for the twenty-two years period i.e. (1961 to 1983), reveals that girls growth rate in enrollment was more (8.73 per cent) than that of the boys (5.89 per cent). A similar pattern is noted also for the period of 1961 to 1986, 1971 to 1983, and 1971 to 1986. It means that girls have always been showing a higher rate of growth than their boys counterpart in going for secondary school education over the last 34-35 years in the country.

It may be noted here that total enrollment in India has gradually gone up with longevity of time. As is indicated in the above table in twelve years period (viz. : 1971 to 1983), it is 4.52 per cent and after another four years (i.e. by 1971 to 1986) it moved up to the tune of 6.01 per cent. Similar has been the trend during the period of twenty-two years (viz : 1961 to 1983) in total enrollments which recorded 6.04 per cent and by 1986 it turned to be 6.98. A similar pattern of growth may also be recorded for thirty-five years (1951 to 1983 and 1951 to 1986). This shows that enrollment rate of secondary school education in India has gone up with the passage of time to a noticeable extent.

Implications, Discussions and Concluding Remarks

It is, thus, obvious that the growth rates of female education at secondary school level has always been higher in India than that of the male counterpart. This implies that in the specific age groups of secondary school education more girls than boys had been and have been going to the secondary schools. Perhaps this is indicative of a strong aspiration and 'motivation' of the parents to send their daughters to the schools, as parents are the deciding factor and authority for the education of girls at this level in particular. However, still less value is attached to the female education in majority of rural part of India. The present trend of result is perhaps indicative of a good demand for female education in the country supported by a strong motive pattern in population. If it is so, the result may have a relevance for the pedagogues and educational administrators in particular in monitoring the system. It can equally be useful to the educational planners and policy makers.

In the practical realm too, in view of the above trend of findings reasons appear, therefore, to believe that careful planning and policy may fetch up more girls/females to the secondary schools. This may in turn be more meaningful for their (the female's) vocational as well as higher education in accordance with the persistent demand in society for the vocational, and female-education in particular.

However, since the secondary education throughout the world is more variable than elementary or higher education, India is not exception to it. The common issues of widespread poverty and a large illiterate population are in marked contrast to those which have highly developed educational systems. India is presently engaged in reformulating its educational policies with emphasis on its relevance particularly of secondary education to the present needs in terms of the issues of desired vocational education, skilled-manpower, or unemployments, or even making people at least literate. Therefore, it has stressed the need to vocationalize secondary education as the key-issue.

This may imply, therefore, that the country perhaps expects the expansion of occupational infrastructure with a new pattern of demands for skilled manpower at the professional, technical and production levels in the near future with a major role to the secondary school education in the production sector. These changes in outlook, therefore, are creating new expectations for secondary schools in both, developing as well as in developed countries—the world over.

So far, there has been an increasing mismatch between the products of secondary education and the economic, political and socio-cultural demands of the community in different countries of the world so in India. Therefore, in most countries the educational systems are being reviewed in an attempt to devise more appropriate objectives of education at secondary level in particular including the females, as this has got the role of preparing students to contribute to society in productive way. Need, thus, remains to address further the reasons of marked contrast with the countries of developed educational systems.

The rapid scientific and technological advances taking place all over the world have made imperative, therefore, that secondary education in the third world countries in particular should cater to the needs of society in the changing world order. It must also respond to the development that have been taking piace in other parts of the world. In such a scenario, environmental psychologists in India should address to some critical issues related to these, like: growing and the massive density of people in the Indian cities and villages at large, as well as bulk of uneducated people particularly women in rural India, the unequal access to resources, land distribution and housing, or opportunities and unemployment at large.

The educational policy and planning thus, can well be positioned at the cross roads of these, not only for the economic but also for social and overall socio-psychological growth of the weaker people in India. Therefore, the individuals today are needed to reassess their aspirations, self-esteem, confidence and attitudes for the new environmental pressures on them to react to.

REFERENCES

Bent, R.K. and Kronenberg, H. N. (1961). *Principles of Secondary Education*, New York : McGraw Hill.

Mukhopadhyay, M. (1981). *Barriers to Change in Secondary Education : Some Case Studies.* Howrah : Education Books UDANG.

Development of Education : 1984-1986 National Report of India. International Conference on Education.40th Session. Geneva. 1986. NCERT. Ministry of Human Resource Development. Government of India.

Report of the Education Commission (1964-66). Education and National Development, Ministry of Education. Government of India. 1966.

Urban poverty in Asia : A survey of critical issues (1994). New York : Oxford University Press.

23

Cognitive Functions of Socio-Culturally Deprived Children

Surendra Nath Dubey

Cognition is a general term covering various modes of knowing such as perceiving, remembering, imagining, conceiving, judging, reasoning and so on. Most of the persons are aware of the intellectual and physical growth of their children but have difficulties in describing the nature of these changes. It was Jean Piaget (1952) who after twenty years of intensive study of cognitive development of the children has described four stages of cognitive development. The Sensory-Motor (birth to 2 years), Preoperational (2 to 7 years), concrete-operational (7 to 12 years) and formal operational (above 12 years) stages. Piaget suggests that many functions, viz., intelligence, memory, visual-motor activities, concept-formation, reasoning, etc., are involved in cognitive development. In the present study intelligence, visual-motor functions and short-term memory (STM) have been studied.

Intelligence is an important cognitive function. It influences every aspect of human life and is being influenced by a number of physical and psycho-social variables. Therefore, the study of this cognitive function has been planned. The visual-motor functions and memory are the other important cognitive functions that influence many psychological functions and at the same time are influenced by physiological, psychological and social factors.

There has been a few studies that show the effect of rural-urban dwelling on cognitive functions of the child. Chatterjee and Paul (1984) have found that urban children were significantly more field independent and better in science achievement than rural children. Nirmala (1990) has reported that cognitive styles, field independence, reflectivity and analytical conceptual style are related to the abstract intelligence. Varma and Sheikh (1992) have investigated a positive relationship between the cognitive styles, achievement and creative thinking of the preuniversity boys and girls. The urban children were found to be more creative than the rural children (Singh,1988). Khan and Singh (1988) found that the rural children were significantly inferior in intelligence, dominance and tendermindedness as compared to the urban children. The rural children were found to be less in intelligence, visual-motor functioning, academic achievement and verbal reasoning as compared to the urban children (Dubey and Dwivedi, 1989; Singh and Dutt, 1988; and Usha Rani, 1990).

Beside the rural-urban dwelling of the subjects, deprivation seems to be another important attribute that influences many psychological functions of the children. Deprivation is primarily an economic concept. There are other factors that tend to form a cluster with the economic, but the nature and composition of these clusters vary from country to country. In our country the situation is compounded by the variable of 'caste'. In a subtle way caste puts the ceiling on educational and occupational achievement, especially in rural areas. Thus, when the child is assessed on a task in which the constrains of his caste act as disadvantages his performance may not reflect his innate potential. The Scheduled Caste persons have suffered the utmost socio-cultural deprivation in our country.

There has been a number of studies that reveal the effect of socio-cultural deprivation on many psychological functions. Agarwal and Misra (1983), Allwood (1983), Coady (1986), Das (1973), Das (1989), Das and Singh (1975), Misra and Shukla (1979), Mishra and Tripathi (1980), Pandey (1970), and Sinha (1977) have reported that Scheduled Caste children were poor in performance on cognitive functions, viz., intelligence, memory, and perceptual abilities as compared to the upper caste children.

The above review of researches suggests that there has been only a few studies in our country showing the effect of socio-cultural deprivation and rural-urban inhabitation separately and in interaction among children especially the rural ones on the psycho-motor functions and short-term memory. Therefore, it seems reasonably necessary to explore these variables.

Methodology

Sample

This study comprises of four groups, viz, SC-rural, SC-urban, upper caste-rural and upper caste-urban. In each group there were 50 children

matched on age, education, sex and income of the parents. The subjects, ranged from 8 to 12 years and they were the students of 3 to 5 standards. The average income of their parents was Rs. 2000 per month. In each group there were 30 boys and 20 girls. The sample of this study was selected from the rural and urban area of Faizabad District. The rural children were selected from the primary schools of villages situated around 20 km. away from the city. The urban subjects were selected from the convent schools of Faizabad city.

Tools

Pass-Along Test

To measure IQ of the children Alexander's pass-Along performance test was used. The test is free from the verbal material. Being interesting to the children and its culture-free nature has directed to prefer it over others available in the field. It is widely used reliable and valid test.

Short-term Memory

To assess the short-term memory of the subjects three lists of 3 to 9 digits numerals were used. In this test the subjects are required to reproduce the correct number immediately after the presentation of the numbers. The numerals were presented to the subjects audio way and the subjects were required to produce in the same mode.

Bender-Gestalt Test

The Bender-Gestalt Test was used to measure the perceptual and visual-motor functioning of the subjects. Bhargava and Sandhu (1987) have reported that the basic rationale of the test lies in the fact that the perception and reproduction of Gestalt figures are determined by biological principles of sensory-motor-action, growth pattern and maturity level of an individual's functional or organic pathological state, education, occupation and social deprivation. Since there is no any test available to assess the visual-motor functions as affected by the socio-cultural deprivation and rural-urban inhabitation of the subjests, the Bender-Gestalt Test is a natural selection. The test has been developed by Bender (1938). It is widely used in all cultures and at every age level. It has nine designs to be administered individually. It is a highly reliable and valid test.

Design

This is a field study comprising of two independent variables, viz., rural-urban inhabitation and socio-cultural deprivation (SC and non-SC) each taking two distinct values manipulated through selection. This satisfies the first criterion of a good design, viz. maximizing experimental variance. The control of extraneous variables, viz., age, sex, education and economic status was achieved through the selection of matched subjects in each group, thus, satisfying the second criterion of a good design, i.e., control of extraneous variance. The situation, sequence and subject relevant variables are minimized by matched selection of the subjects, using same sequence in administration of the test and by using the reliable and valid measures. This fulfils the criterion of minimizing error variance. The dependent measures in this study are IQ, STM and BGT. Since there are two independent variables each taking two forms, the design of this research can be presented under a 2X2 factorial type.

Results and Discussion

In Table 1 the mean and SD of four groups on two variables have been presented.

Table 1

Mean and SD of the Four Groups

Variables	*Scheduled*		*Caste*		*Upper*	*Caste*		
	Rural (N=50)		*Urban (N=50)*		*Rural (N=50)*		*Urban (N=50)*	
	M	*SD*	*M*	*SD*	*M*	*SD*	*M*	*SD*
IQ	70.18	6.84	77.90	6.92	76.73	10.60	93.27	10.02
STM	3.4	0.59	5.2	0.32	6.3	0.90	8.22	0.70
BGT	24.50	5.18	20.84	4.99	20.24	4.99	16.86	4.98

Intelligence

It is clear from the Table 1 that mean IQ scores of the non-SC urban children is highest (M=93.27), followed by SC urban (M=77.90), non-SC rural (M=76.73) and SC rural (M=70.18). To find out the significance of difference between the mean IQ scores of SC-non-SC and rural-urban children, two-way analysis of variance has been carried out.

Table 2

Summary of the Analysis of Variance for the IQ Scores

Source of Variance	*Sum of Squares*	*df*	*Mean squares*	*F-ratio*
Between Deprivation (D)	*7362.90*	*1*	*7362.90*	*128.31**
Between Inhabitation (I)	*6002.79*	*1*	*6002.79*	*104.61***
Interaction: DxI	*971.08*	*1*	*971.08*	*16.92***
Within Groups	*11247.03*	*196*	*57.38*	
Total	*25583.80*	*199*		

* $p<.05$
** $p<.01$

Table 2 shows significant effects of deprivation and inhabitation on IQ. Moreover their interactional effect also came to be significant.

Deutsch (1965), Tiwari (1983), Burg and Belmont (1990), Ogilvy (1990), Fiedler (1995) and Hacker (1995) have shown that sociocultural deprivation and many other variables affect the cognitive functions of the children. There are only a few studies that support our results of the effect of inhabitation on intelligence (Dubey and Dwivedi, 1989; Burg and Belmont, 1990).

Short-term Memory

The non-SC urban children have highest score (M=8.22) on STM followed by rural non-SC (M=6.3), urban SC (M=5.2) and rural SC (M=3.4). To see the significance of difference between the mean STM scores of the four groups, the data has been subjected to a two-way analysis of variance. The summary of ANOVA has been presented in Table 3.

Table 3

Summary of the Analysis of Variance for the STM Scores

Source of Variance	*Sum of Squares*	*df*	*Mean Squares*	*F-ratio*
Between Deprivation	156.65	1	156.65	447.5**
Between Inhabitation	465.13	1	465.13	1328.9**
Interaction : DxI	01.12	1	01.13	3.2**
Within Groups	70.06	196	0.35	
Total	692.96	199		

** p< .01

The results show that the socio-cultural deprivation has affected significantly the STM scores (F=447.5), the non-deprived scoring significantly higher. The rural children have significantly lower scores on STM (F=1328.9) as compared to the urban children. The effect of interaction of socio-cultural deprivation and inhabitation on STM is also significant. There are other studies that reveal the effect of socio-cultural deprivation on STM of the subjects (Templin, 1957; Thomas, 1971; Burg and Belmont, 1990).

Visual-Motor Functions

The higher score is an indicator of poor performance on BGT. The SC rural children have highest score (M=24.50) followed by SC urban (M=20.84), Non-SC rural (M=20.24) and non-SC urban subjects who have the lowest score (M=16.86). These scores are much higher than the normal scores (4.72 to 2.81) of the Indian adaptation of BGT. This suggests that the subjects of this study are intellectually more impaired. Their visual-motor perception, maturation and growth level are much less than worked out for this age group. To see the effect of socio-cultural deprivation and inhabitation on BGT scores the two-way analysis of variance has been carried out. The result of the analysis is given in Table 4.

Table 4

Summary of the Analysis of Variance for BGT Scores

Source of Variance	*Sum of Squares*	*df*	*Mean Squares*	*F-ratio*
Between Deprivation	852.85	1	852.85	32.20**
Between Inhabitation	623.05	1	623.05	23.52**
Interaction : DxI	01.12	1	01.12	0.04
Within Groups	5191.34	196	26.48	
Total	6668.36	199		

** p<.01

The results indicate significant effect of socio-cultural deprivation and inhabitation on BGT but the interaction thereof has not yielded significant effect. Out of all the four groups non-SC urban children have the best performance and the SC rural children are poorest in performance on BGT, whereas non-SC rural and SC urban are similar in their performance. It reveals that non-SC urban children are most mature in their visual-motor perception followed by the Non-SC rural and SC urban children. The rural SC children are found to be least mature among all the four groups. These results find support in the studies conducted by Tiwari (1983), Reissman (1962), Philip (1988), and Deutsch (1965).

The results may be interpreted in the light of socio-cultural environment of the eastern Uttar Pradesh. On the basis of the results supported by the findings of other researches it may be inferred that socio-cultural deprivation and rural-urban inhabitation affect the intellectual ability, STM and BGT scores. It may be because of the fact that the deprivation of rich diet and the absence of challenging environment needed for the development of the cognitive abilities of the children seem to hamper the development of cognitive functions of the SC and rural children in our country. On the contrary, the upper caste and the urban children have got the facilities of taking balance diet and opportunity to face a challenging environment right from the beginning, which in turn, facilitate their cognitive development.

The overall higher score on BGT by all the groups of this study may be attributed to the immaturity, non-seriousness, less intellectual ability, less interest in drawing and any possible emotional disturbances of the children of the eastern part of Uttar Pradesh. The poor performance (indicated by high scores) on BGT may be because of the fact that the socio-cultural environment of the people of this area does not facilitate the interest of the people in such a work that does not result into getting something concrete immediately after the task is complete. Moreover, children are also not interested in doing such a work that they feel useless as far as their emotional and educational satisfaction is concerned.

REFERENCES

Agarwal, S. and Mishra, R.C. (1983). Disadvantages of caste and schooling and development of category organization skill. *Psychologia,* 26, 54-61.

Allwood, C.M. (1983). The relation between culture and human cognition. *Nordisk Psykologi,* 35, 161-69

Bender, L. (1938). *A Visual-Motor Gestalt Test and Its Clinical Use.* New York: American Orthopsychiatric Association.

Bhargava, M. and Sandhu, R. (1987). *Guidelines for Bender Visual Motor Gestalt Test.* Lucknow: Annkur, Psychological Agency.

Burg, B. and Belmont, I. (1990), Mental abilities of children from different cultural backgrounds in Israel. *Journal of Cross-Cultural Psychology,* 21,90-108.

Chatterjee, R.G. and Paul, B. (1984). The study of field independence in relation to science achievement, rural-urban habitat and intelligence. *Indian Journal of Psychology,* 59. 1-13.

Coady, H. (1986). Effect of incentives on learning in middle and lower class children. *Journal of Psychology,* 120, 249-52.

Das, J.P. (1973). Cultural Deprivation and Cognitive Competence, In N.R. Ellis (Ed.), *International Review of Research in Mental Retardation.* Vol. 6, New York: Academic Press.

Das, J.P.(1989). Cognitive style of tribal and non-tribal children. *Psycholingua.* 19 (1) 9-16.

Das, J.P. and Singh, P.S. (1975). Caste, class and cognitive competence. *Indian Educational Review,* 10-18.

Deutsch, C.B. (1965). Education for disadvantaged group. *Review of Educational Research,* 35, 140-6.

Dubey, B.L. and Dwivedi, P. (1989) . A longitudinal study of intelligence of rural children. *Medical Education and Research,* 22, 51-56.

Fiedler, F.E. (1995). Cognitive resources and leadership performance. *Applied Psychology: An international Review,* 44,5-28.

Hacker, W. (1995). Cognitive resources and leadership performance: What about the task requirement? *Applied Psychology: An International Review,* 44,48-50.

Khan, R.H. and Singh, P.N. (1988). Impact of area residence on the development of the different traits of personality in children. *Journal of Psychological Researches,* 33,109-13.

Misra, G. and Shukla, A. (1979). Experiential Deprivation and Development of Serial Memory. *Psychologia,* 22-155-63

Misra, G. and Tripathi, L.B. (1980). *Psychological Consequences of Prolonged Deprivation* . Agra:National Psychological Corporation.

Nirmala, M.L. (1990). Cognitive styles and intelligence — A correlational study. *Journal of Psychological Researches,* 34, 173-76.

Ogilvy, C.M.(1990). Family type and children's cognition in two ethnic groups. *Journal of Cross-Cultural Psychology,* 21, 319-334.

Pandey, R.N. (1970). Differences in Mental Ability among Special Classes. Unpublished Doctoral Thesis, University of Gorakhpur.

Philip, G. (1988). Social class, social disadvantage and child health. *Children and Society,* 2. 9-19.

Piaget, J. (1952). *The Origins of Intelligence in Children.* New York: University Press.

Reissman, F. (1962). *The Culturally Deprived Child.* New York: Harper and Row.

Singh, B. (1988). A comparative study of mathematical creativity and selected personality characteristics of two socio-economic levels of junior high school children. *Journal of Psychological Researches,* 32, 163-7.

Singh, M.P. and Dutt, K. (1988). Effect of malnutrition on cognitive abilities of rural primary school children. *Journal of the Medico Psychological Research Society,* 14, 17-22.

Sinha, D. (1977). Social disadvantages and development of certain perceptual skills. *Indian Journal of Psychology,* 52, 115-32.

Templin, M.C. (1957). *Certain Language Skills in Children: Their Development and Interrelationships.* Minnesota : Minnesota University Press.

Thomas. E.C. (1971). Conceptual development in advantaged and disadvantaged kindergarten children. *Perceptual and Motor Skills,* 32, 711-17.

Tiwari, B.N. (1983). The effect of socio-cultural deprivation and age on perceptual illusion. *Perspectives in Psychological Researches,* 6. 38-41.

Usha Rani. N. (1990). Influence of malnutrition on intelligence and social maturity of rural and urban children. *Journal of Psychological Researches.* 34. 80-84.

Verma. B.P. and Sheikh. G.Q. (1992). Relationships among cognitive style. creative functioning and academic performance. *Journal of Psychological Researches.* 36. 78-84.

24

Modification of Verbal Behaviour in Children

Pradeep K. Khattri

Language and communication are central to human behaviour. Language is a peculiar revealing form of behaviour. It identifies a person more effectively than almost any other form, because it is the result of slow accretion over long period of time, language habits reveal lives past content, they serve as a symbol of home, family, class, state, status and country.

Hindu society is based on caste system and among these the Scheduled Caste people have been treated at the lowest level of social order. They suffer from the feeling of lack of parity with higher caste people with respect to social recognition. They think that social distance among the members of higher caste is very narrow whereas good deal of distance exists between Scheduled Caste and higher caste people. Despite being part and parcel of society they have not been able to claim, equality with other communities and have been not only hated, oppressed and looked down upon but also treated as untouchables and discriminated by the so-called higher ups in the social orders (Anant, 1970; Sinha and Sinha, 1960; Paranjepe, 1970; Singh, 1957). Due to socio-cultural deprivation and degraded social status Scheduled Caste's children have negative self-image and higher degree of frustration (Rath and Sircar, 1960). Frustration leads to aggression in these children. To get rid of aggressiveness and for reducing their tension they use abusive words or name calling. There is a tendency in them to express their hostility and for expressing it they often use the medium of abusive words that goes on increasing in their language. By the time they reach the school-going age, they have a full set of abusive slang at their command. They freely

Positively reinforced groups						
Scheduled Caste	11.05	6.12	4.39	4.14	4.05	3.64
Non-Scheduled Caste	10.64	4.89	4.39	3.05	2.73	2.55

use it among their friends, hence they are thought to be of low breeding and as they grow up people try to avoid them and keep away from them. In this way on account of the use of abusive language they are debarred from many kinds of psychological benefits, which society could otherwise confer upon them. So, aim at the reduction of this language would be fruitful in many ways as deficiency in language development is a serious handicap in social and intellectual

Table 2

Analysis of Variance Table for 2×2 Factorial Experiment with Six Replications.

Sour of variation	*Sum of squares*	*df*	*Mean squares*	*F*	*Sig. level*
Blocks (Trials)	2469.3090	5	493.8618	86.9000	.01
Treatments	119.7604	3	39.9201	7.0243	.01
Caste (Factor A)	23.9201	1	23.9201	4.2089	.05
Reinforcement (Factor B)	90.0035	1	90.0035	15.8370	.01
Interaction (A×B)	5.8368	1	5.8368	1.0270	Insig.
Error	1585.5938	279	5.6831		

N.B

Treatments :

1. Scheduled Caste with positive reinforcement
2. Scheduled Caste with negative reinforcement
3. Non-Scheduled Caste with positive reinforcement
4. Non-Scheduled Caste with negative reinforcement

Table 3

Means of the Four Treatment Combinations

Caste	*Positive reinforcement*	*Negative reinforcement*	*Overall means*
Scheduled Caste	5.5972	4.1944	4.8958
Non-Scheduled Caste	4.7361	3.9027	4.3194
Overall Means	5.1666	4.0486	

Discussion

In the present investigation the 120 trials series were divided into six blocks of twenty trials each. To determine abusive word usage in Scheduled Caste children t-test and ANOVA of the initial block (Table1) were performed. The resulting and t's and F's between positively reinforced Scheduled and non-Scheduled Caste children were t =.694, df =18, F =84, df =18 respectively and between negatively reinforced Scheduled and non-Scheduled Caste children. They were t =.602, df =18, F =.24, df= 18 respectively. They were found insignificant at .05 level. This indicates that all the subjects proceeded from the same starting-point and there was no difference in the readiness with which abusive words were used by Scheduled and non-Scheduled caste children of the present sample. Since the present sample of Scheduled and non-Scheduled Caste children was drawn from a larger sample of 150 socially disadvantaged children selected for an earlier study (Khattri and Gupta,1978), it could be that social disadvantage was a more dominant variable as far as abusive word usage was concerned rather than caste. To test this possibility, abusive word usage of 50 advantage children of 14-16 years of age was observed. The t-test and ANOVA between means scores of advantaged and disadvantaged children was performed to test for differences (mean of advantaged children 8.44, mean of disadvantaged children =10.69; t =12.87; df =98; F =23.6; df =98). Calculated values of t and F were found significant at .01 levels which indicate that abusive word usage was more frequent among the socially disadvantaged children. The reason for the same may be that the poor and uneducated parents talk less to their children, the nature of language used by parents from low socio-economic strata adversely affects the language development of children (Deutsch, 1965; Evan and William, 1972; Jensen, 1963; Judy and Rayan, 1976; Siller, 1957). From what is known about verbal communication in lower class homes it is generally seen that parents use abusive words in communication. Some authors claim that abuse stems from deep feelings of inadequacy or from parental inability to fulfil the roles expected of parenthood (Cohen, Rapling and Green, 1966; Silver, 1968; Fontana, 1964; Johnson and Morse, 1968; Komisaruk, 1966; Steel and Pallock, 1968). Some describe the parents as immature, self-centered and impulse ridden (Cochrance, 1965; Delancy, 1966; Jacobziner, 1964; Ten Bensal, 1963). Hence, abuse, like other behaviours becomes habitual in these children as they learn from the behaviour they witness.

Analysis of variance table for experiment, 2×2 factorial with six replications (Table 2) shows that the treatment combinations (F=7.0243) are significant at .01 level, which shows that the two types of caste and two levels of reinforcement independently interact with each other. Although the treatment combinations for the caste (Factor A) and for the reinforcement (Factor B) were found to be significant at .05 and .01 levels respectively (F=4.2089 and 15.837 respectively). It was observed from the means for caste factor (Table 3) that mean for Scheduled Caste (M=4.8958) is greater than the mean for non-Scheduled Caste (M=4.3194). This clearly shows that the non-Scheduled Caste subjects improved more than the Scheduled Caste subjects.

F-ratio for factor B, reinforcement (F=15.8370) was obtained significant at .01 level, which shows that the effect of levels of reinforcement, i.e., positive reinforcement and negative reinforcement were significantly different. Table 3 shows that the mean for positive reinforcement is 5.1666 and for negative reinforcement it is 4.0486, implying that positive reinforcement is better for both the castes as compared to positive reinforcement. From this table it is also clear that the non-Scheduled Caste subjects improved better (M for positive reinforcement = 4.736 and M for negative reinforcement =3.9027) than the scheduled caste subjects (M for positive reinforcement = 5.5972 and M for negative reinforcement = 4.1944) under both types of reinforcement. However, calculated value of interaction (F = 1.0270, Table 2) was found insignificant at .05 level which shows that caste and reinforcement do not interact to reduce abuse language of the subjects.

Conditioning blocks (F=86.9000) were also significant at .01 level (Table 2) which indicate that the means for different blocks are different and their pair-wise difference is significant. Further, Table 1 shows that the first conditioning block was most effective for both types of reinforcements in both the castes because there was a decrease of 9.10 in negatively reinforced Scheduled Caste, 9.15 in negatively reinforced non-Scheduled Caste and 7.41 in positively reinforced Scheduled Caste and 8.09 in positively reinforced non-Scheduled Caste. The successive blocks also added to improvement in conditioning but at a slower rate which is consistent with the results of other learning experiments. Comparison of the performance between the first and the last blocks for the negatively and positively reinforced groups for both the castes shows that the improvement is somewhat greater in the subjects of the negatively reinforced group (M=9.12) as compared to the subjects in the positively reinforced group (M=7.75).

Conclusion

1. No differences in abusive word usage were observed as a function of caste in the present study. Since all the subjects came from socially disadvantaged group, it appears that social disadvantage is a more dominant factor than caste.
2. Behaviour change can be affected through simple operant conditioning in Scheduled as well as non-Scheduled Caste children.
3. Socially disadvantaged Scheduled and non-Scheduled Caste children react to various types of reinforcement in similar ways. Negative reinforcement was always better for both castes as compared to positive reinforcement. This result clearly shows that the use of punishment for the use of abusive words makes the subject aware of the undesirability of the expressive behaviour and also the lack of social acceptance for the same.
4. The experiment has dealt with verbal behaviour. It seems reasonable to believe that implicit verbal behaviour or thinking and personality

might similarly be affected. Further studies would help answer the question as to whether personality variables themselves as manifested in overt behaviour and as measured by other devices than those involved in the conditioning routine can be altered by verbal reinforcement.

REFERENCES

Anant, Santokh, S. (1970). Caste Hindu attitudes towards Harijans: A study of inter-caste and urban rural differences. *Psychologia*. 13. 42-6.

Kanfer, F.H. (1968). Verbal conditioning : A review of its current status. In T.R. Dixon and D.L. Horton (Eds.). *Verbal Behaviour and General S-R Theory*. New Jersey : Prentice Hall.

Khattri, P.K., and Gupta, P. (1978). Reduction of abusive language in socially disadvantaged adolescents, *Psychological Studies*, 23, 56-60.

Krasner, L. (1958). Studies of the conditioning of verbal behaviour. *Psychological Bulletin*, 55, 148-70.

Paranjepe, A.C. (1970). *Prejudice and the Individual*. Bombay.

Rath, R. and Sircar, M.C. (1960). Inter caste relationship as reflected in the study of attitudes and opinion of six Hindu caste groups. *Journal of Social Psychology*, 51, 3.25.

Saranson, I.G. (1957). Interrelations among individual difference variables, behaviour in psychotherapy, and verbal conditioning. Paper presented at *West Psychological Association*.

Sinha, A.K.P., and Sinha, R.P.N. (1960). A study of prejudice among university students. *Indian Journal of Psychology*. 35, 159-66.

Singh, K.K. (1957). *Pattern of Caste Tension*. Bombay : Asia Publishing House.

Speilberger, C.D. (1962). Role of awareness in verbal conditioning. In C.W. Erikson (Ed.). *Behaviour and Awareness*. Durham: Duke University Press. 73-101.

Taffel, C. (1955). Anxiety and the conditioning of verbal behaviour. *Journal of Abnormal and Social Psychology*. 51, 496-501.

SECTION V

Aged and Others

25

Old Age: A Psycho-Social Perspective

N. Hasnain, Neeru Singh **and** *Sangeeta Sharma*

Aging refers a pattern of changes in the structure and functioning of body and the adjustment of person. Aging, the process of growing old regardless of chronological age, is a continuous process that begins at conception and eventually ends with death. Comfort (1960) described aging as an increased ability to die, or an increasing loss of vigour, with increasing chronological age or with the passage of the life cycle. Aging is a significant portion of life span resulting in difference between the younger and the older individuals in structure and functioning. Bocker (1959) described aging 'as those changes occurring in an individual as the result of passage of time'. These changes are anatomical, psychological, social and economic.

The Government of India has accepted 58 years as the age for retiring a person whereas in USA, UK and other western countries, it ranges from 60 to 65 years. However, a person's chronological age is by no means a perfect index of his physical and mental capacities but nonetheless they are closely associated. The outward and visible signs of aging appear earlier in some individuals than in others. The discrepancies have led research workers to think in terms of physiological age and functional age (Comfort 1969; Baulicre, 1976). It will, therefore, be a mistake to accept chronological age as anything more than a time marker.

Some researchers have tried to define the aged on the basis of chronological age while others distinguish and separate age groups on the basis of social, psychological or physiological characteristics. In sociological sense 'aged' is defined as a person as old when he is unable to carry out some important social functions. Myers (1985) has elaborated the aging of population in the following ways :

(a) Aging may be viewed as a biological process through which an organism is modified from birth to death. In other words, the psychological and social development process of individual including transitions in social position, roles, status and characteristics of persons can be examined.

(b) An extension of this approach focuses on aging of family, a social grouping that is modified over the life cause of its members in characteristics ways.

(c) On a more aggregate level, there is a sense in which aging can be viewed as a critical index of societal or civilizational maturity. The explanation of the concept of aged varies from culture to culture and country to country. It is the age that determines usefulness of a person in society. Aging brings various changes on different physiological as well as psychological characteristics of an individual. Generally, signs of aging tend to become noticeable after the age of forty. Aging is characterized by a general reduction in functional capacities and structural changes in the body. For instance, gradual increase in body weight, degeneration of the elastic tissues of the skin resulting in wrinkling, deterioration in the hearing ability and vision, decline in muscle power, blader control, deterioration of the muscle of the shoulders, loss of elasticity in the lungs resulting in breathing problems, reduced efficiency of heart and circulation of blood, hormone imbalance, deterioration in some areas of the brain affecting learning and memory, etc.

The apparent effects of physical and functional decline due to aging seems to be related in the psychological functioning and mental health of the elderly. The interpretation of aging based on the Adlerian (1870-1937) psychological perspective can be stated as physical decline, loss of status, beauty and other abilities that result in feelings of inferiority and loss of self-esteem in later life which probably make elderly not only more vulnerable and receptive to socially induced attitude of being incompetent but also bring about changes in attitudes, life-styles, coping strategies, personality and mental health of the elderly. Aging is experienced as an inevitable and life-long process. It can, thus, be viewed on a continuum with conception at one end and death at the other. Aging is often defined biologically as well as chronologically, socially and psycologically (Neugaren and Datan, 1973).

Biological and Physiological Aspects

The process of life consists of physical and mental changes characterized by growth and subsequent decline. Aging generally comprises of those changes that take place during the later part of life, when physical and mental capacities decline become more apparent to concerned individual and to society.

During the early years of old age, decline in both physical and mental capacities is generally slow and the individual compensates the loss by past knowledge and reserves. This period of old age is known as 'senescence'. When more or less completed physical breakdown takes place and mental disorganization is seen, this period is known as 'senility'. At this stage the individual is no longer able to do anything from the reserves to meet present needs and thus exposes himself to social and psychological limitations affecting his personal and social adjustment.

Psychological Aspects

Psychological aging consists of general decline in the mental abilities that accompany old age. The psychological changes in respect of individual's concept of the self, the ideas about one's worth as an individual and as member of social groups, feeling about the attitude and behaviour of others towards him and his general view of life and the world including his own place there in, plays significant role in the process of 'psychological aging'. An unfavourable and negative attitude towards the changed physical and social conditions proves not only a hurdle in better adjustment during old age but brings psychological aging even more rapidly.

Social Aspects

Social aging refers to the person's role and habits expected by society for particular ages. A woman who becomes grandmother at the age of 40 years is considered older in social terms than a woman who has just one child at the same age.

Functional Aspects

Functional age refers to a person's ability to work and discharge duties in society and probably reflects biological, psychological and social age. A 85 year old man who lives alone, drives a car is considered much younger in terms of functional age.

The proportion of older adults in society has grown due to improved medical health services, better quality of life, etc. Interest in adult development and aging has increased steadily. Today there are many centres for the study of aging at a number of universities and researches are being carried out in many countries.

The term 'aged', 'older' and 'elderly' are often used synonymously. Different countries adopt different age-specific definitions, often, they go with retirement age. In Japan and Australia, it is between 60 and 65 years. In India the age of retirement for Government employees is 58 years and in semi-governmental institutions it is 60 years. Therefore, in India the term 'aged' could refer to those individuals who are 60+years of age for re-employment after superannuation for a period of five years is given only to a chosen few. Old age is the product of the interaction of multiple influences as are all earlier stages. In India, the attainment of 55 years of age has been mostly accepted for the purpose of classifying aged persons.

Problems of the Aged

Old age presents its special and unique problems but these have been aggravated due to unprecedented speed of socio-economic transformation in the country leading to a number of changes in different aspects of life and living of people. According to Nag (1987) "due to socio-economic changes in the wake of urbanization and increase in the proportion of the aged in the population, the problem of aged has become formidable. With the impact of industrialization in society, the traditional means of earning a livelihood and mutual-aid institutions are rapidly dying out. The ultimate responsibility for supporting the aged is gradually shifting from family to the state".

Gerontology, the scientific study of aging primarily concerned with time between maturity and death divides the problem of gerontology into four major categories:

1. The social and economic problems caused by an increasing number of elderly people in the population.
2. The psychological aspects of aging alone with their reaction to one another.
3. The physiological basis of aging alone with pathological deviations and disease processes.
4. The general biological aspects of aging in all animal species.

The needs of the elderly in India are many and complex. They range from problems of practical and financial nature to the problems of housing, health, isolation and loneliness and lack of services. The far-reaching and rapid changes of modern society have profoundly affected the position of the old people and their ability to deal with their own problems.

The problem of the elderly vary from urban to rural settings. The life of the aged in rural area is a tranquil and simple one. They continue to the extent of their ability to undertake work and their recreational demands are small. They have different sorts of relationship with their families and are better adjusted to the community.

Aging is not a new phenomenon but the problems that occur with aging appear to be a product of the modern age. In the context of dynamic changes taking place in the Indian society, the problems of the aged have assumed grave importance. Since time immemorial most of the traditional families in India have strong belief that since it is the duty of the parents to look after their children, it is equally important for the children to look after their dependent parents. Due to improved health facilities, there is an increase in the longevity of people from 30-40 years some decades ago to 50-60 years now. It is worthwhile here to note the opinion of the World Assembly on the aging held at Vienna in July 1982. This assembly marked a milestone in the world wide concern on the sorry predicament the aged with the steady decline in the incidence of morality and morbidity in most of the developed countries, and the strives made by the family planning drive, in both the developed and developing countries. It is compounded by an increase in the population of the elderly in both the developed and developing societies with higher expectancy of life, leading to a steady rise in the number of aged.

The increasing number of the aged in society is likely to be accompanied by various problems connected with the welfare of the dependent group of population.

The impact of retirement is tremendous as it results in loss of role, status, power, opportunities for interaction and as Miller (1965) states 'loss of an occupational identity', with the result that the individual withdraws from society and has little social interaction. Therefore, retirement, the point demarcating middle age from old age, can lead to low morale, decreased levels of satisfaction, depression, feelings of loneliness and hopelessness.

Social and Economic Problems

The problem of aged is also socio-economic one. According to Philibert (1969) modern gerontology defines a problem as social when difficulties met by a group of people result from:

1. The functioning, organization or structure of society
2. May endanger society at large and
3. Can and should be solved through social policies and political initiative.

In the pre-industrial society, the old people used to get enough opportunities to satisfy their multiple needs. In the societies dominated by agricultural and handicraft economy they participated in productive activities as specialists, directly or indirectly, depending on their physical health and remained financially independent.

However, the present societies do not provide opportunities to its aged members to lead a comfortable, respectful and socially useful life. Modernization and industrialization of societies in effect reduces the role and status of old people (Kooy, 1963). The younger generation replaces the aged people in their positions as productive members leaving senior citizens in a weakened and functionless situation (Simmons, 1959).

Owing to the changing Indian social structure, the old people have been dislodged from the leadership positions in the family, caste group and community (Bhatia, 1964; D'Souza, 1971; Singh, 1969). With the growth of new economic, political and value systems, the integrity and compactness of the joint family and caste group have been weakened and for the leadership in the community, achieved properties like wealth or education have become more important than the ascribed properties like age and seniority in modern society. This is confirmed by the fact that whenever older persons are in the position of leadership, it is mainly due to their education and wealth rather than age (Singh, 1962). Thus aging is not only biological in nature but also a cultural process. Physical, social and emotional changes at this age require readjustment in interpersonal relations in different situations with the members of the family and society (Chowdhry, 1981).

Psychological Problems

The psychological aspects of aging involve a wide variety of problems. The effect of aging on certain needs and motives, the effect of the prior experience in the aging process, the psychodynamics of the emotional life of the elderly, the effect of age upon learning and psychomotor performance, and the role and importance of sensory changes in aging are particularly important. Psychopathology and problem of the adjustment set by the culture are important psychological aspects of aging. Changing adjustment may in turn be a casual condition determined by a variety of personality and other changes with age and also encompasses the psychological aspect of aging process. The emotional needs of the elderly have been studied intensively by a variety of experts in different disciplines, but physiological and medical researches are integral part of these changes. Lemkar (1955) has clarified that old age gradually reduces sharpness of memory and subjects the aged to varied kinds of mental illness.

Old people may be required to make an adjustment with their family members who may increasingly resent their presence. Old people may have to adjust to a life devoid of much activity. This problem is more crucial for the persons who are required to retire from their active life.

The emergence of new forces affecting the roles and status of the older people have become a source of utter frustration and thereby maladjustment for an ever larger group of socially problematic older people in the present Indian society. It is because, as Kuhlen (1957) has said, the adjustment of aging persons depends upon the degree to which these personal and environmental circumstances offer opportunities or pose threats to the satisfaction of these needs. The present technological society creates such an environment for the aged people which compared to that of the primitive society provides less opportunities of need satisfaction and therefore, is less conducive to proper adjustment in old age. Lumpkin (1985) in a study observed that as subjects grow old their health is declined and they become more external in their locus of control.

In India with rapid industrialization and urbanization, the problems of the aged has emerged as a great social problem. The present industrial society, by decreasing the roles and status of the aged people, has started creating an environment for the old which is less conducive to their good adjustment compared to that of the pre-industrial society. Therefore, in India also the number of maladjusted people is increasing gradually. In the course of time the aged face many problems of varied nature. Depression, frustration, hopelessness and loneliness are some common complaints of aged people which arise due to various biological, psychological and social factors.

In the western countries, the institution of family, in particular, has shown changes in its shape and scope. First, it has shifted from extended to nuclear and then from nuclear to companionate family. This change in structure of family has not been conducive to provide shelter to the aged and satisfy their psychological, social and financial needs. However, in India, specially in villages, joint family system still prevails in one form or the other. Whereas in urban areas nuclear family system has come into existence. The problems of aged are not yet as prominent as in economically developed societies. But breakdown of traditional beliefs, attitudes and practices in India would encourage problems among aged and is a matter of great concern.

REFERENCES

Bhatia. R.S. (1964). Rural Social Change and the Problem of the Aged. *Social Welfare. II.*

Chowdhry, P.D. (1981). *A Handbook of Social Welfare*. Delhi : Atma Ram and Sons.

Comfort, Alexander (1976). Age Prejudice in America. *Social Policy*. 73. 3-8.

D'Souza, V.S. (1971). Changes in Social Structure and Changing Roles of Older People in India. *Sociology and Social Research.* 55, 297-304.

Kooy, Gerrit A. (1963). *Social System and the Problems of Aging.*

Kuhlen, Raymong G. (1959). Aging and life adjustment. In James E. Biresen (Ed). Handbook of *Aging and Individual.* Chicago : The University of Chicago Press.

Lumpkin, James R. (1984). The Effects of Retirement Versus Age on the Shopping Orientations of the Older Consumer. *Gerentologist,* 24, 622-627.

Neugarton, B.L. (1982). *Age of Need and Public Policies for Old People.* New Delhi: Sage Publications.

Philibert, N. (1969). Historical and Theoretical Perspective on Current Development in Social Gerentology. *Proceedings of the 8th International Congress of Gerentology,* Washington: International Association of Gerentology.

Singh, Jagjit (1962). *Problems of the Old Man in Burail.* An Unpublished Masters Thesis. Chandigarh : Punjab University.

Singh, N. (1994). A Comparative Study of Retired and Pre-Retired Persons on Certain Personality and Demographic Variables. An Unpublished Ph.D. Thesis. New Delhi : Jamia Millia Islamia.

Singh, R.R. (1969). The Changing Social Structure and the Aged. *Indian Journal of Gerentology.* Oct. 118-124.

Stieglitzs, Edward J. (1951). The Personal Challenge; Biological Changes and Maintenance of Health. In C. Tibbils (Ed.) *Living Through the Older Years.* Michigan : University of Michigan Press.

26

Insecurity and Alienation among Widows and Widowers of Old Age

Mohammad Ghufran and *N. Hasnain*

It is a well-established fact that an individual's physical and mental abilities decline in old age. Due to declining abilities, aged people often face different social and psychological problems. Among the various social and psychological problems, adjustment in old age is studied extensively by different investigators. Mishra (1989) in his study of problems and social adjustment in old age observed that those old people are better adjusted who are leading a life resembling the life of aged people in pre-industrialist society in terms of having financial and physical security, satisfactory family relationships, social interaction and association with various groups of people, involvement in useful creative activities. Anantharaman (1979) found adjustment to be positively related to education, occupation, income and social class but negatively related with age. In their study of adjustment in old age Deoras and Janabandhu (1979) observed that most of the subjects expressed necessity of pension, regular fund, family and proximity of friends. They found in 38 per cent of their sample, religiosity increased, 64 per cent developed anxiety and were feeling insecure, 58 per cent of the subjects were fully prepared for death but 14 per cent were afraid of it.

Psychologically, old age in which people usually retire from their work may be called the transition between generativeness versus stagnation and integrity versus despair. Thus, the evaluation of one's contribution in the occupation and in the family gains importance as a crucial issue in old age. The sense of satisfaction, the sense of having produced something useful and the sense of accomplishment in the occupation as well as in the family are, therefore, sources of a sense of integrity and security during the stage of life conversely, a sense of stagnation and frustration may increase the feeling of insecurity producing in them alienation. But of course, the possibility of generativeness does not end at the old age, nor is the issue of integrity versus despair suddenly important only in the old age. Instead these two stages of the lifecycle overlap; only the relative emphasis on generativeness or integrity distinguishes one stage from another. As other events occur during this period the importance of integrity versus despair increases. These events include the growing awareness of death as something personally relevant; some friends may have died, one's spouse may be ill or deceased, or one's health may be failing. There may be extended periods of mourning over the loss of a friend or spouse, reawakening old memories that lead to a re-evaluation of one's life. In addition there may be a reduction in the variety of meaningful personal interaction after one no longer sees one's friend at work; the sphere of physical life space may be shrinking; there may be change in residence and one may need to establish new social relationships and adjust to unfamiliar surrounding. Each of these is likely to increase the sense of alienation and feeling of insecurity.

The institution of marriage provides not only the satisfaction of biological needs but it is also very important from psychological point of view, particularly from the viewpoint of emotional support. The emotional support which one's spouse provides becomes all the more important during the old age when people become more isolated. It is the wife who consoles the husband in his difficulties and worries. In the same way, the husband provides emotional support to the wife in despair. But when one of the spouses is no longer available due to death, this important source of getting support is no longer available. In such a situation the individual may feel more insecure and may feel alienated.

Feeling of insecurity is an important motivational variable supposed to exercise immense influence on human behaviour and personality in old age. According to Maslow (1953), human desires are arranged in ascending hierarchy of needs. As soon as one need is satisfied the next need in the hierarchy is activated. There are safety or security needs, belongingness and love needs, self-esteem needs, and lastly self-actualization needs or need for personal fulfilment. The primary motivating force of the security need is to ensure a reasonable degree of certainty, order, structure and predictability in one's environment. Barel (1964) conceptualizes insecurity as an inherent striving for reducing environmental situations to cause and effect relationships thus enabling the individual to predict and control his environment. Security is the opposite of insecurity. For Maslow (1954) insecurity refers to a feeling of rejection, of being unloved, isolated, a constant feeling of anxiety, tension and danger.

Alienation seems to be another important variable which affects the behaviour of old age people. Alienation is a psychological state within an individual in which he feels 'no sense of belonging' to his community, group or nation. The alienated person, as described by Fromm (1963) does not experience himself as the centre of his world, as the creator of his own acts but acts and their consequences become his masters whom he obeys, or whom he even worships. Seeman (1959) has synthesized the concept of alienation embodied in the domain of philosophy, sociology and psychology considered that the broad concept of alienation might be conceptualized in five-fold dimensions of powerlessness, meaninglessness, normlessness, isolation and self-estrangement. Later Seeman (1972) revised the categories of alienation in six: (1) powerlessness—the sense of low control versus mastery over events, (2) meaninglessness—the sense of incomprehensibility versus understandings of personal and social affairs, (3) normlessness—high expectancies for (or commitment to) socially unapproved means, (4) cultural estrangement called value isolation—the individual's rejection of commonly held values in the society versus commitments, (5) self-estrangement—the individual's engagement in activities that are not intrinsically rewarding, and (6) social isolation—the sense of exclusion or rejection versus social acceptance (Seeman 1975).

Alienation has been treated as personality variable by many investigators. Erikson (1964) viewed alienation as a natural consequence of identity confusion. Moreover, alienation has sometimes been regarded as a situation relevant variable (Dean, 1961; Gradizons, 1956). Nettler (1957) opines that alienation has an unfortunate psychopathological cannotation and some bearing on emotional sickness, Maslow (1954) observes that even in healthy personality there must be some degree of alienation.

From the above discussion the importance of studying the feeling of insecurity and alienation among widows and widowers of old age becomes self-explanatory. On the basis of the above assertions it is reasonable to hypothesize that widows and widowers of old age will feel more insecure and alienated in comparison to those people of their age with their spouse.

Method

Sample

The total sample of the present study consisted of 97 subjects with age ranging from 60 to 72 years. Among them 57 were widows and widowers, while 60 subjects were such old age people who have their spouses alive. The sample was further divided on the basis of sex. Among 57 subjects there were 27 widows and 30 widowers. Among 60 subjects whose spouses are alive, 30 were females and 30 males.

Tests

1. Short form of Maslow's Security-Insecurity Inventory developed by Srivastava (1976) was used to measure the feeling of insecurity.
2. Hindi version of Dean's Alienation scale prepared by Singh and Sinha (1991) was used to measure the alienation of the subjects.

Procedure

The subjects included in the sample were contacted individually and administered short form of Maslow's security Insecurity Inventory and Hindi version of Dean's Alienation Scale in order to obtain numerical values of their feeling of insecurity and alienation.

Results

The mean scores on the feeling of security-insecurity and alienation scale obtained by four groups of subjects were compared and t-values for various comparison groups were calculated in order to find out the significance of differences between their means.

Table 1

Means, S.Ds. and t-values for Insecurity Feeling

	Groups	*N*	*M*	*SD*	*t*
1.	Subjects with alive spouse	60	13.26	5.63	
					2.35*
2.	Subject with spouse dead	57	15.53	4.82	
3.	Widows	27	14.15	4.06	
					2.42*
4.	Widowers	30	16.84	4.32	

**Significant at .05 level.*

The above table shows that the mean insecurity score of old aged subjects having their spouse alive was 13.26 and the mean score of insecurity feeling of subjects whose spouse was dead was 15.53. The difference between the two means was significant.

In the same way the mean insecurity score of widows was 14.15 and that of widowers was 16.84. The difference between the two means was also significant at 0.05 level indicating that the widows and widowers differ significantly in their feeling of insecurity.

Table 2

Means, S.Ds. and t-values for Alienation

Groups	*N*	*M*	*SD*	*t*
1. Subjects with spouse alive	60	58.02	9.90	
				1.17
2. Subjects with spouse dead	57	60.19	10.26	
3. Widows	27	58.19	10.52	
				1.99*
4. Widowers	30	63.90	11.15	

**Significant at .05 level.*

It is evident from the table that the mean alienation score of subjects having their spouses alive was 58.02 and the mean alienation score of subjects whose spouse was not alive was 60.19. The difference between the two means was not significant. On the other hand, the mean alienation score of widows was 58.19 and that of widowers was 63.90. The difference between the two means was statistically significant.

Discussion

The above results reveal that the t-value for difference in insecurity feeling between old age subjects having their spouse alive and old age subjects having their spouse dead was significant at .05 level of confidence. The greater mean of insecurity feeling of subjects having their spouse dead indicates that during the old age if one of the spouses is no more available, people become more prone to develop a feeling of insecurity. On the other hand, if both wife and husband are alive in old age, they do not develop a feeling of insecurity to such an extent, because they provide emotional support to each other. The miseries and sorrows are shared by both, thus providing less chances to develop a feeling of insecurity.

The value of t for the difference in insecurity feeling of widows and widowers was also statistically significant at .05 level of confidence. The mean insecurity score of widowers was higher than the mean insecurity score of widows. This higher mean insecurity score of old age male subjects who have not married again after their wives' death indicates that such people need consolation and emotional support more than women who have not married again after their husband's death. It is generally observed that in our family set up aged women usually gain more sympathy and support from their sons, daughters, grand children and other relations than old men. Moreover, women seem to have greater tolerance than men. So the chances of developing the feeling of insecurity become less in aged women.

The results presented in Table 2 indicate that the t-value for difference in mean alienation scores of old age subjects having their spouse alive and the subjects having their spouses dead was statistically not significant at 0.05 level of confidence. It means that both groups of old age subjects sense the same degree of alienation spouse's (powerlessness, meaninglessness, self-estrangement, normlessness and isolation). But the t-value obtained for the difference of mean alienation scores of widows and widowers differed significantly at .05 level of confidence. The mean alienation score of widowers was higher than the mean alienation score of widows. This finding suggests that the old age male subjects who are alone after their spouse's death sensed more isolation. In the Indian family set-up, the male members of the family are usually found to be in a dominating position. They exercise more power in comparison to female members of the family. But in his old age when a man remains no longer an earning member of the family he perhaps feels that his power of authority ceases. In such a situation the wife of an old age person is the only member of the family who not only obeys his authority, but also consoles him in despair. Therefore, the widowers become more alienated after the death of their spouse than widows.

REFERENCES

Ananthraman, R.N. (1979). Adjustment and its correlates in old age. *Indian Journal of Clinical Psychology*, 6, 165-68.

Barel, J.C. (1964). Security as a motivation of human behaviour. *Archives of General Psychology*, 10, 105-8.

Dean, D.J. (1961). Alienation : Its meaning and measurement. *American Sociological Review*, 26, 753-8.

Deoras, U. and Janabandhu, D.S. (1979). Adjustment in old age. An introductory survey. *Indian Journal of Applied Psychology*, 16, 44-7.

Erikson, E.H. (1964). *Insight and Responsibility* : New York; Norton.

Fromm, E. (1963). *The Sane Society*, New York : Holt.

Gradizons, M. (1956). *The Loyal and Disloyal*. Chicago : Chicago University Press.

Maslow, A.H. (1943). A theory of human motivation. *Psychological Review*, 50, 370-96.

Maslow, A.H. (1954). *Motivation and Personality*. New York; Harper.

Mishra, S. (1989). *Problem and Social Adjustment in Old Age*. New Delhi : Gian Publishing House.

Nettler, Co. (1957). A measure of alienation. *American Sociological Review*, 22, 670-77.

Seeman, M. (1959). On the meaning of alienation. *American Sociological Review*, 24, 783-91.

Seeman, M. (1972). The signal of 68 : Alienation in precrises France. *American Sociological Review,* 37, 385-405.

Seeman, M. (1975). Alienation studies. In Inkles, J. Coleman and N. Smelsor (Eds.), *Annual Review of Sociology* (Vol.1) Palo-Alto : California Annual Review Inc.

Singh, A.P. (1992). *Alienation in relation to ethnicity, sex and socio-economic status.* Unpublished Ph.D. Thesis. Muzaffarpur : Bihar University.

Srivastava, G.P. (1976). A short form of Maslow security-insecurity Inventory. *Manas,* 23, 115-20.

27

Locus of Control among Retired and Pre-Retired People of High and Low Socio-Economic Status

Neeru Singh and *M.G. Husain*

Aging is natural and universal. It is a multi dimentional phenomenon with an intraction of biological, social and psychological variables. It is difficult to define old age but it may not be difficult to focus those elements which contribute the pathology that may emerge in later life. Decker (1985) defines aging as "those changes occuring in an individual, as a result of the passage of time".

The process of aging leads, inevitably to three major consequences : (a) the loss of physical and mental capacities. (b) gradual withdrawal or abrupt retirement from gainful activities and (c) socio-psychological disturbances. There are at least three other factors which have given three different social problems. They are: (i) the initiating factors, like an increase in life expectancy and subsequent increase in the population of the aged, (ii) the contributory factors, like technological developments and formal rules of retirement, and (iii) the precipitatory factors like change in family.

The age structure of India's population shows unmistakably a trend towards aging. The estimated population over the age of sixty in India in 1991 was 55 million representing 6.54 per cent of the total population.

Old age presents its special unique problems but these have been aggravated due to unprecedented speed of socio-economic transformation in the country leading to a number of changes in different aspects of life and living of people. As a result, some previously unimportant problems of aging—health, income, and leisure—become obvious and the minor ones are aggravated.

The condition in India are some what different. In villages, joint family system still prevails in one form or the other. It does not allow the aged to live a lonely life or at the mercy of non-familial institutions and services. It is, therefore, conceivable that the aged in rural areas may not constitute the social problems of the aged. In urban areas, however, family is said to be changing. The aged do not seem to enjoy a status in the present urban families, as much as they enjoyed in the past.

The bickerings and quibbles among the family members apart, the aged in urban families are left with no role to play and no authority over the men in the family. They seem to live in the family but without family life as such. Although the family in India is accommodating the aged, the aged are less likely to have a smooth sailing in the urban families in India.

Retirement is an important status passage in every society. Retirement from work has without doubt psychological impact on the individual and probably escalades the process of aging. Reduced health, income and a sudden break with a particular kind of professional life result in various types of socio-psychological problems for the individual. Moreover, retirement is viewed as a period of crisis and adjustment, whereas multiplicity of problems confront the individual at the time of retirement.

Sample

The total sample size was 200. Of the total 200 sample 100 pre-retired and 100 retired aged. Half of the subjects in each group belonged to high and middle economic status from both aged groups. The sample were selected from different localities of Delhi/New Delhi representing two different groups and socio-economic classes.

Tool Used

The purpose of the study was to investigate the extent of locus of control among pre-retired and retired elderly from Delhi belonging to two different socio-economic classes. The Indian adaptation of locus of control scale of Rotter (1966) was used in this study. This scale assesses locus of control (Internal, External and powerful others) of the subjects.

The obtained data were analyzed with the help of t-test.

Results and Discussion

Table 1

The Significance of Difference between the Means of two groups from two Socio-Economic Status on the Internal Locus of Control.

	Comparisons	*N*	*M*	*SD*	*t*	*P*
I.	Pre-Retired (HES)	50	11.40	5.470	1.17	NS
	Pre-Retired (MES)	50	12.70	5.640		
II.	Pre-Retired (HES)	50	11.40	5.470	1.74	NS
	Retired (HES)	50	9.56	5.096		
III.	Pre-Retired (HES)	50	11.40	5.470	2.97	.01
	Retired (MES)	50	8.22	5.227		
IV.	Pre-Retired (MES)	50	12.70	5.640	2.92	.01
	Retired (HES)	50	9.56	5.096		
V.	Pre-Retired (HES)	50	12.70	5.640	4.12	.01
	Retired (MES)	50	8.22	5.227		
VI.	Retired (HES)	50	9.56	5.096	1.30	NS
	Retired (MES)	50	8.22	5.227		

In Table 1 comparisons among I, II and VI show that these groups did not differ significantly from one another on the level of their internal locus of control. Comparisons III, IV and V show that pre-retired group from high economic status and middle economic status were highly internally controlled than the retired group from two different socio-economic status. The obtained t-ratios between these groups were highly significant.

Table 2

The Significance of Difference between the Means of two Groups from Two Status on the External Locus of Control.

	Comparisons	*N*	*M*	*SD*	*t*	*P*
I.	Pre-Retired (HES)	50	8.76	4.322	.64	NS
	Pre-Retired (MES)	50	8.16	5.088		
II.	Pre-Retired (HES)	50	8.76	4.322	1.70	NS
	Retired (HES)	50	10.50	5.786		

III.	Pre-Retired (HES)	50	8.76	4.322	2.08	.05
	Retired (MES)	50	11.36	7.732		
IV.	Pre-Retired (MES)	50	8.16	5.088	2.15	.05
	Retired (HES)	50	10.50	5.786		
V.	Pre-Retired (MES)	50	8.16	5.088	2.44	.05
	Retired (MES)	50	11.36	7.732		
VI.	Retired (HES)	50	10.50	5.786	.63	NS
	Retired (MES)	50	11.36	7.732		

In Table 2 comparisons among I, II and VI show that they did not differ significantly from one among other on the level of their external locus of control. But the comparisons among III, IV and V show significance of difference from one other on their external control scores. Retired aged from two different socio-economic status showed that they were highly externally controlled than pre-retired aged from different socio-economic status. The t-ratio of these comparisons among III, IV and V were significant at .05 level.

Table 3

The Significance of Difference between the Means of Two Different Groups from Two Different Status on the Powerful Others Locus of Control.

	Comparisons	*N*	*M*	*SD*	*t*	*P*
I.	Pre-Retired (HES)	50	6.60	4.454	.20	NS
	Pre-Retired (MES)	50	6.76	3.267		
II.	Pre-Retired (HES)	50	6.60	4.454	1.20	NS
	Retired (HES)	50	7.80	5.485		
III.	Pre-Retired (HES)	50	6.60	4.454	1.17	NS
	Retired (MES)	50	7.86	6.188		
IV.	Pre-Retired (MES)	50	6.76	3.267	1.15	NS
	Retired (HES)	50	7.80	5.485		
V.	Pre-Retired (MES)	50	6.76	3.267	1.11	NS
	Retired (MES)	50	7.86	6.188		

VI.	Retired (HES)	50	7.80	5.485		
					.05	NS
	Retired (MES)	50	7.86	6.188		

Table 3 shows that there was no significant difference between the means of two different groups, i.e., pre-retired and retired from two different socio-economic status (HES and MES) on the level of powerful others (locus of control).

The result shows that the retired group is more externally controlled than pre-retired group. The study by Lumpkin (1985) support the obtained results. Lumpkin (1985), in a study on 601 subjects (Mean age 72.5 years), observed that as subjects grow aged their health declined and they become more external in their locus of control. Even after partialing out the effect of age and health subjects with less activity were more external in their locus of control. The present findings are in line with this study.

Lumpkin *et al.* (1986) had related the problems of adjustment in old age with the external locus of control. They conducted a study on 3.009 subjects in the age group of 23-38 years using Rotter's Internal-External Locus of Control Scale. It was found that the elderly people were on the high side of external locus of control than the younger subjects. The present findings fully support their results.

The pre-retired group was found more internally controlled in their mean scores than retired group. There was no impact of socio-economic status on locus of control of aged group. Recent researches indicate that impact of socio-economic status have not been found in both the groups. However, there is not any significant effect of the powerful others control of two different groups from two different socio-economic status.

REFERENCES

Lumpkin, James and Baylor, R. Hankamer U. (1985). *School of Business · The relationship between locus of control.*

Lumpkin, James, R. (1986) *School of Business : A problem of adjustment in old age with the external locus of control.*

Rotter, J.B. (1966). *Internal versus External Locus of Control.*

28

Prejudice and Stereotyping of Weaker Sections: The Ghost in TV

N. Hasnain* and *Talmeez Fatima

Persons prejudiced against members of a certain group evaluate them negatively solely on the basis of their identification with that group. So they dislike persons of a group and evaluate them negatively which is independent of their unique characteristics or behaviours. Baron and Byrne (1977) while reviewing the literature on prejudice have pointed out that the term prejudice has come to have at least three meanings in everyday use : (1) a judgement or opinion formed beforehand without thoughtful examination of the pertinent facts, issues or argument, especially unfavourable irrational opinion, (2) the act or state of holding preconceived opinions, and (3) hatred or dislike for particular group, race, religion, etc.

However, Baron and Byrne have suggested that for the purposes of research, psychologists generally have consensus on it's definition, and prejudice refers to an usually negative attitude towards members of a specific group (racial, ethnic, religious, etc.).

Proshansky *et al.* (1968) have suggested three norms of rationality, justice, and human heartedness to gauge the prejudiced behaviour. Thus, they have defined prejudice as a failure of rationality, justice and human heartedness in an individual's attitude towards members of another ethnic group.

Prejudice against the members of religions, ethnic, caste and regional groups other than their own are prevalent in the Indian social set-up. Prejudice against persons of other groups has been explained in terms of self-prophecy or ego enhancement and group conformity. The individuals have prejudice against others to enhance their ego or just to confirm the beliefs held by the members of their society. Thus, to say that an individual is prejudiced against the members of some group indicates that he or she tends to evaluate such persons in negative manner not on the basis of their individual character or behaviour but because they belong to or can be identified with that group. Thus, persons of other religions have prejudice against Muslims simply because they belong to Muslim group and are Muslims. Therefore, in a sense, prejudice represents a kind of blanket rejection or condemnation, a strong tendency to dislike Muslims and evaluate them negatively which is independent of their unique characteristics of behaviour.

The prejudiced beliefs are often expressed through stereotyping or discrimination against the members of the group. Erikson (1993) has expressed that stereotypes are often mentioned in connection with racism and discrimination. The members of each group had particular notions about the vices and virtues of others and to Erikson when such notions become part and parcel of the 'cultural knowledge' of a group and thus regularly and more or less predictably guide their relationships with others, we may describe them as ethnic stereotypes. Used analytically in social anthropology, the concept of stereotyping refers to the creation and consistent application of standardised notions of the cultural distinctiveness of a group (Erikson, 1993). The stereotyping provides a justification for discrimination. Thus, men may justify discrimination against women by referring them as lazy, careless, irresponsible etc. It is not necessary that stereotypes are always negative. Sometimes they are positive. Positive stereotypes are often seen for primitive people. However, when there is competition between two ethnic or religious groups or they are distinct in terms of majority and minority, dominationing and dominated, negative stereotypes are shown.

The Scene

The huge network of mass media—press, cinema, radio and television disseminate ideas and suggestions. Television being audio and visual has become the most important effective means of information. This is an organized means of reacting a large number of diverse kinds of people quickly and effectively. The present generation is undoubtedly in the grips of television. But unfortunately television presents only a slice of real life of people, particularly of weaker sections and regions. It has often been observed that various television programmes which portray the members of a group in an unfavourable way have all probabilities to have a profound adverse effect on viewers' attitude towards that group. The members of weaker sections of society are repeatedly projected in negative ways. For example, women have unfortunately been taken for granted as sex-symbols. As soon as you put on your television set you are bombarded with various advertisements with nude adolescent girls and women showing the use of various items of cosmetics. It has repeatedly been emphasized by various sections of citizens that women are unnecessarily exposed in advertisements. From needle to computer it is the woman who is shown using the things in romantic ways. Is it justified? Apart from this, the fair sex does not get fair treatment in various serials and movies. You can easily see the Muslim women as prostitute without any bar almost in every programme, serials and films often if and when there is a role of prostitute. As if the story writers and serial and movie makers cannot carve a role other than pros for a Muslim woman. One can understand that it is a product of feudal systems of Nawabs and Jagirdars. But there are periods other than Nawabs and Jagirdars and when those periods are depicted one must be careful for the selection of a names and persons for the role. Razia Sultana, Chand Bibi, Zeenat Mahal, Noor Jahan and Fatima Bibi are Muslim women. Muslim women are sisters, mothers and wives, social workers, intellectuals and every important thing par excellence. The natural question arises that why they are not depicted in these roles? Is it not stereotypes? So much so that women in general are also portrayed as meak, bumble, tolerant, a commodity to be sold. These positive stereotypes are also equally damaging and surely come in the path of making women self-confident and self-reliant. The mod girls roaming aimlessly with nymphomaniac hunger of sex are unjustified portrayals of women. Such treatments of women are against moral and ethical norms, and human heartedness and justice and therefore, prejudiced stereotyped roles of women.

The images of Muslims are in no way portrayed in a real way. Leave the portrayal of conditions of Muslims, Islam itself is always portrayed in an abberated way. It is portrayed in the way opposite of the spirit of Islam. Whenever, the writers and serial, programme and movie makers want to show the Islamic belief they take some mazar, Qawwal singing qawwali and people praying for the fulfillment of their desired things and wishes. The idol worship is portrayed in Mazar worship while showing the Islamic beliefs. The things and prayers shown and depicted as Islamic in films and serials this way are most un-Islamic and anti-Islamic.

The projection of Muslims and Muslim families with at least one dozen children is a common practice of movie and serial makers. The truth is that in Kerala and Pondicherry the rate of family planning among Muslims is much higher compared to other places on account of higher rate of literacy and economic well-being. They practice family planning like their Hindu counterparts (Engineer, 1996). So it is an economic and educational phenomenon and not a religious one. Objectively watch the affluent and educated Muslims around you and compare the size of their families with that of affluent and educated Hindu, Parsi, Christian, Sikh families or family of any community. In the same way the uneducated poor Muslims may be as shabby as Hindus of the same strata.

The roles of goondas and dadas have become the sole propriety of Muslims. Selling and buying girls are the most preferred works of Muslims ascribed by Indian films and serial makers. They are depicted as riot mongers, Dons and no doubt as helpers of poors indicating positive stereotypes. Eriksen (1993) has written that many Europeans have positive stereotypes of 'primitive peoples', arguing that their quality of life is higher than their own. Kurta-pajama and round cap are the pet stereotyped dress of Muslims portrayed in various programmes of T.V. These together are enough to damage the image of Muslims as they themselves are taken as the symbols of rigidity, intolerance and backwardness.

The case of Christians is no more different. A favourite role for Christians searched by film and serial makers is that of drunkerds. They are portrayed as careless and merry-making. Free mixing of adolescent boys and girls and men and women and often free sex in Christians are shown. There may be freedom of mixing between the sexes in Christians of Western countries but then this may be the culture of that country. So far as Indian culture is concerned it does not allow either Christians or any religio-ethnic group for such acts. They are not appreciated in any religion in Indian or for that matter even in western societies.

The images of members of Scheduled Caste and Scheduled Tribe communities are also tarnished by portraying them rough and tough and uncultured, shaky in ideas, filthy, rigid and illiterate. They are depicted as poor with traditional dresses. The makers of various programmes have become almost habitual and perhaps take it as their right to portray the persons of eastern U.P. and Bihar in the role of servant. Whenever, there is a role of servants it is filled by a person speaking Khari Boli, Bhojpuri and a mixture of the two in a shabby way. They are the persons who have perhaps been born for programme and serial makers to portray them in one and only one role of servants. They perhaps can-not see beyond their prejudices and stereotypes and therefore, cannot find literate, executive, intellectuals, and luminaries in the forms of Chandra Gupta Maurya, Chanakya, Sher Shah, Veer Kunwar Singh, Maulana Sadaqat Ali, Rajendra Prasâd and Jai Prakash Narayan.

The Explanation

The enactment of roles of members of weaker sections of society in unrealistic and non-existent ways in advertisements, programmes and T.V. serials are though basically knowingly or unknowingly, intentionally or unintentionally, consciously or unconsciously are the projections of the prejudices and stereotypes of writers, programme makers of the programmes and serials, inculcates also wrong and unrealistic stereotypical images in the viewers. The continuous and repeated projections of members of certain religious, caste and regional groups as poor, dirty, goonda, illiterate, servants, rigid, careless, merry-making, drunkerds and members of a particular sex as obedient, weak, prostitute, shaky, orthodox show the negative feelings and blanket rejection of the realities found in the individual members of these groups. They are portrayed in the way just because they belong to a particular religion, sex, caste, and regional group. These portrayals do not conform the norms of rationality, justice, and human heartedness laid down by Proshansky *et. al* (1968). The projections of the members of these groups in such unrealistic and false roles are blanket rejections of the realities and failure of rationality, justice and human heartedness. Therefore, they are prejudiced and stereotyped projections. Such unrealistic prejudiced portrayals are detrimental in two ways. First, they are injurious and detrimental for the development of healthy self-concept and identity in the members of the concerned groups, and second, they are helpful in developing unrealistic, untrue or half-true and false images (stereotypes) of the members of concerned group in viewers.

After independence we chose to be a secular country but it could not be applied in practice. Discrimination, denial of equality of opportunity, double standard for different communities exists as it existed before independence or for that matter at any point of time. The advocated objective, unbiased and realistic views of various sections of society could not and are not presented through mass media simply because it is in the hands of members of particular group or community. It is in the hands of Brahmins and the Brahministic views of the minorities, women, Scheduled Caste and Scheduled Tribe are portrayed through T.V. programmes, advertisements, serials and dramas. Is it not a Brahministic orientation that many serials related to Hinduism, i.e. *Mahabharat, Shri Krishna,* and *Jai Hanuman, Om Namasshiway, Balaji, Shiv Mahapuran etc.* are shown in the name of *Bhartiya Sanskriti* (Indian culture) Hindu epics? This is a tragedy that the largest media of communication, T.V. is spreading with all its forces and resources prejudices, hatred and negative feelings and attitudes for various weaker sections in a secular country and yet we talk of international brotherhood and *Vasudeva Kutumbbkam.* What is needed is a projection of balanced, honest, actual and real existing socio-cultural, economic and religious conditions of weaker sections so that positive image of them can be developed in viewers on one hand and the persons of these sections can be devoid of developing in them feelings of inferiority, self-depreciation and negative self-concept. This is a universally accepted fact that there are individual differences in abilities and other psychological variables. Therefore, there are as much individual differences in members of weaker sections as in the members of upper class and caste. Duckitt (1992,1994) has pointed out that the major psychological concerns facing researchers and theorists in the area of prejudice have shifted during the 20th century from (a) 'documenting' ethnic minorities' intellectual inferiority to (b) explaining why majority group members were so quick to assume that minorities were inferior, (c) specifying 'universal' mental phenomena responsible for prejudice, etc. This is the case of western countries. In India it is yet awaited.

REFERENCES

Baron, R.A. and Byrne, D. (1977). *Social Psychology : Understanding Human Interaction.* Boston : Allen and Bacon.

Duckitt, J. (1992). Psychology and prejudice : a historical analysis and integrative framework'. *American Psychologist,* 47, 1182-93.

Duckitt, J. (1994). *The Social Psychology of Prejudice.* Westport, Conneticut : Praneger.

Engineer Asghar Ali, (1996). *Minorities and Stereotypes.* Bombay : Centre for Study of Society and Secularism.

Eriksen, T.H. (1993). *Ethnicity and Nationalism.* London : Pluto Press.

29

The Backwardness of Rural Farmers: Practices and Directions

Sohrab Ali

New technology in agriculture increased the production but did not improve the economic condition of rural people. From the beginning of Fourth Five Year Plan (1969), some attempt were made to directly approach the issue of poverty through poverty eradication programmes like Small Farmers Development Agency (SFDA), Drought Prone Area Programme (DPAP) and target groups and target areas. In the Fifth Five Year Plan (1974) minimum needs programmes were introduced to improve the quality of life of the poor. Introduction of micro-level planning was also introduced to take care of space dimension of development. In other words, poor people and those in backward areas became part of the central concern of development programmes and planning.

The failure of these programmes led to more radical programmes on poverty eradication. These were introduced beginning from the Sixth Five Year Plan (1978) and continued through Sixth and Seventh Five Year Plans (1980-85 and 1985-90). These programmes included : (i) employment planning at the block level through National Rural Employment Programme (NREP) and Rural Labour Employment Guarantee Programme (RLEGP), (ii) Integrated Rural Development Programme (IRDP) which extended the scope and content of SFDA, MFALA, etc., and which aimed at real integration of the various programmes, (iii) revised minimum needs programmes, and (iv) special area programme for backward areas etc.

An analysis of developmental work in rural areas reveals a considerable improvement in the approach to development. First, it is realized that general growth does not reach the poor or poor areas, and thus require special attention. This does not mean that general development ought to be neglected. Along with general development, special anti-poverty programmes are to be instituted. Second, anti-poverty programmes are now superior in terms of their technical content, better quality data, sophisticated methods, etc. And third, the contents and scope of all programmes have improved over the years.

There has been substantial improvement in the rural economy, for example, food production has increased from about 50 million tonnes in 1950-51 to 170 million tonnes in 1988-89 and to 190 million tonnes in 1990-95. We no longer need to import food grains. Famine which was a recurrent feature of India's economy has been controlled. There has been great deal of diversification in agriculture. Gross irrigated area has increased from about 18.3 per cent of cropped area in 1960-61 to about 32.7 per cent in 1986-87. Area under high yielding varieties in case of wheat, rice, jowar and maize had increased from 16.7 per cent of the total cropped area in 1970-71 to 56.1 per cent in 1986-87. Rural poverty has been reduced from 54.1 per cent in 1972-73 to 51.2 per cent in 1977-78 and 39.9 per cent in 1984-85.

Current Problems

However, we are yet to modernize the rural economy. The following factors inhibit the modernization of rural economy.

1. The development process has a great deal of regional imbalance. Some states are agriculturally more developed than others. About 80 per cent of total population below the poverty line is accounted for in eight states. These eight states also account for 70 per cent of the total unemployment. Lack of infrastructure and irregular monsoon are main features of these areas.
2. The huge pressure on agriculture has not helped in increasing the productivity of labour. Even now the per capita availability of food is 465.5 kg (1988-89). Investment in agriculture and irrigation has increased the productivity of land but has not affected labour productivity. In 1960 about 73 per cent of the working force was engaged in agriculture. In 1980, it declined to 70 per cent, though the total number has increased substantially due to a rapid increase in population.
3. Although the Government is providing subsidies to the rural people in the sphere of irrigation, fertilizer, electricity, credit and price support. The subsidy in respect of inputs, on an average constitutes about 16 to 17 per cent of Net State Domestic Product (SDP) at Factor Cost (at current prices) annually. But since the level of income is

awfully low, subsidies do not affect the economic scenario. Moreover, subsidies accrue mostly to rich farmers who are a small group.

4. There is growing disparity between agricultural and non-agricultural income largely due to (a) the large proportion of people dependent on agriculture, (b) the average size of holding decreases annually, and (c) the terms of trade between agriculture and industry remain largely unfavourable for the farmer. The classification of workers in rural areas shows that cultivators account for 51 per cent, agricultural labourers 30 per cent and other workers 19 per cent. Among cultivators 56.6 per cent are marginal farmers (below 1 hect.), 18 per cent are small farmers (between 1 to 2 hect.), 14 per cent are semi-medium farmers (between 2 to 4 hect.), 9 per cent are medium farmers (between 4 to 10 hect.) and 2.4 per cent are large farmers (10 hect. and above). This shows that small marginal farmers account for 74.6 per cent of the total farmers and operate only 26.3 per cent of the total cultivated area. Most of the agricultural labourers are not employed throughout the year. A majority of them work in the informal sector on low wages. The average size of the cultivated area in case of marginal and small farmers comes to 0.39 hectares and 1.43 hectares respectively. The average size in case of all farmers come to 1.82 hectares. We also find that prices of industrial goods are higher than agricultural goods. All these reduce the income level of rural areas. In fact, poverty arises in rural areas which is exported to urban areas creating slums in the latter.

5. Finally, there are some sensitive factors in anti-poverty programmes. Firstly, there is poor coordination among various programmes. Secondly, there is poor diagnosis of the poverty and absence of total approach at the strategy level. When subsidies are given to the poor, no attempt is made to meet their consumption needs or seed needs. Subsidies are given to create income generating assets. But beneficiaries use the assistance to meet their basic consumption needs. Thirdly, no attempt is made to reduce the economic and political power of the rural rich. They still influence decision-making. Asset distribution is hardly emphasised. For example IRDP is evaluated mainly on the basis of amount spent on number of beneficiaries or at most the increase in the income level of the beneficiaries.

Future Directions

In the light of aforesaid trends, the following changes are necessary:.

1. To increase irrigation facilities to increase production.
2. To increase emphasis on provision of social consumption goods and

services to rural areas so as to raise the quality of life of the rural sector.

3. Massive production oriented investment in rural infrastructure covering rural electrification and energisation of pumpsets, rural roads, rural communications, soil conservation, social forestry, etc. All these will not only improve capital formation but also increase employment opportunities for the rural poor.
4. To develop cooperative organisation through education in rural areas that may be fruitful for better development of their lives.
5. Upgradation of technology is another area which can help agricultural production. For example, fertilizer consumption in eastern regions comes to only about 21 kg. per hectare (September, 1988). In some of the districts it is 2 to 4 kg. per hectare. The all India average was 48.7 kg. per hectare in 1986-87. In Punjab, it was about 160 kg. per hectare during the same year. All these comparisons show that there is a considerable scope for increasing intensity of agriculture by upgrading technology in agriculture.
6. Modern agriculture requires a large number of inputs like chemical fertilizer, high yielding variety of seeds, pesticides, credit, pumpsets, etc. One of the major difficulties in agriculture is that these inputs are not easily available to them hence they are not able to increase productivity much more than the big farmers. Alongwith these inputs, extension education should also be imported to the farmers regarding the use of these inputs including water management.
7. Development of rural infrastructure, like roads, electricity, pumpsets, skill formation, etc. which will build up social and physical capital for large scale development of rural industries should be available. These rural industries will upgrade the technology of agriculture, increase rural income and provide alternative employment opportunities which will reduce the pressure of population on agriculture and prevent migration of surplus workers to urban areas.

REFERENCES

Bhatia, B.M. (1988). *Indian Agriculture : A Policy Perspective.* New Delhi : Sage Publications.

Bhalla, G.S. and Tyagi D.S. (1989). *Patterns in Indian Agricultural Development: A District Level Study.* New Delhi.

Bhalla, G.S. and Chadha, G.K. (1982). Green revolution and the small peasant : A study of income distribution in Punjab agriculture. *Economic and Political Weekly*, 15 and 22 May.

Dhawan, (1988). Irrigated versus dry farming, *Mainstream*, 19 March.

Sixth Five Year Plan (1980-85). Mid-term Appraisal (1983). p.53, *Planning Commission*. Government of India.

Economic Survey (1988-89). *Planning and Coordination Development*, Government of Orissa.

Gulati, Ashok (1989). Input subsidies in Indian agriculture. *Economic and Political Weekly*, 24 June.

The Times of India, (1986). Farmer's Issue: A survey. 22 October, New Delhi.

Index